A. POUJADE, *I.P.R. d'anglais*
JRC YGLESIAS, *B.A.*

Let's go on!

classes terminales

nouvelle édition

G. Hocmard, *Agrégé de l'Université.*
　　　　　Professeur d'anglais au lycée Descartes - Tours

K. Sheram, *B.A.*
　　　　　National Public Radio - Washington D.C.

R. Smith, *Agrégée de l'université.*
　　　　　Professeur d'anglais au Lycée Molière - Paris

M. Sommers, *Journaliste*

H. Wolff, *B.A.*
　　　　　Professeur d'anglais - Alberta (Canada)

Armand Colin - Longman

103, boulevard Saint-Michel 75005 Paris

ISBN 2-86644-062-5

La loi du 11 mars 1957 n'autorisant, aux termes 2 et 3 de l'article 41, d'une part que les « copies ou reproductions strictement réservées à l'usage privé du copiste et non destinées à une utilisation collective » et, d'autre part que les analyses et les courtes citations dans un but d'exemple et d'illustration, « toute représentation ou reproduction intégrale, ou partielle faite sans le consentement de l'auteur ou de ses ayants droit ou ayants cause, est illicite » (alinéa 1er de l'article 40).
Cette représentation ou reproduction, par quelque procédé que ce soit, constituerait donc une contrefaçon sanctionnée par les articles 425 et suivants du Code Pénal.

© ARMAND COLIN - LONGMAN. PARIS, 1983

PRÉFACE

Ce recueil est une réédition du troisième volet du tryptique **LET'S GO ON**, destiné aux élèves du second cycle de l'enseignement secondaire, publié par Armand Colin-Longman.

Pourquoi une nouvelle édition de ce manuel, de classes terminales, alors qu'il a connu une très large diffusion ?

Précisément à cause de son succès. Ce nouveau manuel garde l'essentiel de son esprit et de son contenu, à savoir une langue authentique en situation de communication, une possibilité d'approche audio-orale au moyen d'interviews, un apprentissage de la langue et un recyclage des connaissances par le biais d'exercices variés et contextualisés, et enfin une étude de la civilisation à partir de textes littéraires et socio-économiques de registres et de niveaux de langues variés.

Mais la rapidité de l'évolution des idées et des faits nous a incités, d'une part à changer un certain nombre de textes pour les remplacer par des documents mieux adaptés à la compréhension de la société américaine contemporaine, et d'autre part à réactualiser bien évidemment les tableaux statistiques.

Comme dans le précédent manuel, ces nouveaux choix ont été surtout guidés par le désir d'être attentifs à la vitalité bouillonnante de ce creuset permanent où toutes les expériences continuent à être tentées.

L'accompagnement pédagogique est conçu dans la même perspective que celui des précédents manuels. Les exercices suggérés ont pour objectif d'abord d'aider les élèves à comprendre un document oral ou écrit et aussi de leur fournir les outils linguistiques nécessaires à l'analyse de ce document et à l'expression de réactions intellectuelles, morales et affectives.

A la fin de chaque chapitre, nous avons gardé « Surveying the Scene », qui n'a aucun caractère contraignant mais qui peut aider certains élèves à faire une synthèse et à approfondir le thème traité. Dans ce but, nous avons allongé la liste des titres de livres et de films.

Puisse cette nouvelle édition de **LET'S GO ON** terminales soutenir le professeur dans sa tâche d'enseignant et encourager l'élève dans son apprentissage de la langue et dans sa découverte des U.S.A.

CONTENTS

A WORLD OF DIFFERENCE

U. S. A.   **U. K.**

──────────────── *Vocabulary* ────────────────

U. S. A.	U. K.
the Carter administration	the Labour government
apartment	flat
automobile	motor-car
ballpoint	Biro
bar	pub
a (dollar) bill	a (pound) note
box car (freight car)	goods van
broiled	grilled
buddy	mate
bus	bus, coach
can	tin
candy	sweets
the restaurant check	the restaurant bill
(potato) chips	(potato) crisps
closet	cupboard
corn	maize
custom-made	made to measure
dessert	sweet
to do the dishes	to wash up
elevator	lift
fall	autumn
faucet	tap
fender (of a car)	wing
first floor, second floor, ...	ground floor, first floor, ...
French fries	chips
garbage can	dustbin
gas	petrol
guy	chap, fellow, bloke
instalment plan	hire purchase
lawyer, attorney	barrister, solicitor
mail	post
motor	engine
movie	film, pictures
one way/round trip (ticket)	single/return (ticket)
pants	trousers
parking lot	car park
pavement	roadway
to quit	to stop
railroad	railway
schedule	timetable
sedan	saloon (car)
sick	ill
sidewalk	pavement
to stand in line	to queue up
store	shop
subway	tube (*or* underground) train

U. S. A.	U. K.
taxi	cab
truck	lorry
trunk	boot (of a car)
vacation	holidays
wheat	corn
windshield	windscreen

Spelling

U. S. A.	U. K.
1. Words in *-or:* color, humor, neighbor	1. Words in *-our:* colour, humour, neighbour
2. Words in *-ense:* defense, offense, pretense (*but* difference)	2. Words in *-ence:* defence, offence, pretence
3. Words in *-ter:* center, theater	3. Words in *-tre:* centre, theatre
4. One *L* before ending: jeweler, traveler, traveling, ...	4. Two *Ls* before ending: jeweller, traveller, travelling, ...
5. Simplified spelling:	5. Traditional spelling:
airplane	aeroplane
catalog	catalogue
check	cheque
curb	kerb
donut	doughnut
draft	draught
gram	gramme
jail	gaol
plow	plough
program	programme
specialty	speciality
tire	tyre
Etc.	*Etc.*
And even in advertisements :	
thru	through
tonite	tonight
while-U-wait	while you wait

Grammar

U. S. A.	U. K.
1. *To do* auxiliary of *to have.* *Ex:* Do you have any children?	1. *To have* conjugated without auxiliary. *Ex:* Have you any children?
2. To get, I got, gotten. *Ex:* I've gotten through a lot of work today.	2. To get, I got, got. *Ex:* I have got through a lot of work today.
3. Like = as, as if. *Ex:* She can't cook like her mother does. He ran like he had seen the devil.	3. Like ≠ as ≠ as if. *Ex:* She can't cook as her mother does. He ran as if he had seen the devil.

7

U.S.A.		U.K.
/r/ : retroflex		/r/ flapped

/t/ tends to become /d/ between vowels.

/'bedər/	better	/'betər/
/'mædər/	matter	/'mætər/
/'wɔdər/	water	/'wɔ:tər/

/h/ slightly pronounced in _wh_-words.

/hwen/	when	/wen/
/hwaɪl/	while	/waɪl/
/hwaɪ/	why	/waɪ/

/æ/ in such words as:		/ɑ:/ in the same words:
/dæns/	dance	/dɑ:ns/
/ɪg'zæmpəl/	example	/ɪg'zɑ:mpəl/
/glæs/	glass	/glɑ:s/
/græs/	grass	/gr'ɑ:s/
/hæf/	half	/hɑ:f/
/'ræθɜ:r/	rather	/'rɑθɜ:r/
but: /'fɑ:θər/	father	

/e/ in such word as:		/æ/ in the same words:
/ket/	cat	/kæt/
/ketʃ/	catch	/kætʃ/
/'hepi/	happy	/'hæpi/
/hev/	have	/hæv/

/ɔ/ in such words as:		/ɔ:/ in the same words:
/kɔl/	call	/kɔ:l/
/kɔt/	caught	/kɔ:t/
/hɔk/	hawk	/hɔ:k/
/sɔ/	saw	/sɔ:/

/ɔ:/ in such words as:		/əʊ/ in the same words:
/blɔ:/	blow	/bləʊ/
/gɔ:/	go	/gəʊ/
/hɔ:m/	home	/həʊm/
/nɔ:/	know	/nəʊ/

/u:/ in such words as:		/ju:/ in the same words:
/du:/	dew	/dju:/
/du:/	due	/dju:/
/nu:/	new	/nju:/
/su:t/	suit	/sju:t/
/tu:n/	tune	/tju:n/

/ɜ:/ in such words as:

/klɜːrk/	clerk
/dɜːrbɪ/	Derby
/ˈbɜrklɪ/	Berkeley

/ɑ:/ in the same words:

/klɑːk/
/dɑːbɪ/
/ˈbɑːklɪ/

/i:/ in such words as:

/ˈiːðəʳ/	either
/ˈniːðəʳ/	neither
/ˈliːðəʳ/	leisure

/ɑɪ/ or /e/ in the same words: /ˈɑɪðəʳ/
/ˈnɑɪðəʳ/
/ˈleʒəʳ/

Secondary stress in long words, with connected vowel changes:

/ˌædvəˈtaɪzmənt/	advertisement	/ədˈvɜːt smənt/
/ˌekstrəˈɔrdneri/	extraordinary	/ɪkˈstrɔːdənəri/
/ˈlæbrətori/	laboratory	/ləˈbɒrətri/
/ˈsəkreˌtəri/	secretary	/ˈsəkretəri/
/luːˈtenənt/	lieutenant	/lefˈtenənt/
/ˈrestərənt/	restaurant	/ˈrestərɔ̃/
/ˈrestərɑnt/		/ˈrestərɒnt/

Pronunciation table

CONSONANTS		VOWELS			
SYMBOL	KEY WORD	SYMBOL	KEY WORD	SYMBOL	KEY WORD
b	back	æ	bad	eɪə	player
d	day	ɑ	*AmE* farm	ə	about
ð	then	ɑː	calm	əʊ	note
dʒ	jump	ɒ	*BrE* pot	əʊə	lower
f	few	aɪ	bite	ɜ	*AmE* bird
g	gay	aʊ	now	ɜː	bird
h	hot	aɪə	tire	i	pretty
j	yet	aʊə	tower	iː	sheep
k	key	ɔ	*AmE* form	ɪ	ship
l	led	ɔː	caught	ɪə	here
m	sum	ɔɪ	boy	o	*AmE* port
n	sun	ɔɪə	employer	uː	boot
ŋ	sung	e	bed	ʊ	put
p	pen	eə	there	ʊə	poor
r	red	eɪ	make	ʌ	cut
s	soon				
ʃ	fishing				
t	tea				
tʃ	cheer				
θ	thing				
v	view				
w	wet				
z	zero				
ʒ	pleasure				

Special signs

/ʳ/ at the end of a word means that /r/ is usually pronounced in American English and is pronounced in British English when the next word begins with a vowel sound

/ɪ̆/ means that some speakers use /ɪ/ and others use /ə/

/i/ means many American speakers use /iː/ but many British speakers use /ɪ/

/ə/ means that /ə/ may or may not be used

/o/ means that American speakers use either /ɔ/ or /əʊ/

/ɑ/ /ɑ, ɔ, ɜ/ are used for American
/ɔ/ English to represent /ɑː, ɔː, ɜː/
/ɜ/

I. THE AMERICAN DREAM...

WHAT DOES IT MEAN ?

An interview with Dr Lee Hertz, 45, director of a scientific laboratory at Stanford University, California.

INTERVIEWER : *What does the expression "the American Dream" mean to you ?*

DR HERTZ : I guess in one way it's the vision of my grandparents. They turned their backs on the poverty and confines of life in Poland in order to integrate themselves and their children into American life.

5 I. : *So the American Dream means getting out of poverty ?*

DR H. : Then it did. However, when they got to America, they realized that the dream wasn't going to happen, that survival was first. So the dream became the potential for their children to live without hardship.

I. : *How could they achieve that ?*

10 DR H. : First through hard work and giving their kids an education. Through education their children would have a choice of being and doing what they wanted. That basically life could be what you made it.

I. : *Do you believe that is true ?*

DR H. : No, but they did.

15 I. : *Do you mean that you haven't benefitted from the idea of the American Dream ?*

DR H. : No, I definitely have. But for me it required rejecting much of the American culture and the kinds of pressure it puts on people. I am talking about financial, material, social and psychological pressures. I haven't wanted to be what my school, my parents and television wanted me to be.

I. : *But you have had the freedom to pick and choose those elements which have brought you some* 20 *success, more than your parents ever had.*

DR H. : America does give you the opportunity to achieve, though it throws hurdles[1] in your way. However, at least there is room for certain groups of people to be what they want to be and be it successfully.

I. : *Why do you say a few people ? Isn't the American Dream an idea everyone can believe in ?*

25 DR H. : Yes. But only because our government wants us to believe it. The term American Dream has become a public relations word used to help promote the capitalistic system. It keeps the bulk of the population working and spending their money to acquire things which make the material of the dream.

I. : *Well, do they achieve this through hard work ?*

30 DR H. : Of course not. But even if they don't, the constant portrayal of the good life in the mass media, especially T.V., shows that the dream can be reached through money. That's how one learns the American Dream. The constant penetration of advertising which tells you to buy and buy so that finally you will reach the dream.

I. : *But if a large part of society doesn't achieve this, why does the idea persist ?*

35 **Dr H.** : Well, since a lot of satisfaction is gained from acquiring things, a considerable amount of people feel they are on the way to achieve what they have been told is available to them through hard work and participation in the American society.

I. : *Would you say that it is this goal which makes the system work ?*

Dr H. : Yes, because people become obsessed with upward mobility, they have to reach the top. They
40 are never satisfied with the status quo. The American Dream is at the end of the rainbow, the end result of the pursuit of happiness. It is the contentment of having sufficient money to buy the things you want, of reaching the status of all the other people who have the money to buy what they want : cars, color T.V.s, washing machines. The American Dream is in one's head and in one's pocketbook.

-----

1. hurdles : obstacles.

A TRUE OR FALSE ?

1. Dr Hertz's grandparents found out that survival came first. 2. Education is more important than hard work to achieve the American Dream. 3. Dr Hertz believes that life is what you make it. 4. Dr Hertz didn't reject any part of American culture. 5. He didn't want to be what his school and parents wanted. 6. People can't achieve the material of the Dream through hard work. 7. T.V. shows that the Dream can be reached through money. 8. Acquiring things is the goal which makes the capitalistic system work. 9. People in the United States are satisfied with the *status quo.*

B ANSWER THESE QUESTIONS :

1. Why did Dr Hertz's grandparents come to the United States ? 2. Why couldn't they benefit from the American Dream ? 3. How could they make sure that their children would not live in poverty ? 4. How has Dr Hertz been able to benefit from the American Dream ? How far do you think he realises that he has ? 5. Why can everybody believe in the American Dream ? 6. Why does the government profit from using the term *the American Dream* ? 7. How does television promote the idea of the American Dream ? 8. Why does the idea of the American Dream persist ? 9. Why are some Americans obsessed with upward mobility ? 10. Why is money an important part of the American Dream ?

C EXPLAIN IN YOUR OWN WORDS

1. They turned their backs on the poverty and confines of life in Poland.
2. America throws hurdles in your way.
3. The term *American Dream* has become a public relations word.
4. People feel they are on their way to achieve.
5. The American Dream is at the end of the rainbow.
6. The American Dream is in one's head and in one's pocketbook.

D DISCUSSION

Why is money such an important part of the American Dream ?

A SLICE OF A CONTINENT

Over 200 million people whose ancestors came from all of the continents, many races, many climates, a land area bigger than all the countries of the Common Market, lakes, mountains, valleys, fields—how can anyone describe America, or what it means to be an American ? John Dos Passos, one of America's great writers, tries. The following is an extract from the introduction to his U.S.A. : The 42nd Parallel.

The young man walks by himself searching through the crowd with greedy eyes, greedy ears taut to hear, by himself, alone.

The streets are empty. People have packed into subways[1], climbed into streetcars and buses ; in the stations they've scampered for suburban trains ; they've filtered
5 into lodgings and tenements, gone up in elevators into apartmenthouses. In a showwindow two sallow windowdressers in their shirtsleeves are bringing out a dummy girl in a red evening dress, at a corner welders in masks lean into sheets of blue flame repairing a cartrack, a few drunk bums shamble along, a sad streetwalker fidgets under an arclight. From the river comes the deep rumbling
10 whistle of a steamboat leaving dock. A tug hoots far away.

The young man walks by himself, fast but not fast enough, far but not far /ɪˈnʌf/
enough (faces slide out of sight, talk trails into tattered scraps, footsteps tap fainter in alleys) ; he must catch the last subway, the streetcar, the bus, [...] register at all the hotels, work in the cities, answer the wantads, learn the trades, take up the jobs,
15 live in all the boarding-houses, sleep in all the beds. One bed is not enough, one job is not enough, one life is not enough. At night, head swimming with wants, he walks by himself alone. [...]

Only the ears busy to catch the speech are not alone ; the ears are caught tight, linked tight by the tendrils[2] of phrased words, the turn of a joke, the singsong fade
20 of a story, the gruff fall of a sentence ; linking tendrils of speech twine through the city blocks, spread over pavements, grow out along broad parked avenues, speed with the trucks leaving on their long night runs over roaring highways, whisper down sandy byroads past wornout farms, joining up cities and fillingstations, roundhouses, steamboats, planes groping along airways ; words call out on
25 mountain pastures, drift slow down rivers widening to the sea and the hushed /hʌʃt/
beaches.

It was not in the long walks through jostling crowds at night that he was less /ˈdʒɒsəlɪŋ/
alone, or in the training camp at Allentown, or in the day on the docks at Seattle, or in the empty reek[3] of Washington City hot boyhood summer nights, or in the meal
30 on Market Street[4], or in the swim off the red rocks at San Diego, or in the bed full of fleas in New Orleans, or in the cold razorwind off the lake, or in the gray faces trembling in the grind of gears in the street under Michigan Avenue[5], or in the /graɪnd/
smokers of limited expresstrains[6], or walking across country, or riding up the dry mountain canyons, or the night without a sleepingbag among frozen beartracks in
35 the Yellowstone, or canoeing Sundays on the Quinnipiac ;

but in his mother's words telling about longago, in his father's telling about when I was a boy, in the kidding stories of uncles, in the lies the kids told at school, the hired man's yarns, the tall tales the doughboys told after taps ;

it was the speech that clung to the ears, the link that tingled in the blood ; U.S.A.

40 U.S.A. is the slice of a continent. U.S.A. is a group of holding companies, some aggregations of trade unions, a set of laws bound in calf, a radio network, a chain of moving picture theatres, a column of stock-quotations rubbed out and written in by a Western Union[7] boy on a blackboard, a public library full of old newspapers and dogeared[8] history books with protests scrawled on the margins in pencil.
45 U.S.A. is the world's greatest rivervalley fringed with mountains and hills. U.S.A. is a set of bigmouthed officials with too many bank accounts. U.S.A. is a lot of men buried in their uniforms in Arlington Cemetery[9]. U.S.A. is the letters at the end of an address when you are away from home. But mostly U.S.A. is the speech of the people.

John Dos Passos, *The 42nt Parallel,* 1930

---

1. subway *(Am.)* : underground *(Eng.).*   **2.** tendrils : *vrilles (de la vigne).*   3. reek : stink.   **4.** Market Street : in San Francisco.   **5.** Michigan Avenue : in Chicago.   **6.** limited express trains : *train express (≠ rapide).*   **7.** Western Union : telegram company.   **8.** dogeared : worn with use.   **9.** Arlington Cemetery : National Military Cemetery near Washington D.C.

A   UNDERSTANDING THE TEXT

1. Is the young man one person ? Justify your answer. Who do you think he represents ?   **2.** Why is he searching through the crowd with greedy eyes and greedy ears ?   **3.** In what sort of a landscape does the scene take place ?   **4.** What do you think the author means when he writes, "one bed is not enough, one job is not enough, one life is not enough" ? Justify your answer   **5.** What does the author seem to suggest about the speech ?   **6.** Why was the young man less alone in the places mentioned than in the stories he used to hear when he was a boy ?   **7.** In what way was the speech essential for the U.S.A. be considered "a slice of a continent" ?   **8.** In what way can the United States be considered "a slice of a continent" ?

B   LANGUAGE AT WORK

Compound nouns

The author uses a lot of compound nouns, for instance :

• **footstep**	(noun + noun)
• **highway**	(adjective + noun)
• **by-road**	(adverb + noun)
• **show-window**	(verb + noun)
• **sleeping-bag**	(-ing form + noun)
• **stock-quotation**	(locution)

Find all those used in the text. Using the last paragraph as a model, give a description of France as for a guide-book, using as many compound nouns as you can.

1. *The first paragraph describes what the "young man" sees. Explain what the author wants to suggest in each of the following sentences :*

a) People have packed into subways.
b) They've scampered for suburban trains.
c) They've filtered into apartment houses.
d) A few drunk bums shamble along.
e) A sad streetwalker fidgets under an arclight.

2. *The third paragraph describes what the "young man" hears. Why do you think the author writes that the "linking tendrils of speech" twine through the city blocks, spread over pavements, grow out along broad parked avenues, speed with the trucks, whisper down sandy byroads, call out on mountain pastures, drift slow down rivers ?*

C FOLLOW UP WORK

1. The author presents one picture of the U.S.A. What does the U.S.A. mean to you ? List all the ideas and images you can think of, making two columns for positive and negative images. Then write a composition on your impressions of the U.S.A.
2. In what ways could the passage be considered more a poem than a narrative ?

The language of discussion

- I really think so.
- You're right, quite right, absolutely right.
- I would agree to a certain extent, but...
- I have the feeling, the impression that...
- On one hand... on the other hand...
- In the first place / To begin with...
- My opinion is that...
- The problem as I see it is whether...
- You may be right, but...

- I don't think so.
- I don't think that's quite right...
- I don't see the question that way...
- I don't quite agree with you.
- There's one point on which I disagree.
- May I just point out that...
- One point on which I am in complete disagreement is...

PARADOX AND DREAM

Americans seem to live and breathe and function by paradox, but in nothing are /bri:ð/
we so paradoxical as in our passionate belief in our own myths. We truly believe
ourselves to be natural-born mechanics and do-it-yourself-ers. We spend our lives
in motor cars, yet most of us—a great many of us at least—do not know enough
5 about a car to look in the gas tank when the motor fails. Our lives as we live them
would not function without electricity, but it is a rare man or woman who, when the
power[1] goes off, knows how to look for a burned-out fuse and replace it. We
believe implicitly that we are the heirs of the pioneers ; that we have inherited self-
sufficiency and the ability to take care of ourselves, particularly in relation to
10 nature. There isn't a man among us in ten thousand who knows how to butcher a
cow or a pig and cut it up for eating, let alone a wild animal. By natural
endowment, we are great rifle shots and great hunters—but when hunting season
opens there is a slaughter of farm animals and humans by men and women who
couldn't hit a real target if they could see it. Americans treasure the knowledge that
15 they live close to nature, but fewer and fewer farmers feed more and more people ;
and as soon as we can afford to we eat out of cans[2], buy frozen T.V. dinners[3], and
haunt the delicatessens. Affluence[4] means moving to the suburbs, but the American
suburbanite sees, if anything, less of the country than the city apartment dweller
with his window boxes and his African violets carefully tendend under lights. In no
20 country are more seeds and plants and equipment purchased, and less vegetables
and flowers raised. [...]

The inventiveness once necessary for survival may also be a part of the national /sər'vaɪvəl/
dream. Who among us has not bought for a song[5] an ancient junked car[6], and with /'eɪnʃənt/
parts from other junked cars put together something that would run ? This is not
25 lost ; American kids are still doing it. The dreams of a people either create folk
literature or find their way into it ; and folk literature, again, is always based on /'lɪtərətʃʊər/
something that happened. Our most persistent folk tales—constantly retold in
books, movies, and television shows—concern cowboys, gun-slinging sheriffs, and
Indian fighters. These folk figures existed—perhaps not quite as they are recalled
30 nor in the numbers indicated, but they did exist ; and this dream also persists. Even
businessmen in Texas wear the high-heeled boots and big hats, though they ride in
air-conditioned Cadillacs and have forgotten the reason for the high heels. All our
children play cowboy and Indian ; the brave and honest sheriff who with courage
and a six-gun brings law and order and civic virtue to a Western community is /'sɪvɪk/
35 perhaps our most familiar hero, no doubt descended from the brave mailed[7] knight /'vɜrtʃu:/
of chivalry who battled and overcame evil with lance and sword. Even the /daʊt/
recognition signals are the same ; white hat, white armor—black hat, black shield. /naɪt/
And in these moral tales, so deepset in us, virtue does not arise out of reason or
orderly process of law—it is imposed and maintained by violence. [...]

A modern cowboy. How do you think Steinbeck would have liked this Texan businessman's outfit?

40   For Americans too the wide and general dream has a name. It is called "the American Way of Life". No one can define it or point to any one person or group who lives it, but it is very real nevertheless, perhaps more real than that equally remote dream the Russians call Communism. These dreams describe our vague yearnings toward what we wish we were and hope we may be : wise, just,
45   compassionate, and noble. The fact that we have this dream at all is perhaps an indication of its possibility.

John Steinbeck, *America and Americans,* **1966**

---

1. power : electricity.   2. cans *(Am.)* ; tins *(Eng.).*   3. T.V. dinners : prepacked meals on a tray.   4. affluence : wealth.   5. bought for a song : bought cheaply.   6. junked car : *épave.*   7. mailed : wearing an armor made of metal links.

A   UNDERSTANDING THE TEXT

1. In what way are Americans most paradoxical ?
2. What does the author think is paradoxical about Americans and cars ?   3. What does he think is paradoxical about Americans and electricity ?
4. According to the author, in what ways do Americans believe they are the heirs of pioneers ? What is his own view ?   5. What does the author believe to be true about American eating habits ?
6. According to the author, do many Americans grow their own vegetables ? Justify your answer.
7. What do American kids do with junked cars ?

8. Who are the three main characters of American folk tales ? Why do you think they endure ?   9. How do many businessmen dress in Texas ? Why do you think they dress that way ?   10. According to the author, who is the ancestor of the "brave and honest sheriff" ? What do *you* think ?   11. According to the author, what is the name given to the American Dream ?   12. What is the author's feeling about the American Dream ? Do you agree with his conclusion ? Justify your answer.

Expressing contrast

Example :

> • We are great hunters, *but* when hunting season opens, there is a slaughter of farm animals and humans.

Steinbeck could also have written :

> • We are great hunters, *and yet* when hunting season opens, there is a slaughter of farm animals and humans.
> • *Although* we are great hunters, when hunting season opens...
> • We *may be* great hunters but when hunting season opens...
> • We are great hunters ; *still,* when hunting season opens...
> • We are great hunters ; when hunting season opens, there is a slaughter of farm animals and humans, *though.*
> • We are great hunters ; when hunting season opens, *however,* there is...

Notice the different constructions. Then read the text again and, on the models above, rephrase the paradoxes pointed out by Steinbeck :

a) We spend our lives in motor cars...
b) Our lives... would not function without electricity.
c) We believe... that we have inherited self-sufficiency and the ability to take care of ourselves, particulary in relation to nature.
d) Americans treasure the knowledge that they live close to nature.
e) Affluence means moving to the suburbs.

Expressing wishes

Examples :

> • The dream describes what we wish we were. If only we were...
> • The dream describes what we wish we had. If only we had...
> • The dream describes the kind of life we wish we could live. If only we could...

Using the above constructions, express some of the dreams which seem common to all Americans.

C FOLLOW UP WORK

1. *"No one can define* (the American way of life) *or point to any one person or group who lives it, but it is very real nevertheless, perhaps more real than that equally remote dream the Russians call Communism."* Do you agree or disagree ? Support your conclusion.

2. What do you think some of the things the French believe about themselves are ? Are they all true ? Are French people paradoxical as well ? Support your conclusion.

The making of
the Declaration of Independence.

THE DECLARATION OF INDEPENDENCE

WHEN IN THE COURSE OF HUMAN EVENTS IT BECOMES NECESSARY FOR ONE PEOPLE TO DISSOLVE THE POLITICAL BANDS WHICH HAVE CONNECTED THEM WITH ANOTHER, AND TO ASSUME AMONG THE POWERS OF THE EARTH, THE SEPARATE AND EQUAL STATION TO WHICH THE LAWS OF NATURE AND OF NATURE'S GOD ENTITLE THEM, A DECENT RESPECT TO THE OPINIONS OF MANKIND REQUIRES THAT THEY SHOULD DECLARE THE CAUSES WHICH IMPEL THEM TO SEPARATION.

WE HOLD THESE TRUTHS TO BE SELF-EVIDENT, THAT ALL MEN ARE CREATED EQUAL, THAT THEY ARE ENDOWED BY THEIR CREATOR WITH CERTAIN UNALIENABLE RIGHTS, THAT AMONG THESE ARE LIFE, LIBERTY AND THE PURSUIT OF HAPPINESS.

THAT TO SECURE THESE RIGHTS, GOVERNMENTS ARE INSTITUTED AMONG MEN, DERIVING THEIR JUST POWERS FROM THE CONSENT OF THE GOVERNED, THAT WHENEVER ANY FORM OF GOVERNMENT BECOMES DESTRUCTIVE OF THESE ENDS, IT IS THE RIGHT OF THE PEOPLE TO ALTER OR TO ABOLISH IT, AND TO INSTITUTE A NEW GOVERNMENT, LAYING ITS FOUNDATION ON SUCH PRINCIPLES, AND ORGANIZING ITS POWERS IN SUCH FORM, AS TO THEM SHALL SEEM MOST LIKELY TO EFFECT THEIR SAFETY AND HAPPINESS.

1. Why did the American colonists believe it necessary to "dissolve (their) political bands" with Britain ? 2. Why did they feel obliged to "declare the causes which (impelled) them to the separation" ? 3. What is a basic truth according to the opening lines of the Declaration of Independence ? Do you believe this ? Justify your answer. 4. According to the Declaration of Independence, what are the unalienable rights of the People ? What is original about this list ? Do you agree with it ? 5. How do you define the "pursuit of Happiness" ? 6. What course of action is justified when a government no longer respects the unalienable rights of the people ? 7. How would you characterize the style ? What does it reveal about the writer's—i.e. Jefferson's—background and training ?

Martin Luther King Sr, at the Lincoln Memorial. Why is it significant that Martin Luther King's father is speaking here ?

I HAVE A DREAM

The following are two of the most famous speeches in American history. The first is the address Abraham Lincoln gave at the dedication of a national cemetery at Gettysburg on the site of one the major battles of the Civil War, four months after thousands had been killed there. The second (slightly shortened) was given a hundred years later by a famous black American, Martin Luther King Jr., underneath the statue of Lincoln before over a million Blacks who had come to Washington to stage a civil rights demonstration.

The Gettysburg Address

Fourscore[1] and seven years ago our fathers brought forth on this continent a new nation, conceived in liberty,
5 and dedicated to the proposition that all men are created equal.

Now we are engaged in a great civil war, testing
10 whether that nation, or any nation so conceived and so

Speech at the Lincoln Memorial

Five score years ago, a great American, in whose symbolic shadow we stand, signed the Emancipation Proclamation. This momentous[3] decree came as a great beacon[4] light of hope to millions of Negro slaves who had been seared[5] in the flames of withering injustice. It came as a joyous daybreak to end the long night of captivity. 5

But one hundred years later, we must face the tragic fact that the Negro is still not free. One hundred years later, the life of the Negro is still sadly crippled by the manacles[6] of segregation and the chains of discrimination... One hundred years later, the Negro is still languishing in the corners of American society and finds himself an 10 exile in his own land. [...]

(The Gettysburg Address)

dedicated, can long endure. We are met on a great battlefield of that war. We
15 have come to dedicate a portion of that field, as a final resting place for those who here gave their lives that that nation might live. It is
20 altogether fitting and proper that we should do this.

But, in a larger sense, we cannot dedicate—we cannot consecrate—we cannot hal-
25 low[2]—this ground. The brave men, living and dead, who struggled here, have consecrated it, far above our poor power to add or detract.
30 The world will little note, nor long remember, what we say here, but it can never forget what they did here. It is for us the living, rather, to be
35 dedicated here to the unfinished work which they who fought here have thus far so nobly advanced. It is rather for us to be here
40 dedicated to the great task remaining before us—that from these honored dead we take increased devotion to that cause for which they gave
45 the last full measure of devotion—that we here highly resolve that these dead shall not have died in vain—that this nation, under God, shall
50 have a new birth of free- dom—and that government of the people, by the people, for the people, shall not perish from the earth.

**Abraham Lincoln,
November 19, 1863**

(Speech at the Lincoln Memorial)

There will be neither rest nor tranquillity in America until the Negro is granted his citizenship rights. The whirlwinds of revolt will continue to shake the foundations of our nation until the bright day of justice emerges. 15

I say to you today, my friends, that in spite of the difficulties and frustrations of the moment I still have a dream. It is a dream deeply rooted in the American dream.

I have a dream that one day this nation will rise up and live out the true meaning of its creed : "We hold these truths to be self-evident ; 20 that all men are created equal."

I have a dream that one day on the red hills of Georgia the sons of former slaves and the sons of former slaveowners will be able to sit down together at the table of brotherhood.

I have a dream that one day even the state of Mississippi, a desert 25 state sweltering[7] with the heat of injustice and oppression, will be transformed into an oasis of freedom and justice.

I have a dream that my four little children will one day live in a nation where they will not be judged by the color of their skin but by the content of their character. 30

I have a dream today.

I have a dream that one day the state of Alabama whose governor's[8] lips are presently dripping with the words of interposition and nullification, will be transformed into a situation where little black boys and black girls will be able to join hands with little white boys 35 and white girls and walk together as sisters and brothers.

I have a dream today.

I have a dream that one day every valley shall be exalted, every hill and mountain shall be made low, the rough places will be made plains, and the crooked places will be made straight, and the glory of 40 the Lord shall be revealed, and all flesh shall see it together.[...]

And if America is to be a great nation this must become true. So let freedom ring from the prodigious hilltops of New Hampshire. Let freedom ring from the mighty mountains of New York. Let freedom ring from the heightening Alleghenies of Pennsylvania ! 45

Let freedom ring from the snowcapped Rockies of Colorado ![...]

Let freedom ring from every hill and mole hill of Mississippi. From every mountainside, let freedom ring.

When we let freedom ring, when we let it ring from every village and every hamlet, from every state and every city, we will be able to 50 speed up that day when all of God's children, black men and white men, Jews and Gentiles, Protestants and Catholics, will be able to join hands and sing in the words of the old Negro spiritual. "Free at last ! Free at last ! Thank God Almighty, we are free at last !"

Martin Luther King, Jr., August 28, 1963

---

exile /'eksaɪl/   Mississippi /,mɪsə'sɪpɪ/   Alabama /,ælə'bæmə/

---

1. fourscore : 4 × 20 years. **2.** hallow : sacred. **3.** momentous : important. **4.** beacon : *phare (fig.).* **5.** seared : burnt. **6.** manacles : *menottes.* **7.** sweltering : hot and humid. **8.** Governor of Alabama : George Wallace at the time.

Martin Luther King Jr. delivering a speech.

A UNDERSTANDING THE TEXT

1. Who is Martin Luther King addressing and in what circumstances ? 2. What happened "fourscore and seven years ago" ? 3. Why had Lincoln come to Gettysburg ? 4. According to Lincoln, what task remained to be accomplished by the survivors of the Battle of Gettysburg ? 5. What was the purpose of the Emancipation Proclamation ? 6. Why do you think Martin Luther King's speech begins in a way similar to Lincoln's Gettysburg Address ? 7. What does Martin Luther King refer to with *this momentous decree* (lines 2/3) ? 8. In what ways was the Negro still not free in the U.S.A. at the time of Martin Luther King's speech ? 9. What did Martin Luther King hope would happen in Georgia some day ? 10. What was Martin Luther King's "dream" regarding his children ? 11. What kind of change did Martin Luther King hope would come about in Mississippi ? In Alabama ? 12. According to Martin Luther King, what had to become true if the U.S.A was to become a great nation ? 13. How do you interpret the last paragraph of Martin Luther King's speech ? 14. Why do you think Martin Luther King uses so many biblical images and allusions ? 15. In what way do you think Lincoln and Martin Luther King express the American Dream ?

A young spectator listening to Martin Luther King in August 1963.

B LANGUAGE AT WORK

Conditions not yet realized

Examples :

> • There will be *no* rest *until* the Negro is granted...
> • There will be *no* rest *as long as* the Negro is *not* granted...
> • There will be rest *only when* the Negro is granted...

Read the text and, using the above models, say what are some of the conditions required for Martin Luther King's dream to come true.

Expressing wishes and hopes

Examples :

> • He wishes to see his children really free one day.
> • He hopes to see his children really free one day.
> • He expects to see his children really free one day.

Using the above patterns, and other means of expressing wishes (see p. 19, 45, 65 and 186), rephrase some of the wishes expressed by Martin Luther King.

The two speeches are in an oratorical style. If Martin Luther King had been giving an interview to a journalist after his speech, he probably would have expressed himself differently ? Compare these sentences :

> • **Five score years ago, a great American in whose symbolic shadow we stand, signed the Emancipation Proclamation.**
> • **Abraham Lincoln signed the Emancipation Proclamation a hundred years ago.**

What would he have said instead of

a) One hundred years later, the life of the Negro is still sadly crippled by the manacles of segregation and the chains of discrimination.
b) The whirlwinds of revolt will continue to shake the foundations of our nation until the bright day of justice emerges.
c) ... one day this nation will rise up and live out the true meaning of its creed.
d) ... the sons of former slaves and the sons of former slaveowners will be able to sit down together at the table of brotherhood.
e) ... even the state of Mississippi, a desert state sweltering with the heat of injustice and oppression, will be transformed into an oasis of freedom and justice.
f) ... the state of Alabama, whose governor's lips are presently dripping with the words of interposition and nullification.
g) ... little black boys and black girls will be able to join hands with little white boys and little white girls and walk together as sisters and brothers.
h) I have a dream that one day every valley shall be exalted, every hill and mountain shall be made low ; the rough places will be made plains, and the crooked places will be made straight, and the glory of the Lord shall be revealed, and all flesh shall see it together.

C FOLLOW UP WORK

1. Martin Luther King represented the forces of non-violence in the black struggle. What does non-violence mean to you ?
2. In what ways do you think Abraham Lincoln and Martin Luther King express the American Dream ?
3. Compare Abraham Lincoln's and Martin Luther King's respective styles.

Here in America are all the wealth of soil, of timber, of mines and of the sea put into the possession of a people who wield all those wonderful machines, have the secret of steam, of electricity ; and have the power and habit of invention in their brain. American energy is overriding every venerable maxim of political science. America is such a garden of plenty, such a magazine of power that at her shores all the common rules of political economy utterly fail. Here is bread and wealth and power and education for every man who has the heart to use his opportunity. **From *Resources* by R. Emerson**

LOVING AMERICA

Loving America is a very special task. No other country makes quite the same demands in being loved, nor presents quite the same difficulties.

IN most other nations, patriotism is essentially the love of family, of tribe, of land, magnified. There may well be an ideological mixture. The France of the Revolution and Napoleon, for instance, proclaimed the rights of man. Liberty, equality, fraternity were useful enough to overthrow an order and kill a king. But France's love of her earth and her produce, her landscape, her language and her money—those are the things French patriotism is really about. So it is with other European nations. The songs and the poetry of patriotism are filled with scenery : with rivers and mountains, with cities longed for, with valleys lost, with castles conquered. American patriotism has much less of this specific sense of place. [...]

It is possible to be deeply moved by the endless American plains, and the settlements defiantly set down in the midst of this vastness, by the coast of Maine or the Rockies or the desert. But that is not loving America. Loving America means loving what it stands for as a political and social vision. Although the great American epic is the conquest and taming of a continent, American patriotism is not concentrated on geography but on a historic event and an idea. The event is the creation of the United States as a fresh start [...]. The idea is freedom. Both notions have been distorted or perverted at times—that happens with all patriotism. But even when it is misused, American patriotism remains ideological more than racial or ethnic.

but more than anything else Americans believed they were fighting for ideas, for a system. It may have been naive to think that other countries were waiting to be given the blessings of democracy, free enterprise and individualism, but that is what Americans did believe.

The U.S. was not born in a tribal conflict, like so many other nations, but in a conflict over principles. Those principles were thought to be universal, which was part of the reason for the unprecedented policy of throwing the new country open to all comers. [...] The millions from other lands and other culture had different loves for many different plots of earth, languages, traditions. The unifying love had to be for America as an idea.

In part, this helps to explain the unusual stability of American institutions. In Europe it is possible to shift loyalties from king to republic, from democracy to dictatorship, and still love one's country. In the U.S. loyalty must be to the institutions themselves. [...]

We still perceive America as something unprecedented in history, as an experiment, and as such something that must "work" in order to prove itself over and over again. Hence America demands that love be given not once and for all, but that it be constantly renewed and reaffirmed. [...] "My country, right or wrong" is not a very American slogan. We Americans have a hard time accepting a situation in which our country is wrong, not because we are more arrogant than other people, but because our country's rightness is our soil, our home. [...]

WHEN the French carved up Germany or the Germans carved up France, it was done for the greater glory of each nation, with firm belief in the innate superiority of their own people. Whenever Americans went to war, they may have been seized by jingoism[1] to some extent,

ONE loves America both for its virtues and its faults, which are deeply intertwined. Indeed, one loves America for the virtues of its faults. One loves the almost obsessive American need to believe, the resistance to cynicism even if that sometimes means oversimplification and moralizing. One loves the unique American restlessness, the refusal to settle for what is, even if that sometimes means a lack of contemplation and peace. One loves the fact that America sees itself as the shaper of its own destiny, both private and public. [...] This rejection of fate, this insistence that everything is possible, is surely the dominant American characteristic, and at the heart of its genius. [...]

In rejecting fate, the U.S. is the ultimate incarnation of Western, Faustian man. [...] Disease, poverty and other ancient afflictions, simply are not accepted as part of the human condition. Perhaps rightly so. And yet the conviction that they can be banished completely is a tremendous burden because each setback, each delay, is seen as a personal or national failure. That is partly why we Americans are so impatient with the study of history—because history is a reminder of fate. We would rather learn to do than learn to know.

One must love this American view of learning as the tool by which man transforms himself. We Americans believe that everything can be learned, including, to a very large extent, to be what you are not. [...] There is something admirable about this, yet nagging questions remain. Where is the line between making the most of one's potential and reaching for the unattainable ? [...]

HE American spirit is deeply divided about money. In one sense the faith in money is pure : it need not, as it does in so many older societies, apologize for its existence. Money is what it is—good in its own right, a sign of success, if perhaps no longer of divine grace. Yet this conflict is at war with an older tradition [...]. The great callings are not trade or commerce but the state or the military or the church or scholarship. The great legendary virtues are not thrift[2]—and its explosive extension, profit—but courage, kindness, faith. [...]

Ultimately all American forces, including money, converge in the passion for freedom. [...]

We tend to think of freedom as a positive and unalloyed good. We speak of "enjoying" freedom. [...] It can be argued that we bear freedom for much of the rest of the world—not only in the sense of material and military support for the cause of freedom as the West understands it, but in the sense of experimenting with freedom in a kind of vast social laboratory. [...]

OR freedom to be workable as a political and social system, strong inner controls, a powerful moral compass[3] and sense of values, are needed. In practice, the contradiction is vast. The compass is increasingly hard to read, the values hard to find in a frantically open, mobile, fractioned society. Thus, a troubling, paradoxical question : Does freedom destroy the inner disciplines that alone make freedom possible ? [...]

One loves America for its accomplishments as well as for its unfinished business. [...] One ultimately loves America not for what it is, or what it does, but for what it promises. [...]

Henri Grunwald in *Time,*
July, 5, 1976

magnified /'mægnɪfaɪd/   mixture /'mɪkstʃər/   defiantly /dɪ'faɪəntli/
conquest /'kɑŋkwest/   ethnic /'eθnɪk/   democracy /dɪmɑkrəsi/
jingoism /'dʒɪŋɡəʊɪzəm/   individualism /,ɪndɪ'vɪdʒʊəlɪzəm/
obsessive /əb'sesɪv/   thrift /θrɪft/   promises /'prɑmɪsɪz/

---

1. jingoism : *chauvinisme.*   2. thrift : being careful with money.   3. compass : *boussole.*

A UNDERSTANDING THE TEXT

1. Why does the writer think loving America is a "very special task" ? 2. How does the writer define patriotism in most nations ? 3. In what way does the writer believe American patriotism is different ? What does he say American patriotism is ? 4. Do you agree with his definition of French patriotism ? Justify your answer. 5. According to the writer, what is one aspect of loving America ? Do you agree that people should love what a country stands for ? Why, or why not ? 6. Why do you think the writer defines the creation of the United States as a "fresh start" ? 7. What does the writer feel is the American attitude towards war ? 8. According to the writer, in what way were Americans naive ? Do you think he is right ? Justify your answer. 9. What does the writer suggest is the difference between the origin of the United States and that of most other nations ? 10. How does the writer compare loyalty in Europe and America ? 11. According to the writer why is it so difficult to love America ? 12. Why does one love America ? 13. How does the writer define restlessness ? Are French people restless as well ? Justify your answer. 14. Do you agree with the writer that America is "the shaper of its own destiny" ? 15. What does the writer believe to be the result of America's rejection of fate ? 16. According to the writer what is the American view of learning ? Do you agree ? Justify your answer. 17. How does the writer justify his view that "the American spirit is deeply divided about money" ? 18. What does the writer think the American virtues are ? Do you agree that these are virtues ? Justify your answer. 19. Why do you think the writer calls America "a vast social laboratory" ? 20. What does the writer think is necessary for freedom to work ? Do you agree ? Justify your answer. 21. Why is this question paradoxical : *"Does freedom destroy the inner discipline that alone makes freedom possible"* ? 22. Do you agree with the writer's conclusion ? Justify your answer.

B LANGUAGE AT WORK

Which and what

Study the following examples :

- **What America stands for is...**
- **What may have been naive was to think that...**
- **Money is important, which is one of the things that irritate Europeans.**
- **American patriotism has very little sense of place, which is surprising to us.**

Using the same constructions as models, what, according to the text, could you say of

a) American patriotism ?
b) Patriotism in Europe ?
c) The reason why America has gone to war ?
d) America's institutions ?
e) Americans' view of history ?
f) American passions ?
g) Legendary virtues. ?

C FOLLOW UP WORK

1. *"One loves America both for its virtues and its faults, which are deeply interwined."* Can the same be said about France ? What do you think some of France's virtues and faults are ?

2. Do you agree with the statement that money is a sign of success ? What does having money mean to you ?

AMERICA — love it or leave it !

SURVEYING THE SCENE

1. Read the passages again. How has each writer defined the American Dream ?
2. To what extent do you think that Dr Lee Hertz might agree or disagree with the other passages ?
3. What do you think Martin Luther King might have said about the second paragraph of the Declaration of Independence ?
4. Compare the two passages *Paradox and Dream* and *Loving America*. Suggest similarities and differences.
5. What is *your* interpretation of the American Dream ?

Some books you might like to read : *The Great Gatsby (Gatsby le Magnifique)* by F. S. Fitzgerald.
The Old Man and the Sea (Le Vieil Homme et la Mer) by E. Hemingway.
Catcher in the Rye (L'Attrape-Cœur) by J.D. Salinger.

A film you might like to see : *How the West Was Won (La Conquête de l'Ouest)* by J. Ford, G. Marshall and H. Hathaway.

MERRITT PARKWAY

*As if it were
forever that they move, that we
keep moving —*

               *Under a wan sky where
as the lights went on a star
       pierced the haze and now
follows steadily
            a constant
above our six lanes
the dreamlike continuum...*

*And the people — ourselves!
the humans from inside the
cars, apparent
only at gasoline stops
          unsure,
eyeing each other*

               *drink coffee hastily at the
slot machines and hurry
back to the cars
vanish
into them forever, to
keep moving —*

II. ...REACHING FOR IT

Houses now and then beyond the
sealed road, the trees/trees, bushes
passing by, passing
      the cars that
           keep moving ahead of
    us, past us, pressing behind us
                      and
            over left, those that come
        toward us shining too brightly
moving relentlessly

      in six lanes, gliding
north south, speeding with
a slurred sound —   Denise Levertov: *The Jacob's Ladder*

WHERE THEY'RE GOING

ALASKA
+ 32

HAWAII
+ 25.3

WASH.
+ 21

ORE.
+ 25.8

IDAHO
+ 32.5

MONT.
+ 13.4

N.DAK.
+ 5.8

MINN.
+ 7.1

WIS.
+ 6.5

M.
+ 4.2

N.H. + 24.8

VT.
+ 15

ME.
+ 13.2

MASS.
+ 0.8

R.I.
- 0.2

CONN.
+ 2.4

N.Y.
+ 3.6

WYO.
+ 41.9

S.DAK.
+ 3.6

IOWA
+ 3

NEB.
+ 5.7

ILL.
+ 2.8

IND.
+ 5.7

OHIO
+ 1.3

PA.
+ 0.5

N.J. + 2.7

NEV.
+ 63.4

UTAH
+ 38

COLO.
+ 30.8

KANS.
+ 5

MO.
+ 5.1

KY.
+ 29.9

W.VA.
+ 11.8

VA.
+ 14.9

DEL. + 8.8

MD. + 7.4.

D.C. -15.7

CALIF.
+ 18.5

ARIZ.
+ 53.1

N.MEX.
+ 27.7

OKL.
+ 18.2

ARK.
+ 18.8

TENN. + 16.9

N.C.
+ 15.5

S.C.
+ 20.4

MISS.
+ 13.7

ALA.
+ 13

GA.
+ 19

TEXAS
+ 27

LA.
+ 15.3

FLA.
+ 43.4

NORTH EAST

WEST

NORTH CENTRAL

SUNBELT

SOUTH

**Population gains
and losses 1970-1980**
NATIONAL AVERAGE : +11.4

MOVING TO THE SUNBELT

*An interview with Jim Studebaker, 39, born in Ohio and trained in New York to be a photographer.
He recently moved to Santa Fe, New Mexico.*

INTERVIEWER : *What made you decide to leave New York ?*
JIM : Well, for one thing, I couldn't stand the rat race[1].

I. : *Do you mean the competition ?*
J. : It was not so much that as the pace of things. In New York with the subway and commuter train
5   schedules[2], I was constantly looking at my watch.

I. : *How are things different now ?*
J. : For one thing, my productivity is sky high. In New York I spent a lot of my life being busy, but
not really doing much, you know. Now I am busy and producing good things. Before I left New York
I had reached the end of my emotional and professional strength. Now, everything about my life
10 seems to have changed. First of all it's more relaxing and informal here. I feel in touch with people
around me. When I got to Santa Fe I found people with casual[3] manners, easy and loose in their
movements instead of the pressurized people and skyscrapers bearing down on me.

I. : *Does that mean that you no longer feel crowded in ?*
J. : Well, yes, that's part of it. People give you a lot of elbow room. And besides the pacing of things
15 is different. Things don't seem so rushed. It's more relaxing and informal here. There's less pressure
on people so they can concentrate more on what they want to really do in life. Santa Fe has given me
more freedom than any place I've ever been.

I. : *But what about the cultural and intellectual stimulation of a place like New York. Don't you miss
that ?*
20 J. : Not really. I visited New York recently but left after two days. That was all I could stand. I started
getting that closed-in feeling again. Here in the Sunbelt there is room to grow. The climate is pleasant.

The Sunbelt... permanent summertime and the livin' is easy...

I. : *Do you think your children are better off here ?*
J. : And how ! This is a great place to raise children. They can get a real sense of freedom, being outdoors, establishing healthy relationships with their environment and us too.

25 **I. :** *So you are happy with your move, you don't miss the movement and attractions of a big city ?*
J. : Not at all. This is really where the action is. People have been saying for years that the Southwest is the new frontier in America, where people can still reach the American Dream. It's certainly been true for me.

---

1. rat race : struggle for success. **2.** schedules *(Am.)* : timetables *(Eng.).* **3.** casual : informal.

A   TRUE OR FALSE ?

1. In New York City, Jim was always thinking about trains and time. 2. He was always busy and productive when he lived in the East. 3. People in the Southwest are relaxed and informal. 4. Jim misses the cultural and intellectual stimulation of New York City. 5. In the Sunbelt it is easy to get a closed-in feeling. 6. The Southwest is still a place where one can reach the American Dream.

B   ANSWER THESE QUESTIONS :

1. Why did Jim leave New York City ? 2. What was his state of mind before he left ? 3. Why does he like Santa Fe ? 4. What didn't he like about New York ? 5. What is the pace of life like in Santa Fe ? 6. How long did he stay when he last visited New York ? 7. Why does Jim feel that living in Santa Fe is good for children ? 8. Why is he happy living in Santa Fe ?

C   EXPLAIN IN YOUR OWN WORDS

1. I couldn't stand the rat race.
2. My productivity is sky high.
3. I feel in touch with people around me.
4. People give you a lot of elbow room.
5. You no longer feel crowded in.
6. Children can have a healthy relationship with their environment.
7. This is where the action is.

D   DISCUSSION

In New York I spent a lot of my life being busy, but not really doing much, you know.'' Do you feel this is true of your life or of the people around you ? Why or why not ?

THE GOLD RUSH

One prime wonder of the California gold rush is that so many people survived it. They poured out of Atlantic seaboard[1] cities, Ohio villages and Southern plantations in abysmal ignorance of the geographic and social obstacles that loomed ahead[2]. Had the deluge dropped onto an unprepared California, the results 5 would have been disastrous. Thanks to the continent's width, however, men who were familiar with the West had a year's grace during which they could attack the knottier problems connected with geology, mining technology, transportation, and political order that were raised by the frenzy.

/əʊˈhaɪəʊ/
/ˈsʌðərn/

Even among experienced Westerners, the madness was acute. "The whole 10 country", wrote one San Francisco newspaper editor, "[...] resounds with the sordid cry of gold ! GOLD ! GOLD ! while the field is left half planted, the house half built, and everything neglected but the manufacture of shovels and pick axes." The alcalde of Monterey described the situation there : "All were off for the mines, some on horses, some on carts, and some on crutches[3], and one went in a litter."

/ælˈkældi/

15 Breathless talk like that suggests, inaccurately, that torrents of people washed immediately through the mountains. Actually, the rush developed slowly. In mid 1848, California's non-Indian population, women and children included, amounted to no more than fourteen thousand. Perhaps half of these were native *Californios,* many of them living on isolated ranches in the south and less 20 susceptible to the fever than the Americans and Englishmen in the towns farther north. Probably there were no more than a thousand people who were directly involved with the initial rush.

New surges soon followed, however, as fast as ships spread the news along the Pacific shores. The first groups appeared during the summer from 25 Hawaii—nineteen vessels in three weeks. Their clamour for supplies sent prices skyrocketing. Flour that sold for twenty dollars a barrel at Stockton early in the summer, soared[4] in the mountains, during moments of pinch, to eight hundred dollars. Eggs at times brought three dollars each. [...]

/həˈwaɪ/
/flaʊəʳ/

Store in Jamestown, Tuolumne, California, today.

Advertisement for a sailing ship from New York to California. How do you think such advertisements helped encourage the Gold Rush ?

GLIDDEN & WILLIAMS' LINE

FOR SAN FRANCISCO

To Sail on or before THURSDAY, March 11th.

THE CELEBRATED EXTREME CLIPPER SHIP

WITCHCRAFT

JOHN W. BOOTH, Commander.

This is one of the fastest ships afloat—has made the passage in 94 days—is in fine condition, and will sail as above. Shippers will oblige by forwarding their engagements promptly. For Freight or Passage, apply to

GLIDDEN & WILLIAMS, 39 Lewis Wharf.
Agents at San Francisco, Messrs. FLINT, PEABODY & CO.

30 The thousand Californians who hurried toward the mountains during that first spring of 1848 lived in pure romance. They climbed from hot valleys into rolling hills dotted with live oaks and vivid with orange poppies[5]. The canyons deepened, singing 35 with water. No rain came until late fall ; they camped in comfort under the flimsiest[6] shelters of brush[7], or under nothing at all. The great drawback was a dearth of food. Hunting took time, and as a result, the 40 length of a man's stay in the diggings was determined by what he could carry with him.

Even the climate cooperated. The annual summer drought shrank the streams, exposing deposits of gold-bearing gravel called bars. These had formed during high water wherever the current was slack : opposite bends in the river channel, behind 45 boulders, and in potholes[8] in the stream bed. Gold had settled with the gravel. Heavier than the sand, it worked its way into cracks and cavities in or near bedrock. Receding water opened these spots to the crude tools of the early miners. Other deposits were found in ancient channels that had been left dry following changes in the stream's course.

50 Rewards were sometimes extraordinary. One lump of gold unearthed at Sonora weighed twenty-eight pounds ; eight other nuggets from the same district exceeded /weɪd/
twenty pounds. A small group of friends from Monterey, aided by hired Indians, took two hundred and seventy pounds from the Feather River in seven weeks. The first five prospectors to reach the Yuba River gleaned seventy-five thousand dollars 55 in three months. In ten days one soldier off on a furlough[9] picked up fifteen /ˈfɜrləʊ/
hundred dollars. These strikes[10] and similar ones in '49 and even '50 were exceptions ; yet even those unoriginal souls who clung near the familiar bars at Coloma, the site of Marshall's[11] discovery, are said to have averaged twenty-five to thirty dollars a day, at a period when skilled labour elsewhere in California 60 commanded about three dollars daily. Under such conditions, a man did not mind standing in icy water all day while a hot sun beat on his head, his shoes turned to pulp, and his stomach, assaulted with insufficient amounts of monotonous food, sent forth calls of distress.

David Lavender, *The Penguin Book of the American West*, 1965

---

1. Atlantic seaboard : the northeastern states.   **2.** that loomed ahead : that would rise and threaten them.
3. crutches : *béquilles.*   **4.** soared : went up quickly.   **5.** poppies : *coquelicot.*   **6.** flimsy : poorly built.   **7.**
brush : *maquis.*   **8.** potholes : *nids de poule.*   **9.** furlough : permission for absence (vacation).   **10.** strikes :
discoveries.   **11.** Marshall : the discoverer of the first nugget.

A UNDERSTANDING THE TEXT

1. Why was it so amazing that so many people "survived" the California gold rush ? 2. What was one good thing about the width of the continent ? 3. What was the major preoccupation of people at the time ? 4. How many people initially went to California ? Why did they go there ? 5. What was one of the immediate results of the gold rush ? 6. Why were the first prospectors fortunate ? 7. What were some of the "extraordinary rewards" ? 8. How does the author describe the working conditions ? 9. What kind of atmosphere do you think there was in California at the time of the gold rush ? 10. How does this passage relate to the whole idea of the American Dream ?

B LANGUAGE AT WORK

If clauses. Conditions not realized in the past

Study these examples :

- *If* the deluge *had dropped* onto an unprepared California, the results *would have been* disastrous.
- *Had* the deluge *dropped* onto an unprepared California, the results *would have been* disastrous.

Do the same using the correct tenses of the verbs in brackets.

a) If it (rain) that first summer, many people (be) without shelter.
b) (Realize) they how hard it was, people (not go) to California to look for gold.
c) If you (be) in California in 1848, it is possible that you too (look for) gold.
d) What you (do), if you (be) there ?
e) (Have) the early miners better tools, they (take out) more gold.
f) If more people (arrive) earlier, there is no telling what (happen).
g) (Be) there a railway line, people (pour) into California.

Do this exercise again using the other form.

All the + comparative + as/since/because

Study the following examples :

- It was *all the more* surprising that so many people survived *as* the conditions of living were really bad.
- It was *all the harder* for them to find gold *because* they had not the required equipment.
- It was *all the more* attractive *because* some rewards were extraordinary.

Using the above constructions as models, express some of the surprising elements in the California gold rush.

C FOLLOW UP WORK

1. How much money represents a fortune to you ?
2. Who do you think made the most money in the California gold rush ? Justify your answer.
3. It is no longer possible to *"strike it rich"*. Support your arguments.

CLÉMENTINE

Moderato

1. In a cav-ern, in a can-yon, Ex-ca-vat-ing for a mine, Dwelt a min-er, for-ty nin-er, And his daughter Cle-men-tine. Oh my darl-ing, oh my darl-ing, oh my darl-ing Cle-men-tine! Thou art lost and gone for ev-er, dreadful sor-ry Cle-men-tine. Light she

1

In a cavern, in a canyon,
Excavating for a mine,
Dwelt a miner, forty niner,
And his daughter Clementine.
   Oh my darling, etc.

2

Light she was and like a fairy,
And her shoes were number nine,
Herring boxes without topses,
Sandals were for Clementine.
   Oh my darling, etc.

Oh my darling, oh my darling,
Oh my darling Clementine!
Thou art lost and gone for ever,
Dreadful sorry Clementine.

3

Drove she ducklings to the water,
Every morning just at nine,
Hit her foot against a splinter,
Fell into the foaming brine.
   Oh my darling, etc.

4

Saw her lips above the water
Blowing bubbles mighty fine,
But alas! I was no swimmer,
So I lost my Clementine.
   Oh my darling, etc.

TALES MY MOTHER TOLD ME

The daughter of pioneers who followed the Oregon Trail[1], Mary Patton Taylor settled with her husband in Fossil, Oregon.

Father and mother's married life began with a romance[2] crossing the plains. Right away mother and father cottoned to one another[3], but grandfather had other plans. There was another young fellow in their train—they came with a big wagon train of sixty wagons in '48—that grandfather liked better than Tom Patton, and
5 that was a young man named Trullinger. When Tom Patton asked for mother, he was told to get out. He got out all right, but mother was just as stiff as grandfather. She said, "If I marry anybody, it's Tom Patton," and when she said that, with her backbone up, I guess grandfather decided he might as well give in. Anyway, they were married.

10 Mother always said they had an awful good time crossing the plains. When they came in '48 there wasn't any Indian trouble or anything, and at night they used to have a lot of fun. All they danced then was square dances[4], and after the camp was settled down for the night the young folks would turn to and dance[5]. Grandfather was religious and awful strict. He didn't believe in dancing, so mother'd go to bed
15 as demure[6] as you please, and as soon as she was sure grandfather was asleep, she'd slip out and dance as big as any of them.

When my folks got to Oregon they settled in the Waldo Hills. They settled on their claim[7] just three days after they arrived. My grandparents got here in September, and in November father and mother were married. The only thing
20 mother had to start housekeeping with was a plate. She paid fifty cents for it, and she earned the fifty cents sewing three days for a woman in the Waldo Hills. Father wasn't much better off than mother. He wasn't twenty-one years old, and so he couldn't take a claim. And he didn't have any money, because all he made crossing the plains was his food and bed and fifteen dollars that he got for driving
25 grandfather's oxen. But he wanted to get married, and, when he got there, he went to work for a man named Nicholas Shrum right away. He split rails[8] for Shrum, and all he got was 37 1/2 a hundred. Can you beat that ? Just as soon as father had $2.25 he thought, maybe that's enough to pay the preacher. When father and mother were married, father paid over $2.25. He must have looked kind of poor
30 about it, for right away Elder[9] Simpson asked him how much money he had left, and father said that was all, and Elder Simpson handed it back to him, telling him he needed it most. But father was gritty[10]. He said, "If my girl's worth marrying, I'm willing to spend all I have to get her". And he made Elder Simpson keep the $2.25.

35 My father's parents had filed on[11] a donation claim of 640 acres[12] and father hoped to get the one adjoining ; but before he was old enough a man named Center got it. That didn't discourage father any. He went to Mr Center and asked him to

---

THE OREGON TRAIL : one of the famous trails (cf. the Mohawk Trail, the Santa Fe Trail) followed by pioneers in their move westward. It went across the Great Plains, through the Rocky Mountains and down the Columbia River toward the Pacific. It was 2,000 miles long.

---

take the claim a mile further on, so he could have the one next to his Pa and Ma. Center must have been pretty good-natured, for he moved along to the next claim. Father gave him a plug of tobacco[13], and everything was all right.

Ann Banks, *First Person America*, 1981

1. trail : *piste*. 2. romance : love story. 3. cottoned to each other : fell in love with each other. 4. square dances : *quadrilles*. 5. turn to and dance : start dancing. 6. demure : reserved, a little prudish. 7. claim : *concession* (here, donation claim : assignment of public land on liberal terms to settlers under act of Congress). 8. rails : long pieces of wood. 9. Elder : Preacher (among Presbyterians and Methodists). 10. gritty : resolute. 11. had filed (on) : *avaient déposé une demande*. 12. acre : *0,4 ha (arpent)*. 13. a plug of tobacco : *une chique*.

A UNDERSTANDING THE TEXT

1. Approximatively, how old were Tom and Mary Patton when they married ? 2. Are Mary Patton mothers' memories of crossing the plains with a wagon train positive or negative ? 3. What were some of the incidents and accidents covered wagons encountered in the stories of the Old West ? 4. What were some instances which show that although she was brought up fairly strictly, Mary's mother could rebel against her father's authority ? 5. What can we imagine about the young woman's personality ? 6. What about her young man's. 7. What was the young couple's financial situation ? 8. Did this depress them ? Justify your answer. 9. According to Mary Patton's memories, what were the relations between the pioneers ? Would you say this is a romanticized or a realistic account ? 10. Considering the story is autobiographical, what is specially interesting about it ?

B LANGUAGE AT WORK

Expressing repetition in the past

Example :

• **Mother would go to bed as demure as you please.**

Using the same construction, rephrase the following sentences :

a) The pioneers crossed the plains in wagon trains of fifty or sixty wagons.
b) At night one of them took out a fiddle, another a mouth organ and they danced square dances.
c) The young folks met every night.
d) Mother slipped out of her parents' wagon and danced.
e) She joined the other young folks.
f) She held hands with her young man.
g) She slipped back into the wagon when the music stopped.
h) Meanwhile her father slept soundly.

C FOLLOW UP WORK

1. How far do Mary Patton Taylor's recollections as told by her daughter suggest both the "innocence" and vitality of Frontier days ?
2. What makes this evocation of pioneers' life both charming and interesting ?

From gadgets to people

America's genius with high technology may have put men on the moon, but there is growing skepticism about its ability to solve human problems closer to home.

In fact, a subtle but significant shift[1] from purely technological solutions is already under way as scientists argue openly for new directions in research.

A growing number of scientists insist that answers to the world's problems will not come from a flashier array[2] of electronics and machines. Instead, as they see it, solutions must evolve from a better understanding of the humans that drive the system and from a fuller appreciation of the limits and potential of the earth's resources.

What this means is an increased emphasis on the life and earth sciences, on sociology, psychology, economics and even philosophy. [...]

More and more of the best minds in science, particularly young researchers, are being drawn into these developing fields. [...]

Industry officials are concerned by a declining rate of innovation in technology. Patent applications[3] by Americans have been dropping in the U.S. since 1971. Yet many scientists seem to be saying : The need for better televisions, bigger power plants and faster airplanes—markers of rapid-fire technological creativity—is becoming marginal at best. The market in the industrialized nations for this kind of technology, it is claimed, is reaching a saturation point. [...]

All this is not to say that technological creativity will not play a critical role in solving energy and food shortages, or that answers to environmental difficulties will not come from further advances in the same technologies that may have helped cause the problems.

Where the real challenge lies, in the view of the new breed of scientists, is in finding ways to produce goods to meet the world's needs, using less of the raw materials that are becoming scarce. [...]

Roger Revelle, a Harvard professor and authority on global food and population problems, maintains that greater efforts to understand all living systems, particularly human beings, must be given a higher priority in the research community.

Mr Revelle, who traveled recently in India and Nepal, points out that America's high technology often has little use when transferred to less-developed nations. Elaborate[4] machinery that works well for an Iowa farmer can be useless for most people who till the soil in India.

What the Indian farmer needs is some innovative "low" technology—for example, a better one-piece plow that can be pulled by a water buffalo.

In the United States many high-technology companies are increasingly reluctant[5] to pursue new twists in research until they have assurances that the experimental work will result in near-term profits.

More and more of industry's research money is going toward improving existing products and toward defending those already on the market against charges that they use too much energy, pollute or pose some other safety hazard[6] to the worker and consumer.

From *U.S. News & World Report*, Nov. 8, 1976

scepticism /'skept sɪzəm/ subtle /sʌtl/ research /rɪ'sɜrtʃ/
scientists /saɪənt st/ resources/ri'zors z/ psychology /saɪ'kalədʒi/
sociology /,səʊsi'alədʒi/ environmental /ɪn,vaɪərən'mentl/ Revelle /rɪ'vel
Harvard /'harvad/ Nepal /ne'pal/

1. shift: move. **2.** array: display. **3.** patent applications: *dépôt de brevets.* **4.** elaborate: complicated.
luctant: unwilling. **6.** safety hazard: danger.

SPACE HARDWARE COMES TO EARTH

The space program was developed to probe the mysteries of the solar system, but it has also contributed to numerous technological improvements here at home.

Take a look at this list of only a few of the secondary applications of aerospace technology :

• Skylab carbon monoxide monitor is currently being used to measure monoxide pollution in urban areas.

• Viking dirt analyzer can help identify poisons in humans by analyzing the patient's blood.

• Heated space suit technology has led to heated protective clothing (boots, gloves, caps) used by construction workers and consumers.

• Control switch developed so immobilized astronauts could operate controls by eye motion now makes it possible for paralyzed patients to control television, book page turner, bed position, lights and other objects.

• Aircraft icing research information was used to reduce ice build up in commercial planes.

• Miniature Viking seisometer and its computer could help predict quakes on earth.

• Rubber tire with low temperature pliability developed for Apollo-14 mission has led to a studless winter automobile tire that provides traction equal to or better than studded tires on slick surfaces. This is especially important in states that are banning studded tires due to poor traction on dry surfaces and destruction of roads.

• Horizontal shower developed for use in long-term bedrest studies related to lengthy space missions can now be used for bathing bedridden patients. Unit consists of horizontal water-tight compartment with multiple shower heads.

The most important and lasting impact of the entire space effort, however, is in the field of education. NASA has played a key role in developing source materials for teaching space-oriented mathematics.

A UNDERSTANDING THE TEXT

1. Why are scientists arguing for new directions in research ? 2. What do many scientists believe is more important than ''a flashier array of electronics and machines'' ? What do you think ? 3. What are young researchers becoming more and more interested in ? Why do you think this is happening ? 4. Why are industry officials worried ? How do scientists seem to feel about this ? 5. What do many of today's scientists feel is the real challenge ? What do you think ? 6. Why is America's high technology not very useful in less-developed nations ? 7. What does the Indian farmer need ? 8. What is most of industry's research money used for ? 9. What do you think is the most important area of scientific research ?

B LANGUAGE AT WORK

Expressing increase

Examples :

> • *A growing number of* scientists insist that...
> • *More and more of* industry's research money is...
> • It means an *increased* emphasis on...
> • *Greater* efforts must be given *a higher priority*...

Read the text again ; then, using the above patterns as models, say what you think are the most urgent technological problems to be solved today.

Emphasizing

Examples :

> • *Where the real challenge lies is* in finding new ways...
> • *What this means is* increased emphasis on...
> • *What the Indian farmer needs is* innovative low technology.

Using the above patterns as models, rephrase as many of the sentences of the text as you can.

C FOLLOW UP WORK

1. What do you think is the most important invention of our time ? Support your argument.
2. In what ways do we, in France, benefit from space technology ?
3. Can we afford space projects while millions are starving on Earth ?

Why are these people protesting ?

ONE WOMAN'S EMPIRE

Katharine Meyer Graham (1917-   ) is the daughter of Eugene Meyer, a self-made millionnaire who was once chairman of the Federal Reserve Board[1]. When the *Washington Post* was auctioned[2] in 1933, Meyer was the mysterious stranger who bid it in for a bargain $825,000. [...]

5   As a young woman, Katharine feared she would never be able to live up to the standards of her family. During and after her college years, she worked as a reporter on the *San Francisco News* as well as on her father's *Washington Post*. In 1940 she retired, without regrets, to marry Phil Graham, a young lawyer. [...]

After the war, Eugene Meyer persuaded Graham to join the *Post* as publisher, /'juːdʒiːn/
10 and in 1948, he sold the voting stock[3] of the paper to the Grahams on their promise /'vɪrəl/
to continue its tradition of "virile, strong, and independent concern for the general
welfare". Meyer and Graham were a good business team, and they set out to /ə'kwaɪəʳ/
acquire properties. They bought the Washington *Times Herald, Newsweek*
Magazine, radio and television stations, and a news service.

15   Then the catastrophe struck which jolted Katharine out of her comfortable life as a Washington matron. Phil Graham suffered increasingly more serious manic-depressive cycles. In 1963 he shot himself to death, leaving Katharine a publishing empire worth hundreds of millions of dollars. She could have sold it, but she had promised her father that she would maintain the *Post*'s tradition of public service.
20 Someone had to take Phil Graham's place, and Katharine nominated herself. [...]

The *Post* thrived[4] under Katharine's management. James Reston, an editor of /θraɪvd/
the *New York Times* and former chief of its Washington bureau, thought it became
"an immensely better paper than it was when she took it over". Word spread that
Katharine was becoming a power, but she resisted the compliment. [...] She worked
25 hard to escape notice, ducking[5] interviewers, and using her knowledge of
journalism to keep herself out of the papers. People in Washington knew about
her, but she was not a national figure.

She gave others the credit but she took the risks herself. It was her decision, in 1971, to publish the controversial Pentagon Papers and thus expose the *Post* to
30 reprisals, if not court action, for printing classified[6] material illegally "leaked[7]" or /rɪ'praɪzəls/
stolen from a government office.

Then came the Watergate scandal. It broke as a local story in the *Post*—a local story that only an alert newsroom would have pursued. Katharine did not interfere or direct, but she followed the story every day. "My role was to make sure we were

Offices of the *Washington Post*.

³⁵ being fair and we were being factual and we were being accurate," she says. "I had to ask every question I could think of because the reputation of the paper was clearly at stake." [...]

Kay Graham has become noticeably more feminist. In 1970, for instance she refused to attend the all-male Gridiron Club[8] dinner because women less important
⁴⁰ than herself were not invited on the same basis as men. She had quietly contributed $20,000 to help found *Ms*[9] Magazine, but it was not until a few years later that she spoke on behalf of the magazine in public.

/mɪz/

Kay Graham is personally modest. [...] She credits the unraveling[10] of Watergate to her staff, to the press in general, to the courts, to Congress—to anyone but
⁴⁵ herself. But it is increasingly difficult even for her to maintain that she deserves no personal credit for what she has done because she fell into her position, as she once put it, "by matrimony and patrimony". Women who inherit large-scale enterprises do not usually undertake to run them personally. For the brilliant performance of the *Washington Post*, Katharine Graham must take some credit herself.

Caroline Bird, *Enterprising Women*

---

1. Atlantic seaboard : the northeastern states. 2. that loomed ahead : that would rise and threaten them. 3. crutches : *béquilles*. 4. soared : went up quickly. 5. poppies : *coquelicot*. 6. flimsy : poorly built. 7. brush : *maquis*. 8. potholes : *nids de poule*. 9. furlough : permission for absence (vacation). 10. strikes : discoveries. 11. Marshall : the discoverer of the first nugget.

A UNDERSTANDING THE TEXT

1. What is Katharine Graham's own family background ? 2. What did she do before she got married ? 3. Under what conditions did Meyer sell the voting stock of the paper to the Grahams ? 4. What did Katharine Graham do after the death of her husband ? Why ? 5. Why did very few people know about her at first ? 6. What two famous stories were first published in the *Washington Post* ? 7. How did Katharine Graham see her role at the time of the Watergate scandal ? 8. Why did she refuse to attend the football dinner ? Do you think she was right ? Justify your opinion. 9. How does the author describe Katharine Graham ?

Expressing regret over past decisions

Examples :

- I'd like to have gone   *(Mild regret)*
- I should/I shouldn't have gone
  I should never have gone   *(Stróng regret)*
  I'm sorry I ever went
- I don't know why I ever went
  I wish I'd never gone   *(Deep regret)*

Phil Graham was alone when he shot himself. Katharine Graham said, ''I wish I'd never left him alone''.

What might the speakers say in the following situations :

a) Someone sold Meyer the *Washington Post* for a bargain. The newspaper has since made a fortune. The former owner said, ''...''.

b) The man who recommended Katharine for the position of Chairman of the Board thought she would not last very long. He had wanted the job himself and had expected to take over from her. He said, ''...''.

c) Katharine Graham used to escape notice. Then she gave an interview to a national magazine. Now she cannot go anywhere without being noticed. She said, ''...''.

d) The all-male Gridiron Club did not realize that Katharine Graham would not attend their annual banquet if she was the only woman invited. The chairman said, ''...''.

e) After the Pentagon Papers were published many people criticized the *Post*. One of the results of this was increased publicity for the newspaper. One of Katharine Graham's competitors said.

f) A journalist arrived late for work the other morning. He/She said, ''...''.

g) There was a very big cocktail party in the press room the other evening. One of the reporters was unable to go. He/She said, ''...''.

C FOLLOW UP WORK

1. To what extent is Katherine Graham typical of a woman living in today's world.

Women can do anything men can do.

WOMEN IN PROFESSIONAL AND MANAGERIAL POSITIONS						
	1900	*1950*	*1960*	*1970*	*1976*	*1982*
Professional and technical workers	434,000	1,794,000	2,703,000	4,298,000	5,522,000	7,645,000
Managers and administrators, exc. farm	74,000	990,000	1,099,000	1,321,000	1,895,000	3,218,000

A graduating class at Howard University.

FACTS AND DATA ON BLACK AMERICANS

1820 : Slavery permitted only South of the Mason-Dixon line (36°40'N), in "Dixie".

1861-1865 : Civil War.

1865-1870 : Reconstruction Acts. 14th and 15th Amendments against discrimination. Foundation of black universities of Atlanta (1865), Howard (1867), and of the Ku-Klux-Klan (1866).

1909 : Foundation of the N.A.A.C.P. (National Association for the Advancement of Colored People).

After World War I : Drift of black population toward industrial centers in the N.E. ; beginning of black ghettos.

1954 : Segregation outlawed by Supreme Court in taxsupported schools and universities and in recreation places. Strong resistance in Southern states.

1955 : Successful boycott of segregated buses in Montgomery. Ala., under the leadership of Martin Luther King Jr.

1963 : March on Washington culminating in mass rally near Lincoln Memorial.

1964 : Civil Rights legislation. Any form of segregation abolished. Political rights secured. Vast federal welfare program for blacks.

1964 : Martin Luther King receives Nobel Peace Prize.

1966 : First black cabinet member appointed. "Black Power" begins when Stokely Carmichael is elected chairman of Student Non-Violent Coordinating Committee (SNCC). The Black Panthers, a militant organization, is formed and begins confrontation.

1968 : Busing of students to insure school desegregation in Berkeley, California, is begun.

1970 : 50 % of black population now living in northern cities.

1971 : Amid controversey, the U.S. Supreme Court rules that busing of school children is constitutional.

1977-78 : Allan Bakke, a white engineer seeking admission to medical school, sues the university for "reverse discrimination", claiming he was rejected because he is white. The case reaches the U.S. Supreme Court, which rules in Bakke's favor.

1983 : Busing of students continues.

"WE'VE COME A LONG WAY, BABE !"

"Like most black Americans, my roots are in the South." So writes Time
Atlanta correspondent Jack White, 30. Here is his personal account of
being brought up under segregation.

My father's father was born a slave somewhere near Savannah, Ga. My mother's   /sə'vænə/
father was the son of a white undertaker and his mulatto concubine in a small town   /mʊ'lætəʊ/
in North Carolina.   /kɑŋkjubaɪn/

Like many other blacks, my parents migrated North to find education and better   /nɔrθ
5 opportunities. My father went to Howard University[1] medical school, and my   ,kærə'laɪnə/
mother went to Howard's nursing school. My parents wanted to shelter their   /'maɪgreɪtɪd/
children from segregation and all its belittling aspects, so they settled in
Washington, which turned out to be as segregated a city as one could find.

Segregated echo. In the 1950s, a clerk in a department store refused to let me   /klɜrk/
10 sip from a water fountain, despite my mother's plea that "he's just a little boy".
Later, when my family got its first television set, I was entranced by the ads for
Glen Echo amusement park. My mother couldn't really explain why she couldn't
take me there. The reason, of course, was that Glen Echo did not admit blacks. Nor
did many restaurants, movie theaters and other public facilities.

15 My deepest realization of what the Old South was really like came in about 1962,
when my father, brother, a friend and I drove South to my grandmother's house in
Stuart, Fla. On the way we were denied a room in a Holiday Inn in Savannah, and   /hor/
wound up sleeping in a "rooming house" (read whorehouse[2]) that hadn't had an
overnight guest in years. In Stuart, my father went into a hardware store[3] to buy a   /'θɜrməs/
20 Thermos bottle. The white clerk asked my dad, a distinguished professor of surgery
at least 20 years his senior. "What you want, boy ?" My father struggled to
maintain his dignity as he told the clerk what he wanted. I felt in my gut, for the
first time, how hard it had been for black men to preserve their self-respect under a
rigid system of white supremacy.

25 **Southern pride.** Because of the civil rights movement, I will never have to
explain to my four-year-old son that he can't go to an amusement park or swim in a
public swimming pool just because he is black. He will never see me diminish in his
eyes because some white man can lord it[4] over me and make me seem like a child.

White Southerners are now taking a great deal of pride in the region's rapid   /'sʌðərnər/
30 adjustment to the post-civil rights era. The fact is that every change was resisted,
every improvement fought, every overture turned back. Though many Southerners
were made uneasy by the oppressive pattern of Southern race relations, most did
little or nothing to change it. [...] Without unrelenting pressure from blacks and the
Federal Government, white Southerners would never have changed. Southern
35 behavior has changed, but the hearts, for the most part, are probably just the same.

White Southerners tend to have a passion for lost causes. The Washington
Redskins, for example, were the South's "adopted" pro-football team. They
remained lily-white, and they retained their Southern constituency[5], even though   /kən'stɪtʃʊənsi/
they were consistent[6] losers. [...] The Redskins' ownership would rather be white
40 than winners.

Then the team's owner, George Preston Marshall, died, and Lawyer Edward
Bennett Williams took over. Wiliams realized that he was in a new day, and the
Redskins began to get black players. Within a few years, they became winners. Now
everybody loves them.

47

45 Much the same thing has happened to the South. It has become a region of winners. Blacks are playing on the team. Points are going on the scoreboard. But is the change permanent ?

My own guess is that the good impulses will win out. The Southern white man, even at his most bigoted[7], always had some noble impulses : loyalty, independence, /ˈbɪɡət̬ɪd/
50 courage. Martin Luther King spoke of the "redemptive power" of nonviolent love, and his followers nodded amen. They believed white Southerners could be redeemed. And if they thought that, after 350 years of oppression, who am I to quarrel ?

From *Time*, Sept. 27, 1976

1. Howard University : prestigious black university in Washington D.C. 2. whore : prostitute. 3. hardware store : *quincaillerie*. 4. lord it : act superior. 5. constituency : supporters. 6. consistent : constant. 7. bigoted : prejudiced.

A UNDERSTANDING THE TEXT

1. How old is Jack White ? 2. Why did his parents move North ? 3. Why did they settle in Washington ? What is a good choice ? 4. What was one of the writer's early encounters with racism ? 5. What was Glen Echo ? How did the writer find out about it ? 6. Why do you think his mother "could not really explain" why he could not go there ? 7. What was the problem the family encountered when they drove South to visit the writer's grandmother ? How did they solve the problem ? Was the solution an altogether satisfactory one ? 8. What was Jack White's father's profession ? What was especially insulting about the way he was addressed ? 9. What was his reaction to being addressed in this way ? How did the writer himself feel about it ? 10. How has the writer's own life been affected by the civil rights movement ? 11. What does he feel made white Southerners change their behavior ? 12. How did the Washington Redskins become a winning team ? 13. Why do you think peoples' attitudes towards black players changed ? 14. How far do you think Jack White's personality and position may induce him to have an optimistic vision of the evolution in the blacks' condition ?

A rare old photograph of actual slaves on a cotton plantation in the South more than a hundred years ago.

State or habit in the past, no longer true

Examples :

> • **The writer's parents... in the South.**
> → **The writer's parents** *used to* **live in the South, but they** *no longer* **do.**

Using the same model, make sentences with the following elements :

a) The writer's father ... a small town.
b) Blacks ... restaurants.
c) Glen Echo ... blacks.
d) The Holiday Inn in Savannah ... blacks.
e) White Southerners ... blacks ''boy''.
f) Blacks ... slaves.
g) The Washington Redskins ... a losing team.
h) George Preston Marshall ... the owner of the Washington Redskins.
i) Blacks ... Southern teams.

Past action or state still valid

Examples :

> • **The South has always been proud.**
> • **Jim has been in Atlanta for quite a while now.**
> • **He has been in Atlanta for quite a few years.**
> • **He has actually been there since he left Washington.**

Read the last section (Southern pride) *of the text again. Then, using the above patterns as models, rephrase as many of Jack White's remarks as you can.*

C FOLLOW UP WORK

1. In what way do you think the writer shares in the American Dream ?
2. What do you think makes people racist ?
3. Blacks in the United States today live better than their counterparts in Africa, even better than some people in Europe. Discuss.
4. In the light of the unemployment statistics below, how can Jack White's view be qualified ?

Faces of America

What kind of people will Americans be 40 years from now ? We already have a pretty good idea. About one-third of the Americans of 2022 are already alive (although not all are in the United States yet), and the parents of most of the Americans of 2022 are alive, even if it is hard to visualize a 3-year-old as a parent. We know the rather widely varying birthrates or different types of people in the society, and we know something—although less than would be desirable—about the numbers and kinds of people who are immigrating.

The big news, announced most recently in a national study prepared by the Center for the Continuing Study of the California Economy, is that a smaller proportion of Americans in 2022 will be white and non-Hispanic than is now the case. The study expects that percentage to decline from 80 in 1980 to 75 in 2000 ; it makes no estimate for 2022, but the percentage seems almost certain to be lower. The study expects the percentage of Asians to increase from 2.5 percent in 1980 to 4 percent in 2000 ; the percentage of blacks is expected to rise from 11.5 to 12.4, and that of Hispanics from 6.4 to 8.6. If there are not many people left who talk openly about such things, we suppose there are some left who worry privately about them. But the fact is that changing ethnic composition, and rising percentages of groups that are discriminated against are as American as apple pie.

In America as in the world generally, poorer people tend to have more children ; most of the children alive at any time in American history have lived in households that were poorer and more likely to be headed by minorities than the national average. Today blacks, Hispanics and Asians tend to have more children than those who do not fall in those groups, just as 50 years ago Irish, Italian, Jewish and Polish Americans had more children than people of British descent. Although each generation of American children tends to come from households with lower socio-economic status than the contemporary generation of adults, there have been rises in real incomes[1] in every generation of America's history. Lower socio-economic status has not proved an insurmountable handicap ; Americans have leapfrogged[2] ahead of each other, generation after generation.

We see no reason to expect that this will not happen again. The population of children in America today is made up of blacks, Hispanics and Asians to a greater extent than the population of adults. It is one of the major tasks of society's institutions to help their parents prepare them to be productive citizens. There is evidence[3]—rising test scores, for example—that whatever America's temporary economic problems, this is happening.

These children will be joined, when they are in their 20s or 30s, by immigrants of the same age in numbers that cannot be precisely predicted, but which are likely, if history is a guide, to be related to the state of the economy. Immigrants are most often people of above-average initiative and flexibility, and they almost always improve vastly their socio-economic status.

The American people are going to look different in 2022, and they will have had different experiences and backgrounds in many cases. But with some luck, and if America has the good sense to draw on the lesson of success that its history teaches, they can be more prosperous, productive and tolerant than the Americans of today.

From *The Washington Post*, Aug. 5th 1982

---

1. real incomes : *revenus en termes réels.* **2.** leapfrog : *saute-mouton :* to leapfrog ahead : *sauter une étape.* **3.** evidence : *des preuves.*

A UNDERSTANDING THE TEXT

1. What do you know about the origins of the people described as Whites and non Hispanics ? 2. In the early '80s, what is the proportion of Whites and non Hispanics in the American population ? 3. According to estimations, will this percentage go up or down ? 4. Why is this estimation worrying some Americans ? Are they right to be concerned ? 5. Compare the number of children in minority groups and among WASPs (White Anglo Saxon Protestants). 6. Which groups may be discriminated against in this decade ? 7. Throughout the history of the United States what has repeatedly happened to each generation of immigrants ? 8. What special qualities do most immigrants have in common ? 9. What profit can they derive frome these qualities ? 10. How does upward mobility work in the American Society ?

B LANGUAGE AT WORK

Expressing probability

Example :

> • ''The numbers of immigrants *are likely* to be related to the state of the economy.''

1. Using information from the text, complete the following sentences on the above model :

    a) According to birth rate statistics, couples with lower socio-economic status...

    b) Considering (given) the rising test-scores in U.S. schools, children from minority groups... when they reach adulthood.

    c) In 2000 the percentage of Asians in the American population...

    d) In 2022 the percentage of blacks and that of Hispanics...

    e) Accordingly, ethnic groups that have been discriminated against... in about forty years' time.

    f) Changing ethnic composition...

    g) Hopefully Americans... in their relationship with one another in the years to come.

One might also have said :

• *In all likelihood* the number of immigrants *will be* related to the state of the economy.
• The number of immigrants *will probably be related* to the state of the economy.

2. Rephrase the statements in the first exercice using the above models.

3. Say what you consider is likely to happen in your own country forty years from now.

C FOLLOW UP WORK

1. What is the writer's optimistic outlook based on ? What does he recommend ? What does he hope for ? 2. How does the title of the article relate to the notions of the American Dream ? 3. Quote a line or two that you personally found most striking and explain why you chose it. 4. Immigrants are necessary for the development of a country.

Signs of the times : A poster in Spanish alongside a California road.

OCCUPATION	1957	1960	1970	1973	1975	1982
BLACK EMPLOYMENT BY OCCUPATION CATEGORY : 1957 TO 1982 (PERCENT DISTRIBUTION)						
BLACK AND OTHER MINORITIES						
Total employed (in 1,000 s)	6,647	6,927	8,445	9,131	9,070	11,624
White-collar workers	12.8	16.1	27.9	31.1	34.2	41.6
Professional, technical, and kindred ..	3.7	4.8	9.1	9.9	11.4	14.1
Medical and other health	0.6	0.8	1.6	2.0	2.7	3.5
Teachers, except college	1.3	1.7	2.9	3.0	3.1	2.9
Managers, administrators, exc. farm .	2.1	2.6	3.5	4.1	4.4	5.7
Salesworkers	1.0	1.5	2.1	2.3	2.7	3.1
Clerical workers	6.0	7.3	13.2	14.9	15.7	18.7
Blue-collar workers	41.8	40.1	42.2	40.8	37.4	33.4
Craftsmen and kindred workers	5.7	6.0	8.2	8.9	8.8	8.9
Operatives	21.2	20.4	23.7	22.2	20.0	17.8
Nonfarm laborers	14.9	13.7	10.3	9.7	8.7	6.8
Service industries	32.0	31.7	26.0	25.3	25.8	23.2
Farmworkers	13.5	12.1	3.9	2.8	2.6	1.7

TO TAKE YOU FURTHER

Invited and uninvited, rich and poor—but mostly poor—foreigners are pouring into the U.S. in greater numbers than at any time since the last great surge of European immigrants in the early 1900s. Indeed, the U.S. today accepts twice as many foreigners as the rest of the world's nations combined. Thanks in large part to the flood of Cuban and Haitian refugees last year, more than 800,000 newcomers were allowed into the country legally in 1980, up from only 526,000 in 1979. In addition, an estimated 500,000 to one million entered illegally. Although their turn-of-the-century-predecessors were mainly Europeans, today's new arrivals are mostly from Latin America and, to a lesser extent, Asia and the Caribbean. They are transforming the U.S. urban landscape into something that it has not been for decades : a mosaic of exotic languages, faces, costumes, customs, restaurants and religions.

They have also touched off growing concern in Congress and elsewhere that the U.S. can no longer afford such generosity. Those huddled masses, it is feared, are robbing native Americans of jobs, straining community services and provoking new excesses of bigotry and xenophobia across the U.S.

One Democratic Senator estimates that, if present trends continue, immigration will add at least 35 million people to the current U.S. population of 229 million by the year 2000. "Those 35 million people will need land, water, energy and food", complains the Senator. "Where are we going to find those resources, unless we ask our citizens to sacrifice more ?"

Of greatest concern to the restrictionists are those who enter the U.S. illegally, some 50 to 60 percent of whom come from Mexico. Most migrate to find a job, any job ; at least 40 percent of the work force in Mexico is either unemployed or underemployed.

What exactly is the economic impact of illegal immigration ? The AFL-CIO argues that every job taken by an illegal alien is a job lost by an American. On the other hand, illegal immigrants have become so much a part of the U.S. work force, some economists contend, that dismissing them would cripple certain industries.

HOW TO BECOME AMERICAN

According to the Immigration Act of 1965, which finally took effect in 1968 :

1) National quotas were abolished. A ceiling now limits immigration to 170,000 from the Eastern hemisphere (and no more than 20,000 from any one country) and 120,000 from the Western Hemisphere, for an annual total of 290,000.

2) Parents, spouses and unmarried children of U.S. citizens are exempted from all quotas, thus increasing total annual immigration to about 400,000, as compared to about 25,000 per year during the 1950s. Some preference is also given to other kinds of relatives.

3) In the Eastern Hemisphere, preference is given to "members of the professions (officially defined as doctors, lawyers, architects, nurses, engineers, and teachers), and scientists and artists of exceptional ability" and then to "skilled and unskilled workers in occupations for which labor is in short supply in the U.S.". (This does not always work out as planned. So many Filipino doctors and nurses have applied for visas that there is a six-year waiting list.)

4) In the Western hemisphere, there is no system of preferences, and visas are issued on a first-come, first-served basis. But since Latin Americans were not part of the old quota system, the ceiling of 120,000 imposes a new restriction on them, and the waiting lists now average 2.5 years.

What is an "American" ?

SURVEYING THE SCENE

1. In what way can Jim Studebaker *(Moving to the Sunbelt)*, the 49ers described in *The Gold Rush* and Mary Patton Taylor's parents *(Tales my Mother Told Me)* all be said to "reach for the American Dream".
2. How far does Katherine Graham's success feed the American Dream ?
3. What is common to the new immigrants described in *Faces of America* and Mary Patton Taylor's parents ?
4. How far are gadgets relevant to the American Dream ?

Some books you might like to read : *L'Or* by Blaise Cendrars.
The Grapes of Wrath (Les Raisins de la colère) by J. Steinbeck.
My Antonia by Willa Cather.

Some films you might like to see : *Deliverance (Délivrance)* by J. Boorman.
Annie Hall by Woody Allen.
America, America by Elia Kazan.

III. THE OTHER SIDE OF THE DREAM

HOW THE INDIANS SAW IT

For many people and for a long time, "a good Indian [was] a dead Indian," and the pain of the Indian as he experienced the death of his way of life was simply not understood. Yet on many occasions Indian people tried to explain their feelings to the white man. Here are a few passages from speeches or interviews in which the Indians speak for themselves.

Ma-ka-tai-ma-she-kia-kiak or Black Hawk, Chief of the Sauk and Fox[1], in 1833 :

We always had plenty ; our children never cried from hunger, neither were our people in want... The rapids of Rock River furnished us with an abundance of excellent fish, and the land being very fertile never failed to produce good crops of corn, beans, pumpkins, and squashes[2]... Here our village stood for more than a hundred years, during all of which time we were the undisputed possessors of the
5 Mississippi Valley... Our village was healthy and there was no place in the country possessing such advantages, nor hunting grounds better than those we had in possession. If a prophet had come to our village and told us that the things were to take place which have since come to pass, none of our people would have believed him.

Chief Luther Standing Bear[3], of the Oglala[4] band of Sioux[5], in the 1930s :

We did not think of the great open plains, the beautiful rolling hills, and winding streams with tangled
10 growth, as "wild". Only to the white man was nature a "wilderness" and only to him was the land "infested" with "wild" animals and "savage" people. To us it was tame. Earth was bountiful and we were surrounded with the blessings of the Great Mystery. Not until the hairy man from the east came and with brutal fenzy heaped injustices upon us and the families we loved was it "wild" for us. When the very animals of the forest began fleeing from his approach, then it was that for us the "Wild
15 West" began.

An old Wintu[6] Woman, in the 1950s :

The white people never cared for land or deer or bear. When we Indians kill meat, we eat it all up. When we dig roots, we make little holes. When we build houses, we make little holes. When we burn grass for grasshoppers, we don't ruin things. We shake down acorns[7] and pinenuts. We don't chop down the trees. We only use dead wood. But the white people plow up the ground, pull down the
20 trees, kill everything. The tree says, "Don't. I am sore. Don't hurt me." But they chop it down and cut it up. The spirit of the land hates them. They blast out trees and stir it up to its depths. They saw up the trees. That hurts them. The Indians never hurt anything, but the white people destroy all. They blast rocks and scatter them on the ground. The rock says, "Don't. Your are hurting me." But the white people pay no attention. When the Indians use rocks, they take little round ones for their
25 cooking... How can the spirit of the earth like the white man ?... Everywhere the white man has touched it, it is sore.

The entrance to Pine Bridge Reservation in South Dakota, site of the Battle of Wounded Knee. Why do you think someone changed the sign ?

**Aleek-chea-ahoosh or Plenty Coups, a Crow[8] chief,
in his autobiography,
published before his death in 1932 :**

By the time I was forty I could see our country was changing fast and that these changes were causing us to live very differently. Anybody could now see that soon there would be no buffalo on the plains, and everybody was wondering how we would live after they were gone. There were few war parties
30 and almost no raids... White men with their spotted buffalo* were on the plains about us. Their houses were near the water holes, and their villages on the rivers. We made up our minds to be friendly with them, in spite of all the changes they were bringing. But we found this difficult, because the white men too often promised to do one thing and then when they acted at all, did another.

T.C. McLuhan, *Touch the Earth*

* *cattle (author's note).*

1. Sauk and Fox : a tribe of Indians of the Wisconsin area.   **2.** squash : a kind of courgette.   **3.** Luther Standing Bear : an example of the christianization of Indian culture.   **4.** Oglala : a tribe of Sioux inhabiting the Teton area.   **5.** Sioux : a generic name for a series of tribes inhabiting the Plains west of the Mississippi.   **6.** Wintu : a people of the Sacramento Valley, Calif.   **7.** acorns : *glands*.   **8.** Crow : a tribe of Sioux inhabiting the region between the Platte and Yellowstone rivers.

American Indians demonstrating in front of the White House.

A TRUE OR FALSE ?

1. All the people speaking are famous Indian chiefs. 2. They all remember their young days and the clashes with the whites. 3. They all give the impression of being savage brutes. 4. They all seem to be happy with their lot. 5. They have all made their peace with the whites.

B ANSWER THESE QUESTIONS :

1. Were the Sauk and Fox Indians hunters ? Justify your answer. 2. What did the Sauk and Fox eat in the days Black Hawk refers to ? 3. Had the Sauk and Fox anticipated what happened to them later on ? Justify your answer. 4. How does Chief Luther Standing Bear convey his conviction that the West became the Wild West only with the arrival of the white man ? 5. How does the old Wintu woman show that Indians were very careful not to waste anything and not to hurt the spirit of the earth ? 6. Why do you think white men blast rocks ? 7. In the view of the present environmental problems, what lesson could the whites learn from the Indians ? 8. How old was Plenty Coups, the Crow chief, when things began to change around him ? Why did this make it more pathetic for him ? 9. According to him what type of changes did the arrival of the white man bring ? 10. What is his main reproach against the white man ?

C EXPLAIN IN YOUR OWN WORDS :

1. We were the undisputed possessors of the Mississippi Valley.
2. We were surrounded with the blessings of the Great Mystery.
3. The Indians never hurt anything, but the white people destroy all.
4. Everybody was wondering how we could live after they were gone.
5. We made up our minds to be friendly with them in spite of all the changes they were bringing.

D DISCUSSION

What can we learn from the Indians today ?

GREER COUNTY BACHELOR

The various "homestead acts" that were passed throughout the 19th century gave anyone who was willing to bring it into cultivation the possibility of getting a piece of land from the government at a very low price. Pioneers were encouraged to settle always further West, but they apparently were not all too happy about their "government claims", as this anonymous ballad suggests.

My name is Tom High, an old bachelor am I,
You'll find me out West in the county of fame,
You'll find me out West on an elegant plain,
A-starving to death on my government claim.

5 My clothes they are ragged, my language is rough,   /ˈræg ḷd/
My bread is corndodgers[2], both solid and tough ;
And yet I am happy and live at my ease,
On sorghum[3], molasses, and bacon and cheese.

Hurrah for Greer county, the land of the free,
10 The land of the bedbug, grasshopper and flea
I'll sing of its praise, I'll tell of its fame,
While starving to death on my government claim.

Hurrah for Greer county where blizzards arise,
Where the sun never sinks and the flea never dies.
15 I'll sing of its praises, I'll tell of its fame,
While starving to death on my government claim.

My house it is built of the national soil,
Its walls are erected according to Hoyle[4],
Its roof has no pitch but is level and plain,
20 I always get wet if it happens to rain.

How happy I am when I crawl into bed,
A rattlesnake hisses a tune at my head,
A grey little centipede, quite without fear,
Crawls over my pillow and into my ear.

25 Now all you claim holders, I hope you'll stay,
Chew your hardtack[5] till you're toothless and grey,
But for myself, I'll no longer remain,
To starve like a dog on my government claim.

Good-bye to Greer county, good-bye to the West,
30 I'll travel back East to the girl I love best.
I'll travel back East and marry me a wife,
Call quits[6] on corndodgers for the rest of my life.

1. Greer County : county in Oklahoma. **2.** corndodgers : *beignets de maïs.* **3.** sorghum : *sorgho.* **4.** Hoyle : a writer on card games ; a house built according to Hoyle : a house of cards. **5.** hardtack : a satless hard biscuit. **6.** call quits : give up.

/kwɪts/

A UNDERSTANDING THE TEXT

1. Who is Tom High and what is his marital status ?   2. What is he doing out West ?   3. Why did he go there ?   4. What reasons has he got to blame the government ?   5. What are his complaints ?   6. What impression does he give of the everyday life of the homesteaders.   7. What impression does Tom High give of the government's propaganda to attract homesteaders ?   8. How does he manage to make us realize the contrast between the arguments used to lure people out West and the realities of their life there ?   9. Do you think Tom High is entirely fair in his complaints ? Justify your answer.

B LANGUAGE AT WORK

Expressing contrast

The posters probably said things like "Come to the land of the free", "Come to the glorious West", yet Tom High is starving to death on his government claim. Suppose that he is reporting what he had heard and comparing it to the reality. He might say things like :

> • **They said it was the land of the free, but I'm starving to death in Greer County.**
> • **It was supposed to be the Golden West, but...**
> • **The soil supposedly was very fertile, but...**

On the same model use expressions such as all the same, although, but, however, nevertheless, still, yet *and the following elements to make up what he might say :*

a) "the country of the free"/toiling day and night ;
b) "the land of golden opportunity"/poor as Job ;
c) "very healthy climate"/lots of insects ;
d) "the land of sunshine"/blizzards in Winter ;
e) "the sun never sinks"/freezing at night ;
f) "fertile plain"/parched and rocky soil.

Reported speech

Example :

> • **I wonder where Tom High is ; I wonder if he is married, etc.**

Read the text, then imagine the questions that one who does not know the real life of homesteaders may ask oneself .

C FOLLOW UP

1. Write a letter as Tom High describing your life to a friend who would like to apply for a government claim.
2. Write a letter as Tom High to announce to your girl-friend that you are coming back. You, of course, make plans for the future...
3. In what way does this ballad contrast with the popular view of the conquest of the West ?

Immigrants arriving in New York at the beginning of the century.

1902 : THEY CAME TO AMERICA

In Ragtime, E.L. Doctorow draws the portrait of the U.S. in the first years of the 20th century. A series of loose sketches, the novel is tied together by the presence in different episodes of the same characters, among whom is a family of Jewish immigrants from Eastern Europe, who appear under the names of Mameh and Tateh, as their young daughter calls them.

Most of the immigrants came from Italy and Eastern Europe. They were taken in launches[1] to Ellis Island[2]. There, in a curiously ornate human warehouse of red brick and gray stone, they were tagged[3], given showers and arranged on benches in waiting pens[4]. They were immediately sensitive to the enormous power of the
5 immigration officials. These officials changed names they couldn't pronounce and tore people from their families, consigning to a return voyage old folks, people with bad eyes, riffraff[5] and also those who looked insolent. Such power was dazzling. The immigrants were reminded of home. They went into the streets and were somehow absorbed in the tenements[6]. They were despised by New Yorkers. They
10 were filthy and illiterate. They stank of fish and garlic[7]. They had running sores[8]. They had no honor and worked for next to nothing. They stole. They drank. They raped their own daughters. They killed each other casually. Among those who despised them the most were the second-generation Irish, whose fathers had been guilty of the same crimes. Irish kids pulled the beards of old Jews and knocked
15 them down. They upended the pushcarts of Italian peddlers[9].

Every season of the year wagons came through the streets and picked up bodies of derelicts. Late at night old ladies in babushkas[10] came to the morgue looking for their husbands and sons. The corpses lay on tables of galvanized iron. From the bottom of each table a drainpipe extended to the floor. Around the rim of the table
20 was a culvert[11]. And into the culvert ran the water sprayed constantly over each body from an overhead faucet[12]. The faces of the dead were upturned into the streams of water that poured over them like the irrepressible mechanism in death of their own tears.

/'ɪtli/
/'jʊərəp/

/'gælvənaɪzd/
/'aɪərn/

But somehow piano lessons began to be heard. People stitched themselves to the
25 flag. They carved paving stones for the streets. They sang. They told jokes. The
family lived in one room and everyone worked : Mameh and the little girl sewed
knee pants and got seventy cents a dozen. They sewed from the time they got up to
the time they went to bed. Tateh made his living in the street. As time went on they
got to know the city. One Sunday, in a wild impractical mood, they spent twelve
30 cents for three fares on the streetcar and rode uptown. They walked on Madison
Avenue and Fifth Avenue and looked at the mansions. Their owners called them
palaces. And that's what they were, they were palaces. [...] Tateh was a socialist.   /'səuʃəlᵢst/
He looked at the palaces and his heart was outraged. The family walked quickly.
The police in their tall helmets looked at them. On these wide empty sidewalks in
35 this part of the city the police did not like to see immigrants. [...]

A crisis came to the family when somebody delivered a letter telling them the little
girl would have to go to school. This meant they could not make ends meet.
Helplessly, Mameh and Tateh took their child to the school. She was enrolled and
went off each day. Tateh roamed the streets. He didn't know what to do. He had a
40 peddler's business. Never could he find a place at the curb that was profitable.
While he was gone Mameh sat by the window with her stack of cut cloth and
pedaled the sewing machine. She was a petite dark-eyed woman with wavy brown   /pə'tiːt/
hair which she parted in the middle and tied behind her neck in a bun. When she
was alone like this she sang softly to herself in a high sweet thin voice. Her songs
45 had no words. One afternoon she took her finished work to the loft on Stanton
Street. The owner invited her into his office. He looked at the piece goods carefully
and said she had done well. He counted out the money, adding a dollar more than
she deserved. This he explained was because she was such a good-looking woman.
He smiled. He touched Mameh's breast. Mameh fled, taking the dollar. The next
50 time the same thing happened. She told Tateh she was doing more work. She
became accustomed to the hands of her employer. One day with two weeks' rent
due she let the man have his way on a cutting table. He kissed her face and tasted
the salt of her tears.

E.L. Doctorow, *Ragtime*, 1977

---

1. launches : small boats.   2. Ellis Island : an island in New York bay for quarantining immigrants.   3. tagged :
labelled for identification.   4. pens : enclosures.   5. riffraff : *de la racaille.*   6. tenements : over crowded cheap
housing.   7. garlic : *ail.*   8. running sores : suppurating ulcers (possibly an euphemism for venereal disease).
9. peddlers : *colporteurs.*   10. babushkas : headscarves as worn by Russian women.   11. a culvert : *une rigole.*
12. faucet *(Am.)* : tap *(Eng.).*

A   UNDERSTANDING THE TEXT

1. Where did most of the immigrants come from ?
2. Why did they have to be taken to Ellis Island ?
What sort of verifications took place there ?
3. Were all would-be immigrants accepted into the
country ? Which of them were rejected and
why ?   4. Why could immigrants be reminded of
home when they arrived in the States ?   5. What
opinion of the immigrants did the New Yorkers
have ? How do you account for it ?   6. Why was it
especially surprising to hear the Irish complain about
the immigrants ?   7. Why did people give the
impression that they went on weeping even after·
they death ? What does the writer want to
suggest ?   8. What signs soon indicated that a
family was on its way up in society ?   9. What
does the author mean by "people stitched
themselves to the flag" ?   10. Why was sending the
little girl to school a tragedy for the family ?
11. What is tragic in the final anecdote ?

B LANGUAGE AT WORK

Expressing hopes and expectations

Examples :

> • **The immigrants hoped to succeed in America.**
> • **They expected their children to have a better life.**
> • **They wanted them to become rich.**

Read the text again and, using the above constructions, say what were some of the hopes, expectations, ambitions the immigrants had when they arrived in America.

Expressing wishes and regrets

Study these examples :

> • *I wish/If only* **he could find a better job... but at least he's got that peddler's business.**
> • *I wish/If only* **we had been able to find a bigger apartment... but we can only afford this room.**
> • *I wish/If only* **you were older, you could go to work and bring back some money... but for the time being you must go to school.**

You are an immigrant. Express your wishes and regrets about the following :

a) bringing Grandma over to America ;
b) not living in a tenement with so many Irish people ;
c) saving some money to move to another section of town ;
d) being younger and getting a job on the waterfront ;
e) becoming rich and buying a mansion on Fifth Avenue ;
f) being able to pay the back rent.

C FOLLOW UP WORK

1. Study the style of the passage and show how the author manages to re-create the climate of New York's Lower East Side in 1902.

2. America has been called "the land of freedom and opportunity". To what extent do you think this was true ? Use information from other texts or from the texts previously studied to support your opinion.

THE GOSPEL OF WORK

In few respects has American culture been as radically transformed as in the relation of the machine to the industrial process, and of the worker to the machine and the job. The greatest change has come about in the "gospel[1] of work". Except for the ante-bellum[2] South there were no Greek notions in America of work as a
5 badge of dishonor, something belonging to a lower caste while the elite cultivates the mind or the graces of living. Freshly wrested from[3] the frontier wilderness[4], the American land was a living reminder of the relation between work and survival ; and as America grew in wealth it was a reminder also of the relation of work to its immediate rewards.

10 And to ultimate rewards also, for the religious spirit of America's Protestant sects reinforced the practical reasons for work by bringing God's reasons to bear[5] as well. The American bourgeois spirit, which existed in its purest form where economic man met religious man, regarded idleness[6] as sinful[7] and the way of work as the good way."Work... while it is day", said Jesus to his disciples. "For the
15 night cometh, when no man can work." In the whole calendar of economic virtues work was the primal source of all the others. Even the rich who did not have to work felt uneasy when they did not, and a life of complete leisure was more likely to be regarded as parasitism in the context of the Puritan tradition than anywhere else in the capitalist world. The gospel of hard work took long to die. But it is clear that
20 Blake's "dark, Satanic mills" do not apply to the factory experience of America, where labor was scarce, technical innovation moved fast, and "scientific management" had an early start. The American factories in the early nineteenth century were very different from their European counterparts ; the early factory owners tried to avoid the excesses of the English and the European experience,
25 including long hours, child labor, poor pay, and scabrous[8] working and living conditions. The idea behind the early American factories was that the American worker was a dignified human being entitled to decent treatment.

The panic of 1837 changed the picture, driving many mill-owners and manufacturers to the wall and giving them a reason for treating the workers in a
30 more exploitative way. The new tides of immigration, by providing a large labor force whose living standards were lower, made the situation worse. Toward the end of the century there were "sweat-shops"[9] in American garment manufacture, there was child labor, and until 1923 there was a seventy-two-hour week in the steel industry. Yet despite these changes the old Protestant-bourgeois work ethic died in
35 America for other reasons than applied to the dirty, crowded factories and the long, exhausting hours of the English Industrial Revolution.

One might say that the old work ethic[10] died because the work became dehumanized and joyless, but this would miss the fact that joylessness in itself might strengthen the Puritan work ethic, making work an end in itself. What did

THE GREAT PANIC OF 1837 : a severe financial crisis in the United States.

THE FRONTIER : it was the line where the settlements ended. Initially the "west" began close to the Atlantic seaboard. On April 22 1889, an Indian reservation in Oklahoma was opened to the settlers. It was the last time ever. The Frontier was gone. It was officially declared closed in 1890.

WILLIAM BLAKE (1757-1827) : English poet.

"THESE DARK, SATANIC MILLS" : a quotation from a famous poem by Blake. The mills mentioned here are the factories (mills) built at the time of the English Industrial Revolution.

A 19th century view
of a foundry.

40 happen was that with the growth of the big corporation[11], work became depersonalized ; and with the change in the immigrant experience and composition, hard work became associated with the foreign-born, the Blacks, the illiterate, and the underlying social strata[12]. The atmosphere of the Big Money and the knowledge that so much of the income comes by way of what the workers consider "easy
45 rackets"[13], all conspired to strip work of its incentives[14]. In the thinking both of the corporate employers[15] and the trade-union members work came to be expressed mainly in money terms. It was cut off from a sense of creativeness and lost much of its dignity and meaning. The idea of the dignity of work died not in the "dark, Satanic mills" but in the well-lighted, ingeniously laid out, scientifically organized
50 assembly-line plants, and in the spacious headquarters and offices of the great American corporations. What has replaced it on the employers' side is the ethic of efficiency and profit and on the workers' side the ethic of security and success.

Max Lerner, *America As a Civilisation,* 1957

---

1. gospel : a) *évangile ;* b) a set of principles that one believes in. **2.** ante-bellum : before the Civil War (1861-1865). **3.** wrested from : obtained by effort. **4.** the frontier wilderness : the wild territories gradually settled by the pioneers in their move westward. **5.** to bear : to exert an influence. **6.** idleness : *oisiveté.* **7.** as sinful : as a sin *(péché).* **8.** scabrous : squalid, filthy. **9.** sweatshop : a place where workers are employed under unfair and unsanitary conditions. **10.** ethic : moral philosophy, rules of conduct. **11.** corporation : *société industrielle ou commerciale.* **12.** the underlying social strata : *les classes les plus défavorisées.* **13.** easy rackets : quick and dishonest ways of getting money. **14.** incentive : *motivation.* **15.** corporate employers : *chefs d'entreprise.*

A UNDERSTANDING THE TEXT

1. What was the common attitude to work in classical cultures ? 2. What made the situation so different in America ? 3. What is meant here by ''the immediate results of work ?'' 4. What is meant by ''ultimate rewards'' 5. How did the religious spirit of American Puritans play an important part in defining the role of work in society ? 6. What were the incentives to work in a Puritan-oriented society ? 7. In the early 19th Century what excesses of the Industrial Revolution in Britain were avoided in the U.S. ? 8. When did things change and why ? 9. How could the successive waves of immigrants enable manufacturers and mill owners to exploit workers ? 10. Which parts of the population did hard work then become associated with ? 11. In the writer's opinion, what are the bosses (corporate employers) interested in ? What about labor leaders ? 12. What is their common goal ? 13. What has been lost in the process ?

B LANGUAGE AT WORK

Past tenses : preterit and present perfect

Examples :

> • ''The American land *was* a living reminder of the relation between work and survival.'' *(in the old days)*
> • ''The greatest change *has come about* in the 'gospel of work'.'' *(in modern times)*

Complete the following sentences choosing the appropriate past tense :

a) In England at the time of the Industrial Revolution workers...   long exhausting hours. (to work)

b) They...   a decent wage. (not to be paid)

c) Great improvements in working conditions...   since then. (to be made)

d) Yet, in many Third World countries child-labor...   (not to be eradicated)

e) The first assembly line...   the industrial process for well over three quarters of a century. (to dominate)

f) Since the advent of Big Technology job-satisfaction...   for those who work ''on the line''. (to disappear)

g) Scientific management...   in the U.S. in the early 20th Century. (to be started)

h) Today work...   its dignity and meaning for many blue-collar workers. (to lose)

i) Still the drive to understand why and how machines work...   whether in the small factory, the school machine shop or the home work-shop. (not to die out)

C FOLLOW UP WORK

1. Stress the relationship between the growth of the big corporation and the depersonalization of work.

2. How can you explain that the idea of the dignity of work has disappeared in modern times ?

3. In the writer's opinion, are the views of the bosses of industry and those of the trade-union members far apart in the U.S. ? What are the bosses (corporate employers) interested in ? What about trade-unionists ? What is their common goal ? What has been lost in the process ?

4. Comment : ''Work was cut off from a sense of creativeness''.

Chicago's El.

NO ONE EXISTS BUT ONESELF

My first glimpse of the flat black stretches of Chicago depressed and dismayed me[1], mocked all my fantasies. (...) The din[2] of the city entered my consciousness, entered to remain for years to come. The year was 1927.

What would happen to me here ? Would I survive ? My expectations were
5 modest. I wanted only a job. Hunger had long been my daily companion. Diversion and recreation, with the exception of reading, were unknown. In all my life—though surrounded by many people—I had not had a single satisfying, sustained relationship with another human being and, not having had any, I did not miss it. I made no demands whatever upon others.

10 The train rolled into the depot. Aunt Maggie and I got off and walked through the crowds into the station. I looked about to see if there were signs saying : FOR WHITE—FOR COLORED. I saw none. Black people and white people moved about, each seemingly intent upon his private mission. There was no racial fear. Indeed, each person acted as though no one existed but himself. It was strange to
15 pause before a crowded newsstand and buy a newspaper without having to wait until a white man was served. And yet, because everything was so new, I began to grow tense again, although it was a different sort of tension than I had known before. I knew that this machine-city was governed by strange laws and I wondered if I would ever learn them.

20 As we waited for a streetcar[3] to take us to Aunt Cleo's home for temporary lodging, I looked northward at towering buildings of steel and stone. There were no curves here, no trees ; only angles, lines, squares, bricks and copper wires[4]. Occasionally the ground beneath my feet shook from some faraway pounding[5] and I felt that this world, despite its massiveness, was somehow dangerously fragile.
25 Streetcars screeched[6] past over steel tracks. Cars honked their horns. Clipped speech [7] sounded about me. As I stood in the icy wind, I wanted to talk to Aunt Maggie, to ask her questions, but her tight [8] face made me hold my tongue. I was

The New York subway.

learning already from the frantic[9] light in her eyes the strain[10] that the city imposed upon its people. I was seized by doubt. Should I have come here ? But going back
30 was impossible. I had fled a known terror, and perhaps I could cope [11] with this unknown terror that lay ahead. (...)

People got on and off the car, but they never glanced at one another. Each person seemed to regard the others as a part of the city landscape.

We went to Aunt Cleo's address and found that she was living in a rented room. I
35 had imagined that she lived in an apartment and I was disappointed. I rented a room from Aunt Cleo's landlady and decided to keep it until I got a job. I was baffled[12]. Everything seemed makeshift[13], temporary. I caught an abiding sense of insecurity in the personalities of the people around me. I found Aunt Cleo aged beyond her years. Her husband, a product of a Southern plantation, had, like my
40 father, gone off and left her. Why had he left ? My aunt could not answer. She was beaten by the life of the city, just as my mother had been beaten. Wherever my eyes turned they saw stricken[14], frightened black faces trying vainly to cope with a civilization that they did not understand. I felt lonely. I had fled one insecurity and had embraced another.

Richard Wright, *American Hunger,* 1944

---

1. dismayed me : filled me with consternation. 2. din : loud continued noise. 3. streetcar : *tramway.* 4. copper wires : *fils de cuivre.* 5. pounding : thumping, striking heavily and repeatedly. 6. to screech : to utter a high, piercing, unpleasant cry. 7. the clipped speech : *le parler pointu (du Nord).* 8. tight : tense. 9. frantic : wildly agitated by anxiety. 10. strain : tension. 11. to cope : to manage successfully. 12. baffled : perplexed, confused. 13. makeshift : temporary. 14. stricken : afflicted.

A UNDERSTANDING THE TEXT

1. When and where did this young man get his first impressions of Chicago ? 2. What immediately struck him about the place ? 3. Why had he fantasized about this city before and why was he moving North ? 4. What do we learn about his background and life in the Deep South ? 5. What struck him in the station a) as a newcomer to the big city ? b) a black boy from the South ? 6. What impressed him about the people he could see on his way to his Aunt's ? 7. Describe his feelings then. 8. Can you imagine why his Aunt's husband had left her ? In what way is this situation typical of many poor black families ? 9. Is the description of Chicago a powerful one ? Explain. 10. What were the different causes of this young man's alienation ? 11. What is both striking and moving about his personality ? 12. What is the tone of the passage ? 13. Why is this text interesting ?

B LANGUAGE AT WORK

Expressing doubt

Examples :

> • "He was seized by doubt, he really could not tell whether he could cope."
> • He did not know whether...
> • He wondered whether...
> • He was not sure whether...
> • He could not tell whether...

Using the above expressions rephrase the variety of things the young man was in doubt about on his arrival in Chicago.

C FOLLOW UP WORK

1. Do you think this young man will get a job ?
2. Nowadays would it be illegal for a Black to sit side by side with a white on public transportation in a southern state ? In what ways has the Civil Rights legislation radically changed the situation ?

3. Explain :
"I had fled a known terror and perhaps I could cope with this unknown terror that lay ahead."
"I had fled one insecurity and had embraced another."

The history of pollution

WASHINGTON. — Everyone talks about water pollution, but no one seems to know who started it. The history of modern water pollution in the United States goes back to February 28, 1931, when Mrs Frieda Murphy leaned over her back-yard fence and said to Mrs Sophie Holbrook, "You call those shirts white ?"

Mrs Holbrook blushed and said, "They're as white as I can get them with this ordinary laundry soap."

— "What you should use is this *Formula Cake Soap* which guarantees against the dull wash-tub grey look that the family wash always had."

Skeptical but adventurous, Mrs Holbrook tried the *Formula* soap, which happily did take the grey out of her husband's shirts. But what Mrs Holbrook didn't know was that after the water was drained from the tub, it emptied into the sewer, which emptied into the Blue Sky River, killing two fish.

Three years later, Mrs Murphy leaned over the fence and said to Mrs Holbrook : "It's none of my business, but are you still using that *Formula Cake Soap* ?

— "Yes, I am."

— "No wonder your husband's shirts always look dirty around the collar."

— "I can never get the dirt off the collar," Mrs Holbrook cried.

— "You can, if you use *Klonk Soap Chips*. They were designed especially for collar dirt. Here, you can have my box."

Mrs Holbrook used the *Klonk* and the next time her husband put on his shirt he remarked : "How on earth did you get the collar clean ?"

— "That's my secret," said Mrs Holbrook, and then she whispered to no one in particular, "and Mrs Murphy's."

But unbeknownst to[1] Mrs Holbrook, the water from *Klonk Soap Chips* prevented any fish downstream from hatching eggs. Four years later, Mrs Murphy was hanging up her shirts and Mrs Holbrook said : "How did you ever get your cuffs so white, surely not with *Klonk* ?"

— "Not ordinary *Klonk*," Mrs Murphy said. "But I did with *Super Fortified Klonk* with the XLP additive. You see, *Super Fortified Klonk* attacks dirt and destroys it. Here, try some on your shirts." Mrs Holbrook did and discovered her husband's shirt cuffs turned pure white. What she could not possibly know was that it turned the river water pure white as well. The years went by, and poor Mrs Murphy died. Her daughter-in-law took over the house. Mrs Holbrook noticed how the daughter-in law used to sing as she hung up her wash. "Why do you always sing ?" asked Mrs Holbrook.

— "Because of this *Dynamite* detergent. It literally dynamites my clothes clean. Here, try it, and then let's go to a movie[2], since *Dynamite* detergent takes the drudgery[3] out of washing." Six months later the Blue Sky River was declared a health hazard.

Finally last year Mrs Murphy's daughter-in-law called over to Mrs Holbrook : "Have you heard about *Zap*, the enzyme giant killer ?"

A few days later, as Mr Holbrook was walking home from work, he accidentally fell into the Blue Sky River, swallowed a mouthful of water and died immediately.

At the funeral service the minister said : "You can say anything you want about Holbrook, but no one can deny he had the cleanest shirts in town."

Art Buchwald
in the *International Herald Tribune*

pollution /pə'lu:ʃən/   sceptical /'skeptɪkəl/   dynamite /'daɪnəmaɪt/
enzyme /'enzaɪm/

---

1. unbeknownst to : jokingly archaic for : unknown to.   **2.** movie : film.   **3.** drudgery : dull repetitive work.

A dam in the Sierras.

A UNDERSTANDING THE TEXT

What is amusing in the writer's statement about the beginning of water pollution in the U.S. ? **2.** The scene where Mrs Murphy leans over her backyard fence and asks Mrs Holbrok ''you call those shirts white ?'' is vaguely familiar. So are the other scenes whenever Mrs Murphy suggests a new detergent to Mrs Holbrook. Where do those scenes come from ? **3.** What, then, is the main reason why housewives always want to have whiter laundry, according to the writer ? **4.** How does advertising play on those feelings ? **5.** To what extent do you think the improved action of the soap powders each time coincide with the change of name ? **6.** What does the writer want to suggest about the growing sophistication of the soap names and of the publicity around them ? **7.** To what extent do you think the improved action of the soap powders coincides with the growing water pollution ? What does the writer want to suggest ? **8.** What changes in society and everyday life does this text reflect? **9.** To what extent do you think advertising reflects these changes ? **10.** What does the writer want to suggest with his final quip ?

B LANGUAGE AT WORK

Expressing absolute opinions

Examples :

• No one can deny	
• The is no denying	that Holbrock had the cleanest shirts in town.
• It's no use denying	

Using the above constructions, imagine the type of arguments Mrs. Murphy might have used each time in order to brainwash poor Mrs. Holbrook into following her advice.

73

Giving advice

Examples :

> • If I were you, I'd use the other soap.
> • What about/How about | using the other soap ?
> | a try ?
> • Why don't you try *Zap* ?
> • I think you should use the other soap.
> • You could use the *Formula Cake* soap, you know.

Read the text again, then using the above constructions, rephrase some of Mrs Murphy's advice to Mrs. Holbrook.

Admitting and conceding

Examples :

> • It may be good/Maybe it is good, but it is lethal for the fish.
> • It is good for shirt cuffs, on the other hand it kills all wildlife in the river.
> • Although they claim it's bio-degradable, it's still noxious.

Using the same models, make up the answers an ecologist could have given each time Mrs. Murphy came to praise a new detergent. First, make up all the answers with may *or* maybe, *then do the exercise over again using expressions such as* although, but, however, on the other hand, still, yet, *etc.*

C FOLLOW UP WORK

1. Give an account of the phenomenon of pollution using the approach of a sociologist. Use what elements you may need in the story, but leave out particular names, jokes, etc. Refer to housewives in general and make complex sentences.
Make the following points :
— the responsibility of the advertisers ;
— the fact that advertising plays on self-esteem ;
— the connection between the growing pollution and the growing sophistication of detergents ;
— the harm done to the environment.
Start like this :
"It can be said that water pollution is directly connected with the growing use of sophisticated detergents. Towards the beginning of the 30's..."

2. The text gives a few examples of brand names of soap powders and of the advertising arguments used to promote them. Notice the gradation and use them as examples to make up 5 successive names and slogans for a brand of cigarettes.
3. Rewrite the same story based on the situations whenever Mr Holbrook arrived at the office with a shirt laundered with a new powder. Use dialogue form and introduce some of the comic devices that occur in the passage.
4. Pollution is inevitable because people are not ready to change their habits.

Daddy, what did you do in the war against pollution?

Of course you can always try to change the subject.

But one answer you can't give is that you weren't in it. Because in this war, there are no 4F's and no conscientious objectors. No deferments for married men or teen-agers. And no exemptions for women.

So like it or not, we're all in this one. But as the war heats up, millions of us stay coolly uninvolved. We have lots of alibis:

What can one person do?

It's up to "them" to do something about pollution — not me.

Besides, average people don't pollute. It's the corporations, institutions and municipalities.

The fact is that companies and governments are made up of people. It's people who make decisions and do things that foul up our water, land and air. And that goes for businessmen, government officials, housewives or homeowners.

What can one person do for the cause? Lots of things — maybe more than you think. Like cleaning your spark plugs every 1000 miles, using detergents in the recommended amounts, by upgrading incinerators to reduce smoke emissions, by proposing and supporting better waste treatment plants in your town. Yes, and throwing litter in a basket instead of in the street.

Above all, let's stop shifting the blame. People start pollution. People can stop it. When enough Americans realize this we'll have a fighting chance in the war against pollution.

 Keep America Beautiful

People start pollution. People can stop it.

HOW TO STRIP A JOB-SEEKER NAKED

In The Naked Society, *Vance Packard denounces the threats to privacy and individual freedom that the improvement of surveillance techniques and the computerized collection of data represent in modern society. In this passage he describes a typical interview being conducted with the use of a lie detector.*

Mr Probe helped Bill light his cigarette and then said, "I know we all have skeletons in the closet, and I'm not trying to dig them up. I'm just asking you to be completely honest with me." He gave as an example the fact that some people lie a little bit about their college backgrounds[1]. Some say they attended college when
5 they went only one semester, and others say they have never stolen before and maybe they have. Then he told his new friend Bill : "I want to be able to write that you have a good, clean, smooth indication of truth. I'll be back of you all the way if that is the way it appears." Then he said, "Okay, Bill ?" And added : "If you can't completely and honestly say 'no' to a question, let me know and perhaps I can
10 rephrase the question".

And so Mr Probe began his *pre*-polygraph questioning.
"Have you ever stolen from previous employers ?" Bill shifted in his chair a little and said, "As far as stealing, the only kind I remember is ten years ago I stole some stationery from a company where I was working." Mr Probe magnanimously
15 waved this aside. He said : "I'm not interested in stationery and paper clips ; there's a little pilferage[2] in all of us." Then he said, more solemnly : "Have you ever taken anything beyond what we discussed ?"
BILL : "No."
MR PROBE : "Ever fired[3] for cause ?"
20 BILL : "Never."
MR PROBE : "Ever drink to excess ?"
BILL : "I've been loaded a few times, but I guess that's not 'excess' so I'll say no."
MR PROBE : "Any mental disorders ?"
BILL : "What do you mean, 'mental disorders' ? I guess I'm nervous at times."
25 MR PROBE : "I mean anything mental that would impair your work and prevent you from being a good salesman for this company."
BILL : "No."
MR PROBE : "Are you in good physical condition ?"
BILL : "Yes, as far as I know, except for sinus trouble."
30 MR PROBE : "Are you seeking permanent employment ?"
BILL : "Well, I guess. What do you mean ?"
MR PROBE : "Do you have any plans to leave in the near future if you get the job ?"
BILL : "Not that I know of."

35 At this point Mr Probe explained that his client was not interested in spending $8,000 to $10,000 to break in[4] a man who would go to some other company. Of course, Mr Probe said, no one can blame a man for going to a much better opening. "But right now do you have any other plans ?"

Bill explained that he did have another job offer, in Boston, and he couldn't
40 positively state that he hoped to have a permanent career with the company to which he was applying, since he had not yet worked for it. But he said he hoped to get the job and at the moment had no other plans.

/'klɔzɪt/

/'sainəs/

A 29-year-old walks the streets to advertise his problem.

MR PROBE : "Have you answered truthfully all the questions on the application ?"
Bill paused and explained that there was that thing about having a college degree.
45 He had attended two colleges in the Midwest for about four and a half years but
had never, to be truthful, finally got the degree.

Now Mr Probe began to explain the mechanics of the machine. He asked Bill to
take off his vest[5], roll up his left sleeve, and sit in the subject's chair. Mr Probe
strapped the accordion-like rubber tubing across Bill's chest (to check his
50 respiration), attached a blood-pressure-pulse band to his arm, an electrode to his
hand to check the sweating of his palm and muscular movement. [...]   /ˈswetɪŋ/

I could see that three needles on the recording machine in front of Mr Probe were
already starting to make their squiggling lines on paper : the first recorded
breathing, the second sweating, the third circulatory responses.   /ˈbriːðɪŋ/

55   And now the questionaire began with the machine in operation. In addition to
the ones given in pre-exam, Mr Probe asked such irrelevant questions as "Do you
ever watch T.V. ?" These presumably are control questions. Twice Mr Probe
admonished Bill not to move about so much. At least two new questions were :
"Have you ever been arrested for speeding or getting a ticket ?" (Bill tried to
60 explain something about an incident in Indiana.)

"Have you ever done something that you are really and truly ashamed of ?" Bill
shook his head. My guide whispered : "That question will sometimes smoke out[6]
the homosexual."

When Mr Probe repeated the question about ever stealing merchandise, Bill said
65 "No." One of the needles drew an emphatic peak line and my guide murmured,
"That doesn't look so good."

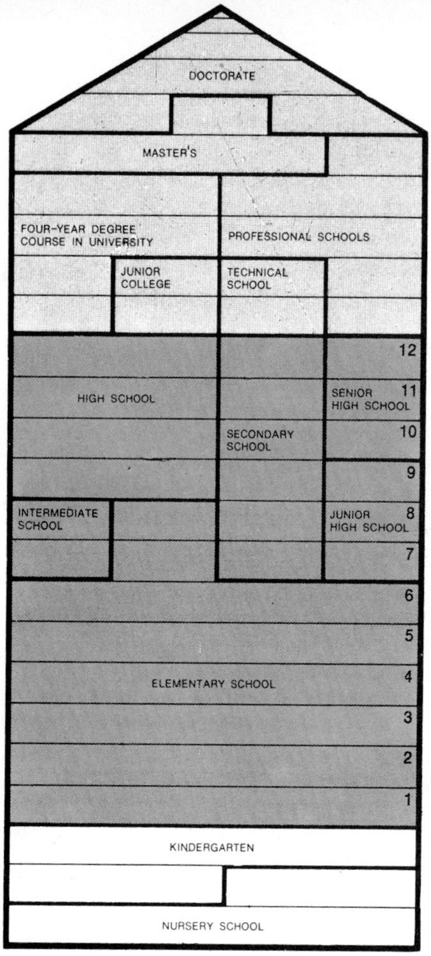
DOCTORATE
MASTER'S
FOUR-YEAR DEGREE COURSE IN UNIVERSITY
PROFESSIONAL SCHOOLS
JUNIOR COLLEGE
TECHNICAL SCHOOL
12
HIGH SCHOOL
SENIOR HIGH SCHOOL
11
SECONDARY SCHOOL
10
9
INTERMEDIATE SCHOOL
JUNIOR HIGH SCHOOL
8
7
6
5
ELEMENTARY SCHOOL
4
3
2
1
KINDERGARTEN
NURSERY SCHOOL

The various streams from infancy to high school graduation and Ph. D.

Now the machine was turned off and Mr Probe was explaining that a couple of Bill's responses did give him a little concern. There was a reference to stealing merchandise. Bill conceded he did feel sort of funny when that one came at him, and he said he had also become nervous when asked about mental disorder. It sort of made him nervous. Also the drinking question. [...]

The examination seemingly was over, and Bill was looking for his hat. Then Mr Probe said pleasantly, "Bill, one more question before you leave. There is nothing personal or offensive about this, but because of the kind of business you are going in and the fact you have been in the summer theater work, I think I should ask it. Are you inclined to be homosexual ?" [...]

The examiners wanted me to watch more tests ; but I said I had had enough. I had had enough to the point of nausea. /'nɔ:ziə/ /'nɔ:ʃə/

Vance Packard,
***The Naked Society*, 1964**

---

1. college backgrounds : *bagage universitaire*. **2.** pilferage : petty thieving. **3.** fired : sacked from a job. **4.** to break in : to train. **5.** vest *(Am)* : usually waistcoat *(Eng.)*, but here jacket. **6.** smoke out : cause to come out of his hole.

A UNDERSTANDING THE TEXT

1. What was Bill in for ? **2.** What is the irony in the name "Mr Probe" ? **3.** Was Mr Probe trying to put Bill at ease simply to be nice ? Justify your answer. **4.** Why do people lie about things such as their college background ? **5.** Why did Mr Probe ask questions about points which did not seem to be important or which were very personal ? **6.** What was the job Bill had applied for ? **7** How does the machine work, and how can it detect lies ? **8.** What worried Mr Probe about some of Bill's responses ? How could these be interpreted unfavorably for Bill ? **9.** Why did Mr Probe want to know about Bill's sexual preferences ? How can this information be of any interest to employers ? **10.** Why had the narrator reached "the point of nausea" ?

Seeking confirmation

Examples :

> • You have been employed at Jones's, haven't you ?
>   — Yes, I have.
> • They specialize in foreign business, don't they ?
>   — Yes, they do.
> • They don't have any connection with Burma, though, have they ?
>   — No, they don't.

Pair work. One student is playing the role of "Mr. Probe" interviewing a prospective candidate to a job, and the other is the candidate, then they reverse. The one doing the questioning asks the other confirmation of a few facts concerning his/her past life, his/her degrees, his/her experience, his/her interests, etc.

Expressing doubts and insinuations

Examples :

> • I have been employed at Jones's.
>   — You have, have you ?
>
> • They specialize in foreign business.
>   — They do, do they ?
>
> • They don't have any connection with Burma.
>   — They don't, don't they ?

Pair work. One student is an attorney cross-examining a witness, and the other is the witness. They should exchange their roles after a while. The witness states

a) that he/she did not see the accused the night of the crime.
b) that he/she does not remember if it was raining or not that night.
c) that he/she did not recognize the accused at first.
d) that he/she never goes to bed later than 10 p.m.
e) that it wasn't midnight.
f) that it was unusual for him/her to go to bed so late that night.
g) that he/she had not realized his/her Venetian dagger had disappeared from where it was, etc.

and of course the attorney remains unconvinced each time.

C FOLLOW UP WORK

1. A friend of Bill's is to be interviewed by Mr Probe for a job with the same firm. Bill gives him a account of the test and of the type of questions asked (used reported speech).

2. Write out the report on Bill which Mr Probe may have sent to his prospective employer after the interview. Write as if you were Mr Probe and give your personal impression of the candidate, the way the interview went, your appreciation of the candidate's responses, and your final recommendation.

3. Tests are essential when hiring employees.

Garden City

Garden City is a real city in Kansas.

Anyone who has made the coast-to-coast journey across America, whether by train or by car, has probably passed through Garden City, but it is reasonable to assume that few travelers remember the event. It seems just another fair-sized town in the middle—almost the exact middle—of the continental United States. Not that
5 the inhabitants would tolerate such an opinion—perhaps rightly. Though they may overstate the case ("Look all over the world, and you won't find friendlier people or fresher air or sweeter drinking water", and "I could go to Denver at triple the salary, but I've got five kids, and I figure there's no better place to raise kids than right here. Swell[1] schools with every kind of sport. We even have a junior college[2]",
10 and "I came out here to practice law. A temporary thing ; I never planned to stay. But when the chance came to move, I thought, Why go ? What the hell for ? Maybe it's not New York—but who wants New York ? Good neighbors, people who care

about each other, that's what counts. And everything else a decent man
needs—we've got that too. Beautiful churches. A golf course."), the newcomer to
15 Garden City, once he has adjusted to the nightly after-eight silence of Main Street,
discovers much to support the defensive boastings of the citizenry : a well-run
public library, a competent daily newspaper, green-lawned and shady squares here   /'kɑmpɪ̪tənt/
and there, placid residential streets where animals and children are safe to run free,
a big, rambling park, complete with a small menagerie ("See the Polar Bears !"   /mɪ̪'nædʒəri/
20 "See Penny the Elephant !"), and a swimming pool that consumes several acres[3]
("World's Largest FREE Swim-Pool !"). Such accessories, and the dust and the
winds and the ever-calling train whistles add up to a "home town" that is probably   /'wɪsəls/
remembered with nostalgia by those who have left it, and that, for those who have
remained, provides a sense of roots and contentment.

25   Without exception, Garden Citians deny that the population of the town can be
socially graded ("No, sir, nothing like that here. All equal regardless of wealth,
color, or creed. Everything the way it ought to be in a democracy ; that's us"), but
of course, class distinctions are as clearly observed, and as clearly observable, as in
any other human hive[4]. A hundred miles west and one would be out of the "Bible
30 Belt", that Gospel[5]-haunted strip of American territory in which a man must, if
only for business reasons, take his religion with the straightest of faces, but in
Finney County one is still within the Bible Belt borders, and therefore a person's
church affiliation is the most important factor influencing his class status. A   /'steɪtəs/
combination of Baptists, Methodists, and Roman Catholics would account for   /'bæptɪ̪sts/
35 eighty per cent of the county's devout, yet among the elite—the businessmen,   /'meθədɪ̪sts/
bankers, lawyers, physicians, and more prominent ranchers who tenant[6] the top
drawer—Presbyterians and Episcopalians dominate. An occasional Methodist is   /ˌprezbɪ̪'tɪərɪəns/
welcomed, and once in a while a Democrat infiltrates, but on the whole the   /ɪˌpɪskə'peɪlɪəns/
Establishment is composed of rightwing Republicans of the Presbyterian and
40 Episcopalian faiths.

Truman Capote, In Cold Blood, 1965   /kə'pəʊt/

---

1. swell : (colloq.) very good.   2. junior college : first two years of university.   3. acres : 1 ha. ≃ 2,5 acres.
4. a bee hive : *une ruche.*   5. Gospel : *Évangile.*   6. tenant : occupy.

A   UNDERSTANDING THE TEXT

1. What does the author want to suggest when he
writes that few people probably remember crossing
Garden City ?   2. What does he want to suggest by
insisting on the fact that Garden City is *in the middle*
of America ? Is he necessarily referring to
geography ?   3. Does the author share the
inhabitants' enthusiasm towards their hometown ?
How does he emphasize his point of view ?   4. How
does he make us realize that life in Garden City is
probably dull ?   5. How does he point out to us the
naive pride of "Garden Citians" ?   6. What
qualities does Garden City possess ? How does the
author convey the type of quiet happiness that
prevails there ?   7. What is the Bible Belt ?
8. What is the criticism the author expresses about
the correlation between religious convictions and
class status ?   9. Why are class distinctions
connected with religious differences ?   10. Is this
your idea of an American town or not ? Justify your
answer.

Expressing moral attitudes

The text exemplifies the type of conformity that can be very strong in a small American community. Notice how it is expressed, i. e. with both general statements and words carrying a moral judgment :

> • "Good neighbors, people who care about each other, that's what counts. Everything else a *decent* man needs — we've got that too."
> • "No, sir, nothing like that here. All equal regardless of wealth, color, or creed. Everything the way it *ought to be* in a democracy."

Using general statements and verbs such as must, have to, should, ought to, *describe the behavior of the ideal citizen as seen by an inhabitant of Garden City.*

Expressing regret or mentionning missed opportunities

Example :

> • I could have moved to Denver. If I had done that, I would have earned three times as much per month.

Using expressions such as might, could, would/if, *describe the type of life that the lawyer thinks he could have had if he had moved to New York.*

C FOLLOW UP WORK

1. You are spending a month in Garden City in the summer as an exchange student. Write a letter to an English friend giving your frank impressions of the place and of the people.
2. Write the text of a pamphlet as might have been commissionned by the Garden City Travel Bureau.
3. It is more pleasant to live in a place like Garden City than in a big town. Discuss.

SURVEYING THE SCENE

1. Say what traditional views of the development of the United States are contradicted by what we learn from
   - *How the Indians Saw it,*
   - *Greer County Bachelor,*
   - *1902 : They Came to America.*
2. To what extent do you think dissenting voices such as the ones heard in the above texts suggest that the American Dream is an illusion ?
3. What vices or shortcomings of the American society are set into relief by
   - *The History of Pollution,*
   - *How to Strip a Job-Seeker naked,*
   - *No one exists but oneself,*
   - *Garden City ?*
4. To what extent do you think the points made in the above texts are sufficient to condemn the American way of life ?
5. In what way can *The History of Pollution* be considered a justification of the Indians' reproaches towards the white man ?
6. What common disillusionment did the immigrants that came to America in 1902 and the young black arriving in Chicago in 1927 experience ?
7. To what extent do you think Mrs. Murphy and Mrs. Holbrook in *The History of Pollution* might be inhabitants of Garden City ?

Some books you might like to read : *U.S.A. (Le 42ᵉ Parallèle ; 1919 ; La Grosse Galette),* by J. Dos Passos.
Black Boy by Richard Wright.
On the Waterfront by Elia Kazan.
The Jungle by Upton Sinclair.

Some films you might like to see : *The Gold Rush* and *Modern Times*, by C. Chaplin.

IV. THE

AMERICAN

MOSAIC

HYPHENATED AMERICANS

For someone like me, whose surname ends in a vowel, Providence, R.I., was a nice place to be born and raised. It is, like a lot of East coast cities, a town where ethnic consciousness runs high, and where one of the dominant values is a belief in the virtues of sticking by one's own kind, whether that means family, neighborhood, or, in a larger context, ethnic group. High school status, I remember, was
5 often conferred on the basis of what ethnic group one belonged to, and what neighborhood one lived in (the "tougher" the neighborhood, the higher the status).

In the parts of Providence where I grew up, the predominant ethnic group was the Italians ; so it was natural that I embraced that part of my heritage. My father is the son of an Italian immigrant, and although I know less about where my grandfather came from and how he got to America than I
10 would like, I have always found the notion of his getting here a romantic and attractive one. In doing so, I undoubtedly slighted[1] my mother's heritage, which was mostly Irish, but that was of no great concern to me at the time ; in Providence there was a great deal of pride associated with being Italian, and as a kid with an Italian surname, it was not something I was about to miss out on.

Away from the peer pressure[2] of those days, I have since come to see myself quite a bit differently. I
15 consider myself a non-ethnic. In saying this, I have no sense that I am rejecting my heritage in order to better blend in with any homogenized mass of white-collar Americans. I am, however, making some distinctions : my past comes out of Rhode Island and America, not Italy, and if I take a certain pride in the accomplishments of my grandfather, or in knowing there is a town in Italy called Nocera (which, without any particular grounding in fact, I have always assumed had something to do with
20 some long-lost ancestors of mine), it is a pride in *personal* past, not a cultural, communal one.

There are many people like me in America, people with "ethnic" surnames[3] but with none of the stereotyped characteristics that are supposed to go hand-in-hand with that particular ethnic group. With each succeeding generation, there are going to be many more, as immigrants die, replaced by the sons of immigrants, and then, the sons of sons of immigrants. A lot of the immigrant culture
25 inevitably dies too. What strikes me as artificial is not the gradual transformation of the generations, but the pressures to preserve the old culture no matter what. That's why I become disconcerted and even vaguely insulted when it is naturally assumed (as it occasionally is) that I should act or think a certain way simply because of that last name I have. I delight in my name, make no mistake, but at the same time, I don't wave my hands around when I talk and I've never been able to arouse any
30 indignation over *The Godfather*. To act as if I did would be false. I had a long conversation a few years ago with a priest who ran the Italian-American Foundation, who insisted on calling me "brother" simply because we both had Italian names. What a tenuous bond[4] on which to hang fraternity !

Joseph Nocera *"The View From Providence"*, *The Washington Monthly,* 1979

tough /tʌf/ undoubtedly /ʌnˈdaʊtədli/

---

1. to slight : to consider unimportant. **2.** peer pressure : pressure from people in the same age group. **3.** surname *(Am.)* : family name *(Eng.)*. **4.** a bond : *un lien*.

"Little Italy".

A TRUE OR FALSE

1. The author is a staunch believer in divine providence.   2. In the town where he was raised, people were considered only according to the image of their ethnic group.   3. He is of Irish descent.   4. He was born on an island.   5. He believes that the immigrants' culture endures and must be cultivated.   6. He is all for putting pressure on the government to save ethnic cultures.

B ANSWER THESE QUESTIONS :

1. What does the author think of his home town ?   2. What seems to be the basic value for immigrants ?   3. What is the author's heritage ? Where did his parents come from ?   4. Did he choose among his parents' origins ? Why ?   5. In what ways does he still consider himself an Italian ?   6. What difference does he make between a "personal past" and a "cultural, communal one" ?   7. To what extent does he consider himself American ?   8. What strikes him particularly among contemporary Italian Americans ?   9. Why isn't he furious at *The Godfather* ? Why should he be or could he be ?   10. Why did he find the priest who called him "brother" a bit ridiculous ?

C EXPRESS IN YOUR OWN WORDS

1. A belief in the virtues of sticking by one's own kind.
2. The "tougher" the neighborhood, the higher the status.
3. The stereotyped characteristics that are supposed to go hand-in-hand with a particular ethnic group.
4. The pressures to preserve an old culture no matter what.
5. I don't wave my hands around when I talk.

D DISCUSSION

It is ridiculous to try to assume a regional past or folklore simply because your parents or grand-parents were born in a given area.

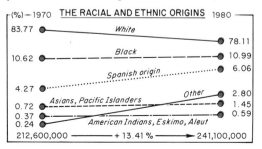

(%) – 1970   THE RACIAL AND ETHNIC ORIGINS   1980

	1970	1980
White	83.77	78.11
Black	10.62	10.99
Spanish origin		6.06
Asians, Pacific Islanders	4.27	2.80
Other	0.72	1.45
American Indians, Eskimo, Aleut	0.37 / 0.24	0.59

212,600,000 ———— + 13.41 % ————▶ 241,100,000

ON THE ROAD

The greatest ride in my life was about to come up, a truck, with a flatboard at the back, with about six or seven boys sprawled out on it, and the drivers, two young blond farmers from Minnesota, were picking up every single soul they found on that road—the most smiling, cheerful couple of handsome bumpkins[1] you could ever wish to see, both wearing cotton shirts and overalls, nothing else ; both thick-wristed and earnest, with broad howareyou smiles for anybody and anything that came across their path. I ran up, said "Is there room ?" They said, "Sure, hop on, 'sroom for everybody."

I wasn't on the flatboard before the truck roared off ; I lurched, a rider grabbed me, and I sat down. Somebody passed a bottle of rotgut[2], the bottom of it. I took a big swig in the wild, lyrical, drizzling air of Nebraska. "Whooee, here we go !" yelled a kid in a baseball cap, and they gunned up the truck to seventy and passed everybody on the road. "We been riding this sonofabitch since Des Moines. These guys never stop. Every now and then you have to yell for pisscall, otherwise you have to piss off in the air, and hang on, brother, hang on."

I looked at the company. There were two young farmer boys from North Dakota in red baseball caps, which is the standard North Dakota farmer-boy hat, and they were headed for the harvests ; their old men[3] had given them leave to hit the road[4] for a summer. There were two young city boys from Columbus, Ohio, high-school football players, chewing gum, winking, singing in the breeze, and said they were hitchhiking around the United States for the summer. "We're going to L.A. !" they yelled.

— "What are you going to do there ?"
— "Hell, we don't know. Who cares ?"

Then there was a tall slim fellow who had a sneaky[5] look. "Where you from ?" I asked. I was lying next to him on the platform ; you couldn't sit without bouncing off, it had no rails. And he turned slowly to me, opened his mouth, and said, "Monta-na".

Finally there were Mississippi Gene and his charge. Mississippi Gene was a little dark guy who rode freight trains around the country, a thirty-year-old hobo but with a youthful look so you couldn't tell exactly what age he was. And he sat on the boards crosslegged, looking out over the fields without saying anything for hundreds of miles, and finally at one point he turned to me and said, "Where *you* headed ?"...

I said Denver.

/ˌmɪnɪˈsotə/

/nəˈbræskə/

/dɪˈmɔɪn/

/dəˈkotə/

/kəˈlʌmbəs/
/əʊˈhaɪo/

/mɑnˈtænə/

/ˌmɪsəˈsɪpɪ/

Two unusual hitchhikers.

— "I got a sister there but I ain't seen her for several couple years." His language was melodious and slow. He was patient. His charge was a sixteen-year-old tall blond kid, also in hobo rags ; that is to say, they wore old clothes that had been turned black by the soot of railroads and the dirt of boxcars[6] and sleeping on the
40 ground. The blond kid was also quiet and he seemed to be running away from something, and it figured to be the law the way he looked straight ahead and wet his lips in worried thought. Montana Slim spoke to them occasionally with a sardonic and insinuating smile. They paid no attention to him. Slim was all insinuation. I was afraid of his long goofy[7] grin that he opened up straight in your face and held
45 there half-moronically[8].

— "You got any money ?" he said to me.
— "Hell, no, maybe enough for a pint of whisky till I get to Denver. What about you ?"
— "I know where I can get some."
50 — "Where ?"
— "Anywhere. You can always folly a man down an alley, can't you ?"
— "Yeah, I guess you can."
— "I ain't beyond doing it when I really need some dough[9]. Headed up to
Montana to see my father. I'll have to get off this rig at Cheyenne and move up
55 some other way. These crazy boys are going to Los Angeles."

/dəʊ/
/ʃaɪˈen/

89

— "Straight ?"
— "All the way—if you want to go to L.A. you got a ride."

    I mulled this over[10] ; the thought of zooming all night across Nebraska, Wyoming, and the Utah desert in the morning, and then most likely the Nevada desert in the afternoon, and actually arriving in Los Angeles within a foreseeable space of time almost made me change my plans. But I had to go to Denver. I'd have to get off at Cheyenne too, and hitch south ninety miles to Denver.

    /waɪˈomɪŋ/
    /ˈjʊta/
    /nəˈvadə/

    I was glad when the two Minnesota farmboys who owned the truck decided to stop in North Platte and eat ; I wanted to have a look at them. They came out of the cab and smiled at all of us. "Pisscall !" said one. "Time to eat !"said the other. But they were the only ones in the party who had money to buy food. We all shambled after them to a restaurant run by a bunch of women and sat around over hamburgers and coffee while they wrapped away[11] enormous meals just as if they were back in their mother's kitchen. They were brothers ; they were transporting farm machinery from Los Angeles to Minnesota and making good money at it. So on their trip to the Coast empty they picked up everybody on the road. They'd done this about five times now ; they were having a hell of a time[12]. They liked everything. They never stopped smiling. I tried to talk to them—a kind of dumb attempt on my part to befriend the captains of our ship—and the only responses I got were two sunny smiles and large white corn-fed teeth.

Jack Kerouac, *On the Road*, 1957

---

1. bumpkins : rustics. **2.** rotgut : *tord boyau*. **3.** their old men : (colloq.) their fathers. **4.** hit the road : away. **5.** sneaky : furtive. **6.** boxcars : freight cars. **7.** goofy : idiotic (cf. Walt Disney's character). **8.** half-moronically : half-idiotically. **9.** dough : (slang) money. **10.** mulled over : thought over. **11.** wrapped away : (colloq.) ate up. **12.** a hell of a time : (colloq.) a lot of fun.

A UNDERSTANDING THE TEXT

1. How did the author get what was going to be the greatest ride in his life ? 2. What was his welcome on the flatboard of the truck ? 3. How many boys were there on the truck ? Who were they ? Where were they all headed ? 4. Why does the author refer to the man with a sneaky look as "Montana Slim", and to Gene as "Mississippi Gene" ? 5. What was the author's opinion of the reason why Mississippi Gene's charge had hit the road ? 6. Why did Montana Slim speak to Gene and the boy with a sardonic and insinuating smile ? 7. What was Montana Slim's way of getting money when he needed some ? 8. Can you suggest why this passage appears in the chapter called *The American Mosaic* ? 9. What different aspects of America did the different boys on the platform represent ? 10. What elements give a poetic quality to this passage ?

B LANGUAGE AT WORK

Reporting questions

Examples :

- "Is there room ?" → I asked whether/if there was room.
- "Where are you headed ?" → They asked where I was headed.
- "Where are you from ?" → I asked where he was from.

Notice the changes in verb tenses, pronouns, and word order.

1. Suppose the author arrives in Denver, Colorado. He describes his journey to his friends, and the conversation he had with the others on the flatboard. Give 10 examples of reported questions, starting with I asked, he asked, *or* they asked.

2. Suppose the author, once alone, wonders about the people he has met, about their past and future, etc. Give 10 examples of reported questions starting with I wonder.

Expressing probability

Examples :

- They may have crossed the Black Hills on their way.
- They perhaps/probably crossed...
- They are likely to have crossed...
- They must have crossed...
- They can't have stopped at Mount Rushmore.
- They very likely didn't stop at Mount Rushmore.
- They probably didn't stop at Mount Rushmore.

Read the text. Then, using the above constructions, give accounts of the probable life and past experiences of the various boys on the platform.

C FOLLOW UP WORK

1. At a party later on, someone asks the author why this ride was the greatest in his life and he tries to explain.

2. What different aspects of America did the different boys on the platform represent ?
3. Hitch-hiking is the only intelligent way of travelling.

NIKKI-ROSA

childhood remembrances are always a drag[1]
if you're Black
you always remember things like living in Woodlawn[2]
with no inside toilet
5 and if you become famous or something
they never talk about how happy you were to have your mother
all to yourself and
how good the water felt when you got your bath from one of those
big tubs that folks in Chicago barbecue in   /'bɑrbɪkju:/
10 and somehow when you talk about home
it never gets across how much you
understood their feelings
as the whole family attended meetings about Hollydale[2]
and even though you remember
15 your biographers never understand   /baɪ'ɑgrəfər/
your father's pain as he sells his stock[3]
and another dream goes
and though you're poor it isn't poverty that
concerns you
20 and though they fought a lot
it isn't your father's drinking that makes any difference
but only that everybody is together and you
and your sister have happy birthdays and very good Christmases
and I really hope no white person ever has cause to write about me
25 because they never understand Black love is Black wealth and they'll
probably talk about my hard childhood and never understand that
all the while I was quite happy

Nikki Giovanni, *Black Judgment*

---

1. a drag : a burden.   2. Woodlawn, Hollydale : parts of the Chicago ghetto.   3. stock : shares in companies.

A UNDERSTANDING THE TEXT

1. Why are childhood remembrances "always a drag if you're Black" ? 2. What were the child's reasons for being happy ? 3. Why do you think she had her mother all to herself ? 4. What is difficult for a black to make white people understand when he/she speaks about home ? 5. What was the reason "father had to sell his stock" ? How far does this go against the stereotyped view of the condition of blacks ? 6. What does the poet want her readers to understand by writing "though you're poor it isn't poverty that concerns you". 7. What does she mean by "it isn't your father's drinking that makes any difference" ? 8. Why does she write that she hopes no white person will ever have cause to write about her ? 9. What human truth does she want her readers (especially white ones) to understand ? What attitude on their part does she reject ?

B LANGUAGE AT WORK

Expressing simultaneity

Examples :

> • *While* she was ill, her mother stayed home to look after her. .
> • *During* her illness, her mother stayed home to look after her.

Use either during *or* while *to make up sentences corresponding to the following situations :*

a) They lived in Woodlawn for a few years and they had no inside toilet.
b) She was a child then, and her mother did not go to work.
c) After that, they lived in East Chicago for a few years and her father took to drinking.
d) The depression came and her father had to sell his stock.
e) They attended a meeting in Hollydale once and an incident occurred.
f) The family once took a vacation on Lake Michigan and she shared a room with her sister.
g) In college she studied philosophy.
h) Her parents fought a lot and broke a lot of plates.

Reported questions

Examples :

> • They never talk about how happy you were.
> • It never gets across how much you understood their feelings.

Notice the order of the words. Then, using the same pattern, point out some of the things white people seem never to understand about blacks.

C FOLLOW UP WORK

1. Why does the poet object to the way white people generally visualize a black childhood ?
2. To what extent do you think the poem is autobiographical or refers to black experience in general ?
3. What gives a poetic quality to this text.

Could this be Mike ?

MIKE

Mike Kostelnik is a 36-year-old window-washer with a wife and two children. They live in a residential suburb of a mid-Western town. Mike is explaining to the interviewer why he is happy to have bought a house in such a district.

MIKE : You see, when you're owning individual property, you have a community feeling. Everyone's more interested because they have more at stake. And when you come outside, I mean, there's Joe Blow[1] or whatever his name is, he's doing a concrete job. Well, the thing is to go over and give
5 him a hand. I've got a neighbor across the way, well, he can't do heights[2], so I cut his trees. So the next time the guy comes over my house, he's gonna do my plumbing.

/ˈplʌmɪŋ/

INTERVIEWER : *But doesn't this create obligations ? Don't you think the community imposes a kind of conformity ?*
10 **M :** Look, we had our street paved where we were living. Now everybody had to do this, because you wanted the block to look right, you know. And if you didn't—'cause a couple were real slow at it—all the rest of the people looked at them : "Hey, when are you going to get yours ?" A month or two and you see the guy's not doing it, so you, well, you sort of look it over
15 every time you go by. You give the guy a subtle hint that this should be done. You know. "Lookit, uh, why should you leave it this way ? You like

the area ? That's why you moved here. You like the area ? Keep it up." I
mean, why should you go into an area that you pick and then right away let
the weeds grow, you know ? Why should I be a nonconformist ? You have
20 to conform to society.

I : *How do you explain that blacks are not more numerous in a neighborhood like this ?*

M. : What makes people scared of the blacks is they're scared of
deteriorating property. Now if these people just go ahead and show that
25 they're intelligent enough... And there are a lot of wonderful people. I've
done work for black lawyers, educated people, and you couldn't find a
better group of people. These people don't like their own type, they don't
like their own people in their own race. Now there must be a reason for it. I
have quite a few black friends. I've discussed this basic thing with them. I
30 know a parking-lot fella[3] here. I've met a lot of wonderful black people,
don't get me wrong. It's never a question of color, it's the way a lot of
them live. So why should anybody tell me, the property I'm sweating for[4]
right now and I'm working every day and sweating for, why should I be
told who to sell it to ? Where are *my* civil rights[5] ? There's the twister. Why
35 should I be told what I sweated for and earned—this is against the
constitution actually—how I should dispose of it ? Don't you think that's
wrong ? I don't want to infringe on any man's freedom. But I also don't
want mine infringed on.

I. : *Suppose a neighbor left and sold his house to a black ?*
40 M. : I would not run. But I tell you one thing, he'd better keep up his
property, because then I'd get disturbed. I'd be one of the first guys on the
phone and keep on calling City Hall and telling them : "Here's your man
now, let's see how he keeps up his property." 'Cause I bought my property
and I want my property value to be up. I'm taking care of mine and so are
45 all my neighbors. Now if this gentleman conforms to this type of situation,
there's no restriction. Of course, his moral code I would watch out for,
too...

/,nɑn kən'fɔrmɪ̜st/

/'beɪsɪk/

/'swetɪŋ/

Adapted from *Division Street* by Studs Terkel

---

1. Joe Blow : *Monsieur Tout-le-monde.*   **2.** he can't do heights : *il a le vertige.*   **3.** parking-lot fella : parking-lot attendant ; fella : fellow.   **4.** sweating for : working hard.   **5.** civil rights : allusion to the 1964 equal rights legislation for blacks.

A   UNDERSTANDING THE TEXT

1. What is Mike's job ?   **2.** According to Mike, why do people have a community feeling when they own individual property ?   **3.** What sort of relationships does Mike have with his neighbors ?   **4.** In the place where Mike lived before, what sort of tactics did people use in order to convince some of their neighbors to have the sidewalk paved in front of their houses ?   **5.** What do you think of such an action ?   **6.** In what way does Mike try to avoid giving the impression that he is racially prejudiced ?

7. What is the main argument of middle-class property-owners against having black neighbors ?   **8.** What are Mike's main objections to having black neighbors ?   **9.** What in Mike's words shows the effect of the Federal Government's action in favor of racial integration ?   **10.** How does Mike rationalize his position ?   **11.** To what extent do you think Mike could be typical of homeowners in other countries ?

Forbidding and persuading not to

Depending on the circumstances, his closeness to the other person involved, their reciprocal knowledge and appreciation of each other's social status, Mike could say things like :

- *Don't/You mustn't* **let your dog foul the sidewalk.** *(Interdiction)*
- **You** *don't have* to let your dog... *(Appeal to reason, rather sour tone)*
- *If I were you, I wouldn't* let... . *(Conciliatory tone, advice)*
- *You shouldn't* let... . *(Moral reproach)*
- **Look/Listen,** *you'd better not* let... . *(Threat)*

Using the same models, according to the situation and the special emphasis he (you) might want to give to his (your) remark, say what Mike could say to or about

a) a neighbor who never mows his lawn ;

b) someone up the street who hasn't painted the outside of his house in three years ;

c) a newcomer who generally keeps his T.V. blaring late at night ;

d) some homeowners who haven't had the sidewalk paved in front of their house yet ;

e) the policeman who lives next door and who never says anything when children come cutting across the backyards from a neighboring playing field ;

f) his son who has parked his car in front of a fireplug ;

g) his wife who talks with the wife of a neighbor whom Mike doesn't like ;

h) the newspaper boy who throws the paper from the road and doesn't care where it falls ;

i) the kids from the house across the road who are playing baseball in the middle of the road ;

j) the children next door who always throw their frisbee into Mike's backyard.

C FOLLOW UP WORK

1. Mike has just heard that the house next door has been bought by a black family and he writes a letter of complaint to the mayor or to his congressman.

2. The black family moved in yesterday and Mike has not seen them yet. He is in his backyard, it is Saturday and his new neighbor says hello to him above the fence with a bright smile. Make up the dialogue.

THE LAST COWBOY

Henry Blanton turned forty on an April day when the first warm winds of spring crossed the Texas Panhandle and the diamondback rattlers[1], fresh and venomous from their winter sleep, came slipping out from under the rock of the Canadian River Breaks[2]. It was a day full of treachery and promise, the kind of day that
5 Henry would have expected for the showdown[3] in a good Western. Henry was particular about Westerns. When he was a boy and hired out in the summer—for fifty cents a day and the privilege of keeping a local rancher's thirsty cows from ambling downriver from their summer pasture—he saved his pay in a rusty tin-bank shaped like a bull and planned a winter's worth of Westerns at Amarillo's movie
10 houses. At night, summers, with the covers pulled tight above his head, Henry braved the moaning ghosts who rode the river breeze past the camp where he slept alone—and the way he did it was by fixing his thoughts on calm, courageous movie cowboys. He never summoned up the image of his father, who once had been as fine a cowboy as any man in the Panhandle, or the image of his Granddaddy Abel,
15 who had made the long cattle drive[5] to Wyoming back[5] when Indians were still marauding and a rustler[6] with a long rope would as often as not shoot a trail boss[7] who rode out looking for his strays[8]. Henry, deep in his bedroll, shoring up courage[9] against the river's dead, called on John Wayne, Gary Cooper, and Glenn Ford. Especially Glenn Ford. He was convinced then that for "expressin'right[10]",
20 as he put it, there had never been a cowboy to equal Glenn Ford—and he was still convinced of this at forty. (...)

Henry had lived on ranches where his camp was thirty or forty miles from a paved road ; ranches where Betsy had to cart water from a spring to do the dishes or wash her babies' diapers ; ranches where even the best cowboy was worth no

/'tretʃəri/

Poujade — Let's go on!... terminale — 4

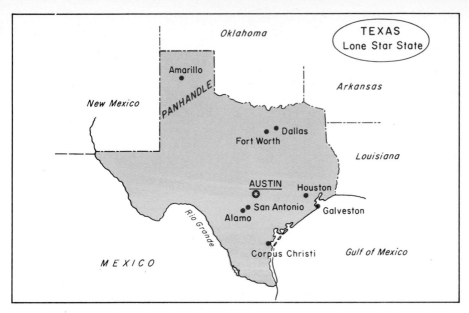

TEXAS
Lone Star State

Oklahoma

Amarillo

PANHANDLE

New Mexico

Arkansas

Dallas
Fort Worth

Louisiana

AUSTIN
Houston

San Antonio
Alamo

Galveston

Rio Grande

Corpus Christi

Gulf of Mexico

MEXICO

25 more to his boss than a hundred and fifty dollars a month in wages, a shack for a
home, and the meat from steers[11] that were too scrawny to send to auction. He did
not like to complain about his life now ; in a neat prefabricated house with
electricity and a telephone and running water—a house with a highway only twelve
miles away down a negotiable dirt road[12]. But a rancher could trust his foreman
30 with ninety thousand or nine hundred thousand acres and still regard him as a kind
of overgrown boy who was best protected from himself by a stern paternal hand
guiding him through a life's indenture[13].

The movies Henry loved had told him that a good cowboy was a hero. They had
told him that a cowboy lived by codes, not rules—codes of calm, solitude, and
35 honor—and that a cowboy had a special arrangement with nature and, with his
horse under him and the range[14] spread out around him, knew a truth and a
freedom and a satisfaction that ordinary men did not. But the movies were
changing—they were full of despair lately. And Henry, turning forty, had little to
show for his life as a cowboy except a hand-tooled[15] saddle and a few horses. Betsy
40 had baked a cake, but she was not speaking to him that birthday morning. His
daughter Melinda, washing for school, had used up all the hot water. Henry began
his forty-first year with a hangover[16] and an icy shower, and, pulling in his boots,
he brooded[17] about the future. The West was full of fences and feedyards[18] now. It
was crowded with calf traders and futures brokers[19], college boys who didn't know
45 a Hereford from an Angus[20], and ranchers who commuted from London or the
South of France—and, whatever the movies once promised, there was not much
chance, in a showdown, for a hero on a horse.

Jane Kramer, *The Newyorker,* 1977

---

1. rattlers : *serpents à sonnettes.* **2.** breaks : *falaises.* **3.** showdown : *confrontation dramatique.* **4.** cattle-drive : a driving of cattle overland. **5.** back when : in the old days when. **6.** rustler : cattle-thief. **7.** trail : track made by passage through a wild region (cf. cattle trail). trail-boss : one in charge of a herd *(troupeau)* fit to be driven from the range to market. **8.** strays : *bêtes égarées.* **9.** shoring up courage : *prenant son courage à deux mains.* **10.** ''expressing right'' : doing the right thing according to a traditional cowboy's code of honor. **11.** steer : bouvillon. **12.** negotiable dirt road : *chemin de terre praticable.* **13.** indenture : *contrat.* **14.** range : large open stretch of grazing ground. **15.** hand-tooled : hand-made. **16.** hangover : *gueule de bois.* **17.** to brood : to think long and deeply. **18.** feedyards : *parcs à bestiaux.* **19.** futures broker : *opérateur sur les marchés à terme des marchandises.* **20.** Hereford, Angus : various breeds of cattle.

A UNDERSTANDING THE TEXT

1. What can we guess about Henry's background and upbringing ? **2.** What did he use to take pride in ? **3.** How can you explain Henry's partiality to Westerns ? **4.** Who else, closer to him, could he have identified with rather than Glenn Ford, John Wayne or Gary Cooper ? **5.** How could the movies have told him "that a cowboy lived by codes, not rules." **6.** Which, of his past and present living conditions, are more gratifying for him and why ? **7.** What seems to be a typical rancher's attitude to cowboys ? **8.** What did Henry resent about his present day bosses ? **9.** What is wrong with his working conditions now ? **10.** Why did Henry find it difficult to adjust to his changing world ? **11.** What is pathetic about his situation ?

B LANGUAGE AT WORK

Traduction de "Faire faire"

Example :

> • **Nostalgia for the Old West made him feel the blues.**

On the same model, say

a) What made young Henry summon up his courage.
b) What made the boy pull covers tight over his head in his lonely camp.
c) What made the boy save his pay when he was hired out in the summer.
d) What made him brood over the future now he had turned forty.

Stressing contrasts between past and present

Example :

> • **He used to be young but now he feels tired.**

Complete the following sentences :

a) He used to live in a shack but now...
b) His wife used to cart water from a spring but now...
c) He used to enjoy going to the movies...
d) He used to feel proud of being a cowboy...
e) He used to be confident and hopeful...
f) He used to get on with his wife...
g) The West used to be just wide open spaces...
h) He used to understand what life was about...

Read the text again, then try and find a few more things that could be said, using the same construction as above.

C FOLLOW UP WORK

1. Comment : "The movies were full of despair lately."
2. Draw a portrait of the man and explain how you think he will end his life.
3. Would you accept such a summer job as Henry's when he was a boy ?
4. "Westerns are only for morons."

DREAMS ARE MY REALITY

In his new boots, Joe Buck was six-foot-one and life was different. As he walked out of that store in Houston something snapped in the whole bottom of him : a kind of power he never knew was there had been released[1] in his pelvis and he was able to feel the world through it. Brand-new muscles came into play in his buttocks[2]
5 and in his legs, and he was aware of a totally new attitude toward the sidewalk[3]. The world was down there, and he was up here, on top of it, and the space between him and it was now commanded by a beautiful strange animal, himself, Joe Buck. He was strong. He was exultant. He was ready.

"I'm ready", he said to himself, and he wondered what he meant by that.

10 Joe knew he was no great shakes as[4] a thinker and he knew that what thinking he did was best done looking in a mirror, and so his eyes cast about for something that would show him a reflection of himself. Just ahead was a store window. Ta-click ta-click ta-click, his boots said to the concrete, meaning power power power power, as he approached the window head on, broad-shouldered, swaggering[5], cool and
15 handsome.

Lord, I'm glad I'm you, he said to his image—but not out loud—and then, Hey, what's all this crap[6] ? What are you ready for ?

And then he remembered...

Over the door of the Sunshine Cafeteria was a big yellow sunburst with a clock
20 (twenty to seven) set in it, and on the face of the clock, it said TIME TO EAT.

As Joe approached the place he saw enacted in his mind the following scene :

He goes into the Sunshine. His employer, a pink man in a soiled gray suit, is just inside the door holding his pocket watch in his right hand and shaking the forefinger of his left at Joe. "You're due here at four o'clock, four to midnight,
25 understand !" he shouts. Customers stop eating and look up. Joe Buck takes the pink man by the ear and leads him past the astonished diners and into the scullery[7]. A number of cooks and counter girls and dishwashers pause in their work to watch as Joe shoves the pink manager against the dishwashing machine. Joe takes his time lighting a cigarette, lifts a brilliantly booted foot and rests it on a dish crate[8]. Then,
30 exhaling a puff of smoke, he says, "They's something about that dishwashing machine been bothering me. Been bothering me a long time. Yes it has. What I been wondering is whether or not that dishwashing machine would fit up your ass". "What, What ? Are you crazy ?" the pink man protests. Joe remains dangerously still, looks out from under dark eyebrows : "Did you call me crazy ?" "No, no,
35 no, I only meant..." The man bends over and Joe sees a billfold sticking out of his hip pocket. "Believe I'll take my pay", he says, removing the money, "plus help m'self to a little bonus". He stuffs a great wad of money into his pocket and walks out of the place, all eyes upon him, wide open and profoundly impressed. But no one dares follow him or in any way impede his exit. In fact, just to play it safe, the
40 pink man himself remains bent over for several days after Joe has gone.

That was the way Joe imagined it. This is what actually took place : he clicked across the street, pushed through the revolving door and into the Sunshine Cafeteria, swung his new body past the tables and toward a door that said EMPLOYEES ONLY on it. This door marked the end of the air conditioning ;
45 inside it was hot and steamy. He passed through another doorway that led into the

/'hju:stən/

/ʃʌvz/

scullery. A colored man of middle age was filling a tray with dirty dishes. Joe watched as the man filled the tray and placed it on a conveyor belt that would carry it through the dishwashing machine. Then he smiled up at Joe and nodded toward a mountain of dish-filled wire baskets stacked[6] on the floor. "Look at that shit, will you, ?" he said.

Joe stood next to the man. "Listen, uh, it looks like I'm headin' East." He lit a cigarette.

The man looked at Joe's suitcase. "You ain't coming to work ?" "Naw, I don't guess. I just come to say goodbye, tell you I'm headin' East."

"East ?"

"Yeah. Oh hell yeah. Thought I say g'bye, take a look around the place."

A door opened and a fat woman with a splotchy[10] face stood there shouting "Cups !" at the top of her voice. Then she closed the door and was gone.

The colored man put his hand forward. "Well. Goodbye."

James Leo Herlihy, *Midnight Cowboy,* 1965

---

1. to release : *(ici) déclencher.*   2. the buttocks, the ass (slang) : the bottom.   3. the sidewalk *(Am.)* : the pavement *(Eng.).*   4. he was no great shakes as : he was not much worth anything as.   5. swaggering : *roulant des épaules.*   6. crap (slang) : *excrément.*   7. the scullery : *l'office.*   8. a dish crate : *un panier à vaisselle.*   9. stacked : piled up.   10. a splotchy face : *un visage boursouflé.*

A   UNDERSTANDING THE TEXT

1. In what state does the scene take place ? 2. What has Joe just bought ?   3. What is his job ? 4. Why do you think he is exultant ?   5. Why does he need to look at himself in a mirror ?   6. Why does Joe imagine a farewell scene at the Sunshine Cafeteria such as the one described ? What does it reveal about him ?   7. How far was the reality of his farewell call at the cafeteria different from what he imagined ?   8. Could he possibly have copied his behavior during his imaginary call at the cafeteria from something ? Can you suggest what ? 9. What does his exchange with the black man at the cafeteria reveal ?   10. Why does Joe Buck feel it necessary to go and say goodbye ? What is he expecting ?   11. Where is he going when he says : "I'm headin' East" ?

B LANGUAGE AT WORK

Expressing appearances

Examples :

> • It *seems/looks/sounds as if* his boots had transformed Joe's personality.
> • Joe *feels as if* he had changed personalities by buying a cowboy's outfit.

Judging from the text and using the above constructions, imagine Joe's impressions of what awaits him in the East.

Expressing hopes and expectations

Examples :

> • Joe wants people to believe he is a real cowboy.
> • Joe expects people to respect him now.
> • Joe hopes to succeed in New York.

Judging from the text and using the above constructions, imagine what could be some of Joe's hopes and expectations as he prepares to board the bus.

C FOLLOW UP WORK

1. How do you account for Joe's behavior ? In what way is he more to be pitied than laughed at ?

2. Using the same device as the author and opposing an imaginary episode to reality, describe a student's late arrival at school as he might dream it and as it really is most of the time.

3. There is no future for a young man or woman outside a big town, where it is easy to succeed. Discuss.

AN OLD, OLD WOMAN ASKED ME

An old old woman asked me if I could walk with her to the end of the block. As soon as I said it was all right she latched on to[1] my clean white shirt with collier's[2] hands : filthy palms, black like shoe polish, and her fingers were quite strong too. They dug into my forearm. We began walking up the long block from Columbus
5 Avenue to Central Park West. At first she did no talking. She was quite short, came up to the middle of my shoulders, with blown-up swollen ankles and thick black shoes. I wondered if she might be a derelict, a bag lady[3] ; that is, I wondered what I had got myself into. She was a little too well-dressed to be a bag lady. She had on a spring coat and a sweater, though the temperature was in the nineties[4]. We were
10 walking so slowly it was more like swimming. Tiny step by tiny step. And the heat waves dancing in the air on this hot June day made it even more like feeling one's

way underwater. People swerved[5] around us. She became voluble, and told me that
all sorts of good things would happen to me as a direct result of helping her. Things
I hadn't ever wished for. It had come true with almost everyone who had helped
15 her. I got the impression she was trying to pass herself off as an elf. She began to
reminisce. She told me she'd been so sickly a child in Ireland, who would have
believed she would live so long ? While the others all were dead. The others back in
Ireland, and here too. What was the difference between here and the old country ? I
asked. Oh, the people in Dublin keep the streets much cleaner than they do in New
20 York. Looking down at her hands, I thought she was no one to talk. Suddenly she
asked, "Are you married ?"

"No, I'm single."

"Just like me !" she replied.

We had gone only three-quarters of the way up the block, but she told me she
25 could manage all right by herself the rest of the way. "God bless you," she said,
and then, as I nodded and started walking away, she added, with a certain
stubbornness, a certain cockiness[6], "God *will* bless you."

Philips Lapate, *Bachelorhood,* 1978

---

1. latched onto : clung to. **2.** a collier : a coal miner. **3.** a bag lady : a homeless woman : *une clocharde.* **4.** 90° Fahrenheit : 32° Celsisus. **5.** swerved : changed direction. **6.** cockiness : effrontery, cool confidence.

A UNDERSTANDING THE TEXT

1. Where did the scene take place ? 2. In what ways was this old woman different from a bag lady ? 3. Was there anything extraordinary about her request ? 4. What was both strange and pathetic about *a)* the way she looked ; *b)* the way she acted when her request was granted ? 5. How did the writer feel as the pair were walking down the street together ? 6. What did her sudden volubility reveal ? 7. What may have led her to ask the writer's help ? 8. What was her problem basically ? 9. What is your comment on the phrase : "They are all dead" ? 10. What is typical of life in big cities especially where elderly people are concerned ? 11. The American Society is a mobile society. To what extent might this be relevant here ? 12. What insight do we get into this old lady's life and personality ? Would you say her case is an isolated one ?

B LANGUAGE AT WORK

Preposition + verb + *ing*

Example :

• **Good things would happen to me as a direct result** *of helping* **her.**

Using -ing *forms, complete the following sentences :*

a) The narrator took her for a bag lady on first...
b) When the old woman's dirty fingers dug into his forearm, he felt like...

A bag lady.

c) As they went down the street he felt a bit strange since he was not accustomed to...

d) She thanked him for...

e) Before... him, she blessed him.

f) Instead of..., she looked cocky and stubborn.

g) She insisted on...

h) After... her, he could never get her out of his mind.

i) We can help elderly people by...

C FOLLOW UP WORK

1. What elements in the story make us believe it is true ?

2. What makes this story different from the usual sad, rather stereotyped accounts about old people ?

3. Describe the incident as briefly as possible.

4. What is interesting about the way the story is told ? What do you think the author feels about his encounter ?

5. Elderly people ("senior citizens") have an important role in our society. How do you react to this statement ?

6. The old lady goes over the day's major event. Write a sequel to the story.

Big Money, Hard Job

ANCHORAGE, Alaska (NYT).—Pat Schnabel is 27, and she's a construction worker. For the past 16 months she has worked in Alaska as a crane operator[1] helping to build the oil pipeline now under construction across the state. During the next year she expects to earn more than $56,000 working 12-hour days and seven-day weeks.

Miss Schnabel looks tough, her brown, shoulder-length hair hangs limply. Her jeans are baggy, her construction boots coated with mud, her blue work-shirt hangs loosely, denying any defined shape beneath it. While Miss Schnabel's appearance seems to lack arrangement, her "look" has been carefully conceived and calculated. "I always wear jeans, three shirts, no make-up," she said. "I de-emphasize my feminity. I have to. The men totally resented me, they totally resent the thought of any woman making as much money as a man."

She admits that the only reason she is out there operating a crane in the mud, in the snow, in the rain, in subzero temperatures, is that the money is good. And there is no other job in the world that is going to give her that kind of money.

While no one is keeping track of the figures, oil pipeline officials estimate that women "man" about 10% of the 20,000 jobs. Most of the women are in traditionally female occupations. They are employed as clerks or secretaries, as kitchen helpers, in the laundries. A smaller percentage work "on the line", driving trucks, operating cranes, working as security guards, drillers or riveters.

Like men on the pipeline, the women are largely motivated by the money. But that's not all. While many men first came to Alaska for the adventure, for money, to get away from bad personal situations back home, women now "escape" to the pipeline for the same reasons.

Most pipeline workers work 82-hour weeks for up to nine straight weeks, then take one or two weeks off. Those who work inside the camps, particularly those in the Arctic north where temperatures may fall to 50 below[2], may not venture out of doors for weeks on end. Construction workers leave their camps each morning with their crew and the group is bused to that day's worksite. After 12 hours, the bus, generally wall-papered with *Playboy* center-folds[3], comes rumbling back to take them back to the camps for the evening. Workers do not pay for room or board, nor for their flights back to Anchorage on their time off. So if they're lucky and the Internal Revenue Service doesn't take too much in taxes, they can save a lot while working on the line.

Hilary Hilscher has saved a lot and thanks to the pipeline she is now settled cozily into the homesteader's log cabin she and her boyfriend, a construction foreman[4], bought in Fairbanks with their "oil money". Miss Hilscher, 27, is typical of many young people on the pipeline. Last fall she left an already well-paying professional job in Juneau where she served as deputy director of telecommunications in the governor's office. "I saw all my friends making these incredible sums of money, and I guess like the rest of the young people up here, I decided to get it while I could," Miss Hilscher said.

The pipeline life bears "little resemblance to the real world". The hours, the surroundings, the living conditions are no less real than the money. As one woman pointed out, very few women stay "single" in the camps—"living together" is tacitly approved.

Some women link up with a man purely as a means of survival—if they are "taken", the other men won't hassle them as much[5].

As one woman puts it : "You're living in a space capsule. It's like being on the moon. You don't live in the camps, you just exist. The only thing that gives a sense of normalcy in your life is a relationship."

From *The New York Times*, 1977

Anchorage /ˈæŋkərɪdʒ/   Alaska /əˈlæskə/   tough /tʌf/
temperatures /ˈtempərətʃərˈ/   loosely /ˈluːsli/   clerks /klɜrks/
guards /gɑrds/   riveters /ˈrɪvɪ̯tərˈ/   capsule /ˈkæpsəl/

---

1. crane operator : *grutière*.   **2.** 50 below : in °F = 45 °C.   **3.** centerfolds : pictures of pinups on the middle pages, that unfold.   **4.** foreman : *chef d'équipe*.   **5.** won't hassle them as much : *ne vont pas autant les embêter.*

A UNDERSTANDING THE TEXT

1. What is especially hard about the work on the Alaska pipeline ?   2. Why do the women working on the line dress sloppily ?   3. Why are men resentful of the women working on the line ? 4. How many women work on the pipeline altogether ?   5. Are they all employed in the construction of the line ? Justify your answer. 6. What are the motivations of the women who come to work on the line ? To what extent do you think they are the same as for men ? 7. Why can people save a lot of money while working on the line ?   8. What, in the case of Hilary Hilscher, shows that the salaries for work on the pipeline are exceptionally high and attractive ? 9. Why do most of the women "link up with a man" ? 10. What sex do you think the author of the article is ? Why ?

B LANGUAGE AT WORK

Like and as

1. Example :

> • **Pat Schnabel works as construction worker on the pipeline.**

Using the same construction, give an account of the difficulties experienced by the different girls in the text as women doing a job traditionally considered as a male's job.

2. Examples :

> • She works like a man.
> • She has saved a lot, as many people have done.

Using the same constructions, compare the life of the women working on the Alaskan pipeline to that of male construction workers.

Past and perfect

Examples :

> • She got her job on the line 16 months ago. She is still working on the line.
> → She has been working on the line for 16 months/since 19... .
> • She got her job in June '76 and left it in October '77.
> → She worked on the line for 16 months./She spent 16 months working on the line.

Using the same models make sentences with the following elements :

a) Pat Schnabel was hired as a crane operator in 1976. She is still working on the line.

b) She doesn't remember when she started wearing jeans. She just loves wearing them all the time.

c) When construction started 4 years ago, the company hired some 2,000 women. They are still employing as many as that.

d) Last year, the temperature reached 58 below one night. Four weeks later it still had not risen above that.

e) Before she got her present job on the line, Hilary had a job as deputy director of telecommunications in the governor's office. She kept it two years.

f) Hilary and her boyfriend moved into their log cabin six months ago. They just love it there.

C FOLLOW UP WORK

1. Mrs Hilscher is worried about her daughter. She cannot understand why Hilary left a good, steady office job to go to work on the line. Write the letter that Hilary might write home to explain.

2. How would *you* like to have a job on the pipeline ? Why or why not ?

3. There are jobs wich are either for men or for women only. Support your argument.

Jumble sale.

SURVEYING THE SCENE

1. What elements in this chapter justify its title ?
2. Which character in this chapter is the most representative of your idea of a typical American ? Justify your answer.
3. What do you think Mike would feel about the women that go to work on the pipeline ? Justify your opinion.
4. What stereotypes do both Joseph Nocera and Nikki-Rosa denounce ?
5. What do you think Jack Kerouac (On the Road) and the narrator of A Walk Across America have in common ?

Some books you might like to read : On the Road (Sur la route) by J. Kerouac.
Travels with Charley by J. Steinbeck.
Tortilla Flat and Cannery Row by John Steinbeck.

Some films you might like to see : West Side Story by R. Wise.
Nashville by R. Altman.
Coal Miner's Daughter (Nashville Lady) by Michael Apted.

Painting by Norman Rockwell.

Sculpture by Claes Oldenburg.

LIVING ON CREDIT

An interview with Patricia Higgins, a young housewife living in New York City. Her husband is in television and they travel extensively.

INTERVIEWER : *Why did you start using credit cards in the first place ?*

MRS HIGGINS : Well, the first credit card came in the mail, without even being solicited. It was from a bank, a Bank Americard I think, or Master Charge. Later on it turned out to be illegal to send cards like that without the customer asking for them. Anyway, it was a way for the banks to hook people,
5 and we got hooked.

I. : *What do you mean by "hooked" ?*

MRS H. : You see, after that we got used to using the credit card. It's kind of a fantasy. It's as if you're spending money that's not real. You know, Monopoly money. After a while we realized that you couldn't do enough with one card, so we decided to get a bigger, more international and
10 important credit card.

I. : *What do you use these cards for ?*

MRS H. : Take vacations[1] for example. I can buy my ticket, pay for the hotel, rent a car and do all my shopping on vacation without having any cash.

I. : *It certainly sounds as if life is much easier that way.*
15 MRS H. : Yes, everything is paid for until the bills come.

I. : *What happens then ?*

MRS H. : They cancel your credit card if you don't pay the bill. But if you have planned it well, you already have gotten[2] another card from another company, which you get when your credit is still good.

20 I. : *When do things finally catch up with you ?*

MRS H. : Eventually you wind up suffering more than enjoying because you have to pay more than you ever imagined you spent. When reality hits you in the face, life becomes very difficult.

I. : *Can you imagine living without your credit card ?*

MRS H. : It's very difficult to live without those damn cards. I learned the hard way once after getting
25 in over my head in debt. I forced my husband to stop using the cards by taking scissors and cutting up all our cards into little pieces.

I. : *So you were able to stop after that ?*

MRS H. : In a way yes, but not completely. I wound up getting more cards eventually. I find it almost impossible to live without them, but now I try harder not to be ridiculous about fulfilling every
30 fantasy immediately. I try to use more checks because you know if you have money in the bank. But a credit card is like magic. You are billed at the end of the month and even then you don't have to pay. They take it over to the next month and even to the third month and only then will they start to sue.

I. : *What did you mean about fulfilling every fantasy ?*

Mrs H. : Well, say you go into a store to buy a vacuum cleaner and it's something that you need but
35 you know you're going to pay with your credit card. It's possible that you will come out with a color
T.V. which you can charge with your card.

I. : *At that time you are aware that you don't have the money ?*

Mrs H. : Yes, you know, but you don't think about it realistically. You figure you're going to get the
money somehow. You get caught up in the idea of buy now and pay later. So in the end you wind up
40 spending much more money and buying things you don't really need, and would never have bought if
you were paying cash.

I. : *Do you think some day credit cards will no longer be available ?*

Mrs H. : I would like to believe that but I can see how I've gotten hooked on them. The whole
consumer society is based on them. Without credit cards there would have to be a complete
45 transformation in people's minds in terms of money and what they need. I don't see that happening in
the near future. Like they say, time is money and credit cards give you both for free !

---

1. vacations *(Am.)* : holidays *(Eng.).*   **2.** gotten *(Am.)* : got *(Eng.).*

A   TRUE OR FALSE ?

1. It is easy to get hooked on using credit cards.
2. The Higgins were content just to use one credit card. 3. In some ways credit cards made life easier for the Higgins.   4. With credit cards the Higgins know exactly how much money they spend. 5. Mrs Higgins is very happy about living on credit. 6. When she goes into stores Mrs Higgins uses her cards just to buy necessities. 7. The consumer society couldn't function without credit cards. 8. One has to pay credit card bills every month or lose the cards. 9. Credit cards give you time and money for free.

B   ANSWER THESE QUESTIONS :

1. Under what conditions was it ruled illegal to send credit cards in the mail ?   2. Why does Mrs Higgins say that credit card money is like Monopoly money ? 3. Why are credit cards cancelled ? 4. Why do credit cards cause suffering ? 5. How did Mrs Higgins stop her husband from using the cards ? 6. Why does she use more checks now ? 7. Why does one spend more money with credit cards ? 8. What would happen if there were no credit cards ?

C   EXPLAIN IN YOUR OWN WORDS :

1.   Without being solicited.
2.   To be hooked.
3.   To pay cash.
4.   When they catch up with you.
5.   Getting in over my head in debt.
6.   Fulfilling every fantasy.
7.   To charge a T.V. with your card.

D   DISCUSSION

Credit cards are no good. Support your arguments.

PLASTIC WORLD

American cities are like badger[1] holes, ringed with trash—all of them—surrounded by piles of wrecked and rusting automobiles and almost smothered[2] with rubbish. Everything we use comes in boxes, cartons, bins, the so-called packaging we love so much. The mountains of things we throw away are
5 much greater than the things we use. In this, if in no other way, we can see the wild and reckless exuberance of our production, and waste seems to be the index. (...) This is not said in criticism of one system or the other, but I do wonder whether there will come a time when we can no longer afford our wastefulness in the rivers, metal wastes everywhere, and atomic wastes and chemical wastes buried deep in the
10 earth or sunk in the sea. When an Indian village became too deep in its own filth, the inhabitants moved. And we have no place to which to move. (...)

I had promised my youngest son to say goodbye in passing his school at Deerfield, Massachusetts, but I got there too late to arouse him, so I drove up the mountain and found a dairy, bought some milk, and asked permission to camp
15 under an apple tree. The dairyman had a Ph. D.[3] in mathematics ; and he must have some training in philosophy. He liked what he was doing and he didn't want to be somewhere else—one of the very few contented people I met in my whole journey (...)

Not far outside of Bangor[4] I stopped at an auto court and rented a room. It
20 wasn't expensive. The sign said "Greatly Reduced Winter Rates". It was immaculate ; everything was done in plastics—the floors, the curtain, table tops of stainless, burnless plastic, lamp shades of plastic. Only the bedding and the towels were of a natural material. I went to the small restaurant run in conjunction. It was all plastic too—the table linen, the butter dish. The sugar and crackers were

25 wrapped in cellophane, the jelly in a small plastic coffin[5] sealed with cellophane. It
was early evening and I was the only customer. Even the waitress wore a sponge-off
apron. She wasn't happy and then she wasn't unhappy. She wasn't anything. But I
don't believe anyone is a nothing. There has to be something inside if only to keep
the skin from collapsing. This vacant eye, listless[6] hand, this damask cheek[7] dusted
30 like a doughnut[8] with plastic powder, had to have a memory or a dream.

On a chance, I asked, "How soon you going to Florida ?"
"Nex' week", she said listlessly. Then something stirred in that aching void.
"Say, how d'you know I'm going ?" (...)
"Maybe I guessed. Like it down there ?"
35 "Oh, sure. I go every year. Lots of waitress jobs in the winter."
"What do you do down there, I mean for fun ?"
"Oh, nothing. Just fool around."
"Do you fish or swim ?"
"Not much. I just fool around. I don't like that sand, makes me itch."
40 "Make good money ?"
"It's a cheap crowd."
"Cheap ?"
"They rather spen' it on booze[9]."
"Than what ?"
45 "Than tips. Just the same here with the summer people. Cheap."

Strange how one person can saturate a room with vitality, with excitement. Then
there are others, and this dame[10] was one of them, who can drain off energy and
joy, can suck pleasure dry and get no sustenance from it. Such people spread a
greyness in the air about them. I'd been driving a long time, and perhaps my energy
50 was low and my resistance down. She got me. I felt so blue and miserable I wanted
to crawl into a plastic cover and die. What a date she must be, what a lover !... For
a moment I considered giving her a five-dollar tip, but I knew what would happen.
She wouldn't be glad. She'd just think I was crazy.

I went back to my clean little room. I don't ever drink alone. It's not much fun.
55 And I don't think I will until I am an alcoholic. But this night I got a bottle of
vodka from my stores and took it to my cell. In the bathroom two water tumblers[11]
were sealed in cellophane sacks with the words : "These glasses are sterilized for
your protection." Across the toilet seat a strip of paper bore the message : "This
seat has been sterilized with ultraviolet light for your protection." Everyone was
60 protecting me and it was horrible. I tore the glasses from their covers. I violated the
toilet seat with my foot. I poured half a tumbler of vodka and drank it and then
another. Then I lay deep in hot water in the tub and I was utterly miserable and
nothing was good anywhere (...)

I remember an old Arab in North Africa, a man whose hands had never felt
65 water. He gave me mint tea in a glass so coated with use that it was opaque, but he
handed me companionship, and the tea was wonderful because of it. And without
protection my teeth didn't fall out, nor did running sore[12] develop. I began to
formulate a new law describing the relationship of protection to despondency[13]. A
sad soul can kill you quicker, far quicker, than a germ.

John Steinbeck, *Travels with Charley*, 1961

---

1. badger : *blaireau*. 2. smothered : thickly covered with. 3. Ph. D. : *doctorat*. 4. Bangor : a town in
Maine. 5. coffin : *cercueil*. 6. listless : *(ici) mollassonne*. 7. damask cheek : *joue vermeille*. 8. doughnut :
beignet. 9. booze : slang for liquor. 10. dame : woman (ironical). 11. tumbler : *gobelet*. 12. running
sores : *ulcères*. 13. despondency : despair.

A UNDERSTANDING THE TEXT

1. How does the author describe American cities ?
2. Do Americans use more or less than they throw away ? What is the "index" of American production ? 3. According to the author, how does America compare with Indian villages of the past ?
4. What problem is America likely to have which the American Indians did not have ? 5. What was special about the dairyman ? Why did Steinbeck appreciate meeting him ? 6. What was Steinbeck's room at the motel like ? 7. What was his reaction to the restaurant and the waitress there ? What does he mean by "she drained off energy and joy" ?
8. Some customers might not be as negative as he was about this doll-like waitress. What might they consider as attractive about her ? 9. Why does Steinbeck say that "the jelly was in a small plastic coffin" ? 10. What did he do when he returned to his room ? Why did he react this way ? 11. What can be said in favor of this motel and restaurant ? 12. What idea is the author trying to express with his story about the old Arab ? Explain why you agree or disagree with him. 13. Why do you think Americans like things that come in packages ? 14. Do you think it is cleaner and more economic for a restaurant to have disposable or reusable items (glasses, napkins, etc.) ?

B LANGUAGE AT WORK

Comparisons

Notice how the author uses a simile to describe America (1) and how he gives descriptive examples of this simile (2).

> • American cities are like badger holes (1).,.ringed with trash, surrounded by miles of wrecked and rusting automobiles, and almost smothered with rubbish (2).

1. *Using similes such as* hospital, cell, laboratory, plastic factory, *and descriptive adjectives such as* artificial, inhuman, antiseptic, impersonal, sterilized, pre-packaged, dehumanizing *to go with them, make similar sentences to describe the author's room and the restaurant where he ate.*

2. *The author could have written descriptions like these :*

> • America is as filthy as a badger hole.
> • The hotel room was more impersonal than a prison cell.
> • The restaurant was as antiseptic as a hospital.

Using the same model make sentences, matching one element from list A with one element from list B, to describe the food at your school, the coffee in a restaurant along the expressway, a self-service restaurant, a food dispensing machine and the sandwiches in it.

List A : tasteless, greasy, stale, friendly, impersonal, appetizing, elegant, hard.
List B : a rattlesnake, a rock, motor oil, old socks, yesterday's chewing gum, last week's news, robot, laundromat.

C FOLLOW UP WORK

1. Do you agree or disagree with Steinbeck's condemnation of a sterilized, plastic motel ? Why or why not ?
2. There is no way of preventing modern society from becoming a "plastic world".

PERPETUAL CARE

Dennis passed through and opening the door marked 'Inquiries' found himself in   /in'kwaɪəriz/
a raftered[1] banqueting-hall. The 'Hindu Love-Song' was here also, gently
discoursed[2] from the dark-oak panelling. A young lady rose from a group of her
fellows to welcome him, one of that new race of exquisite, amiable, efficient young   /ɪl 'skwizɪt/
5 ladies whom he had met everywhere in the United States. She wore a white smock
and over her sharply supported left breast was embroidered the words, *Mortuary*   /ɪm'brɔɪdəd/
Hostess.

    "Can I help you in any way ?"

    "I came to arrange about a funeral."

10 "Is it for yourself ?"

    "Certainly not. Do I look so moribund ?"

    "Pardon me ?"

    "Do I look as if I were about to die ?"

    "Why, no. Only many of our friends like to make Before Need Arrangements.
15 Will you come this way ?"

    She led him through the hall into a soft passage. The *décor* here was Georgian[3].
The 'Hindu Love-Song' came to its end and was succeeded by the voice of a
nightingale. In a little chintzy[4] parlour he and his hostess sat down to make their
arrangements.

20 "I must first record the Essential Data."

He told her his name and Sir Francis's.

"Now, Mr Barlow, what had you in mind ? Embalmment of course, and after that incineration or not, according to taste. Our crematory is on scientific principles, the heat is so intense that all inessentials are volatilized. Some people did
25 not like the thought that ashes of the casket[5] and clothing were mixed with the Loved One's. Normal disposal is by inhumement, entombment, inurnment, or immurement, but many people just lately prefer insarcophagusment. That is *very* individual. The casket is placed inside a sealed sarcophagus, marble or bronze, and /sɑrˈkɑfəgəs/ rests permanently above ground in a niche in the mausoleum, with or without a /nɪtʃ/
30 personal stained-glass window[6] above. That, of course, is for those with whom price is not a primary consideration."

"We want my friend buried."

"This is not your first visit to Whispering Glades ?"

"Yes."

35 "Then let me explain the Dream. The Park is zoned. Each zone has its own name and appropriate Work of Art. Zones of course vary in price and within the zones the prices vary according to their proximity to the Work of Art. We have single sites as low as fifty dollars. That is in Pilgrims' Rest, a zone we are just developing behind the Crematory fuel dump[7]. The most costly are those on Lake Isle. They /ˈlekˈaɪl/
40 range about 1,000 dollars. Then there is Lovers' Nest, zoned about a very, very beautiful marble replica of Rodin's famous statue, the Kiss. We have double plots there at 750 dollars the pair. Was your Loved One married ?"

"No."

"What was his business ?"

45 "He was a writer. "

"Ah, then Poets' Corner would be the place for him. We have many of our foremost literary names there, either in person or as Before Need Reservations. You are no doubt acquainted with the works of Amelia Bergson ?" /əˈmiljə
"I know of them." ˈbɜrgsən/

50 "We sold Miss Bergson a Before Need Reservation only yesterday, under the statue of the prominent Greek poet Homer. I could put your friend right next to her. But perhaps you would like to see the zone before deciding."

"I want to see everything."

"There certainly is plenty to see. I'll have one of our guides take you round just

55 as soon as we have all the Essential Data, Mr Barlow. Was your Loved One of any
special religion ?"
"An agnostic."
"We have two non-sectarian churches in the Park and a number of non-sectarian
pastors. Jews and Catholics seem to prefer to make their own arrangements."
60 "I believe Sir Ambrose Abercrombie is planning a special service."
"Oh, was your Loved One in films, Mr Barlow ? In that case he ought to be in
Shadowland."
"I think he would prefer to be with Homer and Miss Bergson."
"Then the University Church would be most convenient. We like to save the
65 Waiting Ones a long procession. I presume the Loved One was Caucasian[8] ?"
"No, why did you think that ? He was purely English."
"English are purely Caucasian, Mr Barlow. This is a restricted[9] park. The
Dreamer has made that rule for the sake of the Waiting Ones. In their time of trial
they prefer to be with their own people."
70 "I think I understand. Well, let me assure you Sir Francis was quite white."
As he said this there came vividly into Dennis's mind that image which lurked
there, seldom out of sight for long ; the sack of body suspended and the face above
it with eyes red and horribly starting from their sockets[10], the cheeks mottled in
indigo like the marbled end-papers of a ledger[11] and the tongue swollen and
75 protruding like an end of black sausage.
"Let us now decide on the casket."
They went to the show-rooms where stood coffins of every shape and material :
the nightingale still sang in the cornice.
"The two-piece lid[12] is most popular for gentlemen Loved Ones. Only the upper
80 part is then exposed to view."
"Exposed to view ?"
"Yes, when the Waiting Ones come to take leave."
"But I say, I don't think that will quite do. I've seen him. He's terribly
disfigured, you know. "
85 "If there are any special little difficulties in the case you must mention them to
our cosmeticians. You will be seeing one of them before you leave. They have never   /ˌkɑzmə'tiʃən/
failed yet."

Evelyn Waugh, *The Loved One*, 1948

---

1. rafters : *chevrons (dans la toiture)*. 2. discoursed : being emitted. 3. Georgian : eighteenth century
architectural style in England. 4. chintzy : cheap and in bad taste. 5. casket : fancy word for coffin. 6.
stained-glass window : *vitrail*. 7. fuel dump : oil tank. 8. Caucasian : of the white race. 9. restricted : here,
euphemism for segregated. 10. eyes sockets : *orbites*. 11. ledger : account book. 12. lid : cover.

A UNDERSTANDING THE TEXT

1. What were the mortuary and the hostess like ?
Why was Dennis taken aback ? 2. What choice of
burial methods did the client have ? 3. How was
the cemetery divided ? Why was this so ? 4. Was
the cemetery integrated ? Explain. 5. Why was
Dennis worried about the coffin ? 6. Who were
the cosmeticians and what were they going to do ?
7. What was the Dream and who was the
Dreamer ? 8. Why do you think the mortuary was
run the way it was ? 9. How does the author
communicate his idea that the mortuary and
Whispering Glades were ridiculous ? 10. What is
humorous about the text ?

B LANGUAGE AT WORK

Using euphemisms

Euphemisms are often used to soften the meaning of a strong or unpleasant word or image. In this reading there are several. Match the euphemism on the left with a word or phrase on the right that means the same.

1. gentlemen...	a) customers
2. the Park...	b) prepaid funeral
3. guide...	c) the dead person's name and address
4. the Loved One...	d) men
5. friends...	e) the corpse
6. cosmeticians...	f) the family of the dead person
7. Pilgrim's Rest...	g) the boss
8. Before Need Arrangements...	h) the cemetery
9. the Dreamer...	i) the cheap section of the cemetery
10. Essential Data...	j) the expensive section of the cemetery
11. Lake Isle...	k) salesman
12. restricted...	l) segregated
13. Waiting Ones...	m) embalmers

Faire + Infinitif

Examples :

> • She wants to make Dennis pay for expensive things.
> • Dennis wants to have his friend buried.
> • She suggests having Sir Francis placed in a sarcophagus.

Read the text again, then, using the above construction, describe all the things that the salesgirl suggests to Dennis.

C FOLLOW UP WORK

1. Write an advertising brochure for Whispering Glades. Use expressions such as *Loved One, Before Need Arrangements, perpetual care, eternal garden, natural beauty, pleasant rest, permanent home, restricted park,* to describe the facilities and explain why the client should choose *the Dream.*

2. Organizations like *Whipering Glades* are useful and relieve the dead persons' families of all sorts of trouble at the same time as they cater to their tastes.

3. Should people give their bodies to medical science and parts of their bodies to people in need ? Would you do the same ? Why or why not ?

THE PRAYING BUSINESSMAN

"I'm glad you could come, gentlemen," Curtis O'Keefe informed them, as if this meeting had not been planned weeks ahead. "Perhaps, though, before we begin our business it would benefit all of us if we asked the help of Almighty God."

As he spoke, with the ease of long practice the hotelier slipped agilely to his
5 knees, clasping his hands devoutly in front of him. With an expression bordering on resignation, as if he had been through this experience many times before, Ogden Bailey followed suit[1] and, after a moment's hesitation, the younger man Hall assumed the same position.[...]

"Almighty God," Curtis O'Keefe intoned, his eyes closed and pink-cheeked,
10 leonine face serene, "grant us, if it be thy will, success in what we are about to do. We ask thy blessing and thine active help in acquiring this hotel, named for thine own St. Gregory. We plead devoutly that we may add it to those already enlisted—by our own organization—in thy cause and held for thee in trust by thy devoted servant who speaketh." Even when dealing with God, Curtis O'Keefe
15 believed in coming directly to the point.

He continued, his face uplifted, the words rolling onward like a solemn flowing river : "Moreover if this be thy will—and we pray it may—we ask that it be done expeditiously[2] and with economy, such treasure as we thy servants possess not being depleted[3] unduly, but husbanded[4] to thy further use. We invoke thy blessing also,
20 O God, on those who will negotiate against us, on behalf of[5] this hotel, asking that they shall be governed solely according to thy spirit and that thou shalt cause them to exercise reasonableness and discretion in all they do. Finally, Lord, be with us always, prospering our cause and advancing our works so that we, in turn, may dedicate them to thy greater glory, Amen. Now, gentlemen, how much am I going
25 to have to pay for this hotel ?"

O'Keefe had already bounced back into his chair. It was a second or two, however, before the others realized that the last sentence was not a part of the prayer, but the opening of their business session. Bailey was first to recover and, springing back adroitly from his knees to the settee, brought out the contents of his
30 briefcase. Hall, with a startled look, scrambled to join him.

Arthur Hailey, *Hotel*

---

1. followed suit : did the same thing.   2. expeditiously : promptly and efficiently.   3. depleted : reduced.
4. husbanded : used prudently.   5. on behalf of : in the name of.

Teach boys to be manly for Christ!

TRAIN BOYS TODAY TO BECOME MEN GOD CAN USE TOMORROW!

Now available for the first time, the "Man In Demand" Training Program, by Wayne and Emily Hunter, gives practical yet inspirational instruction on how to achieve total manliness to answer the challenge of dynamic Christian leadership in tomorrow's world. Teaches boys how to develop physical and spiritual fitness, good conversational skills, manly manners, a good appearance, self-confidence and a worthwhile self-image. Gives ways to avoid social embarrassment, to cope with sexuality, to keep a clean thought-life, to master damaging habits and to achieve TOTAL CHRISTIAN MANLINESS--morally, mentally, socially, and spiritually.

Teach girls to be lovely for Christ!

Christian Charm Course*

BY EMILY HUNTER

Also available in Spanish.

Gives methods for improving the outward appearance along with spiritual instruction for developing the true beauty which comes from a heart surrendered to the Lord Jesus Christ! Teaches Christian principles of modesty and femininity. Girls love it! Proven results!

BOTH COURSES OFFER...

● Unique "Teaching Bridge" approach leading from the physical to spiritual.
● Illustrated Student Manuals with diagrams, charts, quizzes, spiritual challenges, inspiring verse, "self-inventories."
● Easy-to-follow Teacher Books with word-for-word class instruction, directions for special activities, demonstrations and spiritual correlations.
● Christ-centered, life-changing teachings ideally suited for ages 12 to 17.

A UNDERSTANDING THE TEXT

1. Who was Curtis O'Keefe and what was he trying to do ? 2. How did O'Keefe begin each business meeting ? 3. What was the tone of O'Keefe's prayer ? 4. What was unexpected about his prayer ? 5. What are some examples in the prayer where O'Keefe tries to manipulate the situation ? 6. How and why did Bailey and Hall react to O'Keefe ? 7. What is the author's opinion of O'Keefe and how does he communicate it to the reader ? 8. To what extent do you think O'Keefe was a successful businessman ?

B   LANGUAGE AT WORK

Register

Formal language is common in prayers because it shows respect. Write the meaning of these words or phrases from the prayer.

a) ... grant us ... success in what we are about to do.
b) ... in acquiring this hotel ...
c) ... named for thine own St. Gregory.
d) We plead devoutly ...
e) Moreover, if this be thy will ...
f) ... we ask that it be done expeditiously and with economy ...
g) We invoke thy blessing ...
h) ... thou shalt cause them to exercise reasonableness ...

As if

Examples :

> • *As if* **this meeting had not been planned weeks ahead**
> • *As if* **he had been through all this before**

Suppose you were present at the meeting. Use the above construction to explain to a friend what happened and how people behaved.

Anticipation

Examples :

> • **Grant us success in what** | **we are about to do**
> | **we are going to do**
> | **we are on the point of doing**

The text shows us a piece of O'Keefe's strategy. Using the constructions above, say what you think he is up to next.

A leaflet handed out on the sidewalk during the Republican National Convention, 1976.

PRAYER
AND THE COMING
ELECTION
by
Don W. Hillis

That nation which loses its sense of values and sets its focus on gold, silver, stocks, bonds, houses, lands, property and pleasure *needs prayer*.

That nation in which laws are flagrantly broken, crime is winked at, justice is scorned, riots, drunkenness, pornography, dope and immorality are tolerated *needs prayer*. And to pray is exactly what every Christian is exhorted to do. Supplication, prayers and intercession are to be made for all in authority (I Timothy 2:1,2). It is doubtful that America has ever stood in more need of prayer for those in places of political leadership than today.

Let us not be like Israel of old. She prayerlessly chose Saul to be her first king on the basis of externals. He looked good. He appeared to have the qualifications. But he failed miserably. He was not God's choice. The child of God ought to seek the mind of Him whose choices are not made on the low level of outward appearance, but on the rightness of heart.

It is a tragic fact that many people in America are first Democrats or Republicans and then Christians. They place their party politics above their Christianity. They prayerlessly vote for men purely because they are in the same party and not because they are men of Christian conviction or moral character.

There is plenty of evidence in the Bible that God responds to the earnest prayers of His people with regard to national interests. He has His own sovereign ways of raising up and setting aside rulers.

God was quite ready to hear Abraham's prayers for wicked Sodom and Gomorrah. He is no less ready to hear our prayers for America.

Consider the impact of Daniel's prayer life on the godless rulers of the great Babylonian Empire. God's man of prayer was the instrument through which Nebuchadnezzar and Belshazzar learned that God rules in the kingdom of men and "giveth it to whomsoever He wills" (Daniel 4:25).

Think of the effectiveness of Nehemiah's prayers in the restoring of a defeated, scattered and decadent nation. Basic to Nehemiah's courageous leadership and hard work was continual prayer.

Take a second look at Mordecai and Queen Esther. The doom of Israel had been sealed by Haman's plot and signed by the king. But prayer reversed the whole situation (Esther 4:15-17). Surely God is ready to hear the desperate cries of His children for America today.

And how do you pray for the coming election?

Ask God to put in authority men who will allow us to live peaceable, godly and honest lives.

Ask God for rulers who will in no way hinder the proclamation of the Gospel in this country or other countries.

Ask for wisdom in voting that His will may be done on earth as it is done in heaven.

Pray for America. Pray before you vote. Pray in the assurance that He will answer. "If my people which are called by my name, shall humble themselves, and pray, and seek my face, and turn from their wicked ways, then will I hear from heaven, and will forgive their sin, and will heal their land" (I Chronicles 7:14).

Gospel Tract Society, Inc.
P.O. Box 1118
Independence, Mo. 64051

C FOLLOW UP WORK

1. Religion teaches certain standards of ethics. Make a list of these standards, then discuss each one separately, explaining why you do/do not agree.
2. What ethics of behavior do you think businessmen should follow ?
3. Certain states in the United States have ''blue laws'' which forbid stores to be open on Sundays. Write two ''Letters to the Editor'' of a large newspaper—one from a preacher who is in favor of these laws and one from a stewardess who is against them.
4. Compare the two courses offered on page 122 and discuss the following : religious teaching reinforces sexual stereotypes.

Dear God,
Are boys better
than girls, I
Know you are one
but try to be
fair.

Sylvia.

DEAR GOD, - MY
FATHAR SAID KIDS IS
THE BEST TIME IN
LIFE. PLEASE TELL
HIM WHAT GOOD is it
IF WE NEVER GET TO STAY
UP AND WATCH ANYTHING.
JO

SELLING AMERICA

PRO

Ross Pelletier is 56 years old. He works for one of the largest advertising agencies in the world. As a child he wanted to be a baggageman on a train. Later, when he began to realize how much money he would earn doing that, he started to think that perhaps he could do a little better...

(adapted)

What do you think of advertising ?
Advertising is a very fascinating business to me. We think it's a very important business, sometimes not fully understood. [...] But advertising has been so important in mass consumption. [...] There's no sense producing if people are not going to consume what you produce in masses. You need mass consumption to make use of the goods that are turned out by the dozens in the store, you know.

Does advertising try to manipulate people ?
A product must stand up in the consumer's hands. I could, by advertising, maybe induce you to try a product. But you will not make a repurchase if it is not satisfactory. [...] So you cannot put anything over—at least, not more than once. And who wants to stay in business putting something over once ?

How do you try to reach a potential customer ?
You have to tell a real story. One, is to sell him. But it's to let him know he has a choice. Our economy is an economy of choice. We, in this country, under this wonderful system we have, despite the fact that it has some faults, of course, have a tremendous choice. In worldly goods. And while life is more to it than just worldly goods, still, this man has appetites and needs. And here we have this great choice. [...]

A UNDERSTANDING THE TEXT

1. Why did Ross Pelletier decide not to become a baggageman on a train ?   2. According to Pelletier, why is advertising so important in a country like the United States ?   3. What does he feel is the best way to sell a product ? Is he conscientious ? Use evidence from the text to support you answer.
4. How does he describe the American system ?
5. What does he mean when he says that ''you must be on your toes'' in the American system ?
6. How does Charlie Landesfahr characterize the American consumer and the advertising business ?   7. What potential does he see for American products on the world market ?
8. According to Landesfahr, what is the essence of his job ? How do you think consumers have come to be ''conditioned'' to think that products are different ? 9. Why do you think Landesfahr hates his job ? 10. To what extent do you think the two opinions expressed here are typically American ?

SELLING AMERICA

CON

Charlie Landesfahr is 34 years old. He is copy chief at a middle-sized advertising agency. He was graduated from an Ivy League college[1], and toured Europe as a drummer in a jazz band. On occasion, he writes freelance articles for national magazines.

(adapted)

How do you, as an advertising man, see the consumer ?

The consumer is a great big gaping-jaw we're all trying to fill up with whatever we can cram down there, and the great hope is that that jaw will keep getting wider and wider. And the more products there are, the more, you know.

What segment of the population is potentially the most profitable one for advertising ?

The population explosion is a grand thing for business, of course. My God, think of all the machines we can sell to more people. A third of the population is going to be under the age of twenty in another year or two, I imagine. They got all the money to spend, that's great. We can sell them records and we can sell them cars and dresses and brassieres[2] at that age, and the whole bit. We can make the whole world like us very fast and make a lot of money on it. We can make it an American middle-class universe.

What exactly do you do in your job ?

Sell this product against that product. And what you do is try to find reasons why yours is better. If you can't find those, God help you. It takes time to realize they're identical. We're all conditioned to think this soap is different from that soap, until we go to the factory and see them coming off the same production line. There are times when I still believe they're different. It's a belief we have to hold on to.

Do you like your job ?

Do I like my job ? No. I deplore it. I hate it. I come home sick at night about it. I'm a pretty unhappy guy some nights. And a pretty mean father. I'm not able to divorce myself at five o'clock from what's happened to me all day long—or what I've been making happen to other people. As a consequence, evenings are not always pleasant.

Studs Terkel, *Division Street*

brassiere   /brəˈzɪər/

---

1. the Ivy League : association of the oldest and most prestigious colleges in the East (Harvard, Yale, Princeton, etc.).   **2.** brassière : *soutien-gorge.*

How does each of these airlines try to sell its services ?

The airline built for professional travelers.

It takes a level head and a loving heart to be a Delta professional.

You meet all kinds of people with all kinds of travel problems in a Delta ticket office. And you have to know all the answers.

But not just pat answers. You try hard to come up with a lower fare, an easier connection, a faster route, a free stopover, whatever's best for the customer.

You could get by with less. A lot of folks wouldn't know the difference. But when it comes to people, a Delta professional couldn't care more. ▲ DELTA
The airline run by professionals

Ticket Sales Agent Sandy Johnakin.   *A 15-year Delta professional.*

Delta is ready when you are.®

★★ United's ★★
Four Star Dining

Charge it.

Four Star Dining is our top line of food service. And you can charge it, along with any of the other fine meals, on your Diners Club Card. Naturally, the price includes your flight to any of the 113 cities we serve. No tipping required.

United Air Lines.

You can stop over in Florida for just $5 when you fly me between coasts.

Boston
New York
Newark
Washington
Philadelphia
Baltimore

(Airline of your choice)

San Francisco
Los Angeles
San Diego
Las Vegas

(Airline of your choice)

Houston
New Orleans

or one of 11 other Florida cities.
Miami

I'm Kathy.
And I have Triangle fares between 4 West Coast cities, 2 Gulf Coast cities and 6 East Coast cities.
Whichever triangle you choose, you fly National to or from Miami or 11 other Florida cities and the airline of your choice between coasts. You can stop in Florida either coming or going and stay as long as you like.
Between most cities, the additional airfare is just $5 — NY to Florida to L.A., for instance. For some the price ranges from $11 to $21.
Add a little Florida sun to your next trip. With my Triangle Fare, I'm going to fly you like you've never been flown before.

I'm Kathy. Fly me. ☀ Fly National.

129

B LANGUAGE AT WORK

Superlatives

You have just found a summer job where you must sell laundry detergent door to door to housewives in your neighborhood. Using superlatives such as best, brightest, cleanest, cheapest, most economical, longest lasting, mildest, gentlest, fastest acting, strongest,... in the world, try to sell your product.

More and more

Example :

> • The hope is that the jaw will keep getting wider and wider.

Use the above pattern to express some of the assumptions advertising is working on.

The more, the more

Example :

> • The more products there are, the more necessary advertising is.

Use the above pattern to express the vicious circle to which the affluent society is condemned.

C FOLLOW UP WORK

1. Contrary to what Charlie Landesfahr said, the population "explosion" in the States is slowing down (as shown in the charts). At the same time, people are living longer. Describe the consequences which these demographic changes might have upon the choice of products on the market and their advertising.
2. Advertising helps you to decide what product to buy.
3. Do you think France has become an "American middle-class universe". Why or why not ?

Charts based on U.S. Census projection assuming fertility rate of 2.1 children per woman

Newsweek, Feb. 1977

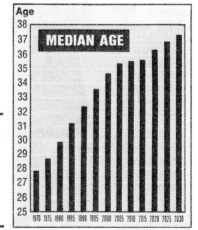

A CHANGING PROFILE

If the birth rate stays low, the nation's demographic profile will change shape and the median age (half the population older, half younger) will rise.

BLACK ELECTED OFFICIALS IN THE UNITED STATES 1970-1982

Year	Total	Numerical increase since previous year	Percentage increase since previous year	Percentage increase since 1969
1970	1,469	284	24	24
1971	1,860	391	27	57
1972	2,264	404	22	91
1973	2,621	357	16	121
1974	2,991	370	14	152
1975	3,503	512	17	196
1976	3,979	476	14	236
1982	5,160	1,181	30	335

BLACK ELECTED OFFICIALS *by Region and Level of Office, 1983*

Région	Repartition of black pop.	Total	Federal Officials	State Officials	County Officials	Municipal Officials	Judicial and Law Enforcement Officials	Education Officials	Black Mayors
Northeast . . .	11 %	577	3	56	16	185	91	216	10
North Central .	21 %	1 090	7	85	75	462	114	271	50
South	61 %	3 140	4	161	364	1 523	287	648	153
West	6 %	308	4	22	10	58	71	124	10
Virgin Islands .	1 %	45	0	0	0	0	0	0	0
Total . . .	100 %	5 160	18	324	465	2 228	563	1 259	223

Source : Joint Center for Political Studies, Washington D. C.

There are 21 black U. S. Representatives and ño U. S. Senator.
There is 1 black in the Cabinet.
The U. S. Ambassador to the United Nations is black.

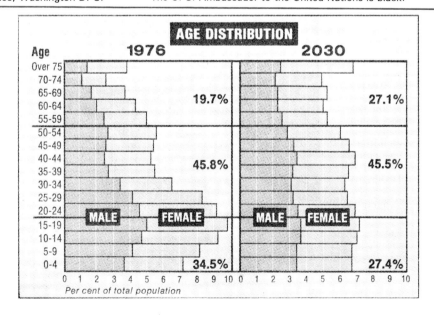

AGE DISTRIBUTION

Age — 1976 — 2030

Over 75, 70-74, 65-69, 60-64, 55-59, 50-54, 45-49, 40-44, 35-39, 30-34, 25-29, 20-24, 15-19, 10-14, 5-9, 0-4

1976: 19.7% / 45.8% / 34.5%
2030: 27.1% / 45.5% / 27.4%

MALE FEMALE   MALE FEMALE

0 1 2 3 4 5 6 7 8 9 10 0 1 2 3 4 5 6 7 8 9 10
Per cent of total population

GOLDEN ULCERS

"Nobody ever went broke[1] underestimating the taste of the American public."
H.L. Mencken, 1880-1956

"The consumer isn't a moron[2], she is your wife."
David Ogilvy, Madison Avenue executive, 1963

It is sometimes said that the tone of American civilization is set by the advertising executives[3] who work on New York's Madison Avenue. Here, at the heart of the American advertising industry, where nearly half the advertising expenditure[4] in the entire country is controlled, they like to claim that their craft is the "sparkplug[5]" of
5 the American economy, a necessary part of the business machine that brings comfort, luxury, and ease to millions. And they often quote approvingly the words of Winston Churchill to the International Advertising Conference of 1924. "Advertising," he said then, "nourishes the consuming power of men. It creates wants for a better standard of living. It sets up before man the goal of a better
10 home, better clothing, better food for himself and his family. It spurs individual exertion and greater production." (...)

"The decade in wich Churchill spoke was one of the golden ages of American advertising, the start of the great consumer-led boom of the twentieth Century in which American advertisers[6] increased their expenditures by over 50 percent. It is a
15 surprisingly small world, this state known as Madison Avenue. The part that houses the advertising industry runs for only about a mile, concentrated between the 200 and 800 blocks of the handsome Avenue, an area known to the cynics as "Ulcer Gulch[7]". In all, perhaps 25,000 people work here, about half of them women. There are creative writers who turn up at the office, invariably late, wearing trendy
20 clothes and showy psyches[8] (one twenty-nine-year-old, hired at a salary of $65,000 a year, reported to work on his first day carrying a golden typewriter). There are account executives[9], those who actually meet the clients, who tend to be more sober and conservatively dressed. There are space buyers[10], artists and TV producers, media specialists and PR men[11], whose talents, even in the 1970s, can command
25 salaries of $80.000 a year and more.

The highest rewards commonly go today to those who work in the power-houses[12] of the agencies, the so-called creative departments, which are staffed by an odd and often bizarre breed of conforming non-conformists. One has the feeling that most of them secretly, or even openly, despise the jobs that pay them so
30 handsomely. But the idiosyncrasies[13] of the creative staffs are benignly tolerated at most advertising agencies. They are the ones, after all, who bring in the bread and butter, and it is recognized on Madison Avenue that the creative juices are not stimulated by regular office hours or conservative clothes. (...) At one agency a leading copywriter[14] is known to curl up under his desk when he is thinking
35 particularly hard. "My God," complained an executive at another agency, "we hired a new copywriter the other day—a very good copywriter, too—and he came to work in bare feet." (...) And David Ogilvy himself one of the most successful creative advertisers of all, has written of his craft :

"I hear a great deal of music. (...) I watch birds. I go for long walks in the
40 country. And I take frequent vacations, so that my brain can lie fallow[15]—no golf, no cocktail parties, no tennis, no bridge, no concentration, only a bicycle. While thus employed in doing nothing, I receive a constant stream of telegrams from my unconscious, and these become the raw material for my advertisements. But more is required, hard work, an open mind, and ungovernable curiosity."

"Ulcer Gulch."

45   The rewards for such activity are high : Ogilvy has made himself a multi-millionnaire and lives for much of the year in a twelfth-century French chateau he bought from the proceeds[16] of the telegrams he received from his unconscious.

    But there is another side to the coin, and that is fear. It is not for nothing that Madison Avenue's best-known luncheon club is called The Golden Ulcers, with the
50 cynical motto, "What good is happiness if it doesn't bring you money ?" This is the original home of the twentieth-century rat race[17], and the insecurities of the advertising world are inseparable from the rewards that come to its successful practitioners. "The advertising industry is a great business of compromise," says one Madison Avenue man. "But you compromise the wrong things—your peace of
55 mind, health, sanity." (...) It is accepted as a basic truth here that unless you own the business, you are going to get fired some day. And on Madison Avenue it may be today.

Robert Hargreaves, *Superpower*

---

1. broke : bankrupt. **2.** moron : very stupid person. **3.** executives : *cadres.* **4.** expenditure : *dépense ;* advertising expenditure : *budget publicitaire.* **5.** sparkplug : *bougie d'allumage (ici, moteur).* **6.** advertiser : *annonceur publicitaire (plus rarement, publicitaire, cf. ligne 35)* **7.** gulch : ravine. **8.** showy psyches : flamboyant personalities. **9.** account-executives : *chef de publicité.* **10.** space-buyer : *acheteur d'espaces (publicitaires).* **11.** PR men : Public Relations men. **12.** power-house : *ici, centre moteur.* **13.** idiosyncrasies : eccentricities (here). **14.** copywriter : *rédacteur publicitaire.* **15.** fallow (land) : *(terre) en friches.* **16.** proceeds : *revenus.* **17.** rat race : fierce, violent competition ; struggle for success.

A UNDERSTANDING THE TEXT

1. What do we learn about New York's Madison Avenue ?   2. What do advertising executives claim about their "craft" ?   3. What part does advertising play in the American economy, and what kind of economy is it ?   4. What did Winston Churchill say in support of advertising ?   5. Why were the twenties one of the golden ages of American advertising ?   6. What type of society is described by Winston Churchill here ?   7. What do you think of the proportion of women employed on Madison Avenue ? Why is the figure quoted here ? 8. What are the various activities connected with the advertising industry ?   9. Do you consider that advertising executives are generally speaking well paid ?   10. What does this imply about the advertising industry ?   11. Who are the best paid people in the ranks of those who work in advertising ? 12. According to you, why do creative people in advertising dress and behave in an outrageous way ? Why does the writer refer to them as "conforming non conformists" ?   13. The business community is fairly conservative. Why is such unusual behaviour tolerated on Madison Avenue ? 14. How does David Ogilvy, a famous advertising man, view his expertise as well as his own person ?   15. Is there anything that sounds slightly ridiculous about his statements ?   16. The writer is an Englishman. What is typical of his comment on David Ogilvy ?   17. Explain : "There is another side to the coin." What is paradoxical about the situation on Madison Avenue ? 18. What price has to be paid to fame and money in the advertising industry ?   19. What do many advertising executives fear ? What are they caught in ? 20. Explain the name given to this luncheon club "The Golden Ulcers".

B LANGUAGE AT WORK

Introducing restrictions

Rephrase the following sentences using the most suitable expressions among :

though - although - unless - in spite of.

a) Creative advertisers command high salaries.
   They despise their jobs.
b) They get the highest rewards.
   They arrive late and dress in an outrageous way.
c) Creative advertisers are brilliant people.
   Creative advertisers know they can be fired any day.
d) David Ogilvy takes frequent vacations so his brain can lie fallow.
   David Ogilvy does not feel inspired.
e) You compromise your peace of mind, health, sanity.
   You cannot stay in the running.
f) Insecurity and fear are part of the game.
   You own the business.
g) There is no lack of brilliant people eager to join the rat race.
   Jobs are insecure in the advertising industry.
h) The advertising industry is flourishing.
   There is no such thing as job security among advertising executives.
i) The advertising industry is claimed to be essential to the American economy.
   The advertising industry has many detractors.

C FOLLOW UP WORK

1. Is the rat race restricted to advertising ?
2. Considering the high financial rewards, do you consider it worth while to join in the rat race ?
3. What good is work if it doesn't bring you money ?

A Shorter Workweek ? No !

Critics of the four-day week—the latest experiment in work schedules[1]—are starting to come forward.

Labor.

Joseph Cointin, a regional official of the Machinists Union in St Louis is one of these objectors. In a recent comment, he argues that unions should be working toward a four-day week of 32 hours at 40 hours' pay and "not a backbreaking compression of four days into 40 hours." [...]

"This business of working 10-hour days strikes at the heart of what our unions have accomplished for us over the years, and the shift[2] to four 10-hour days in a workweek that is taking place in many sections of the country can only wreak havoc[3] in the universal 8-hour day that unions so long fought for. [...] Management, Mr Cointin contended[4], hopes to "make a higher profit off their labor" by saving the expenses of opening the plant for the fifth day and by "cutting overtime costs to the bone".

Criticism also came from a University of Michigan labor relations expert, Thomas K. Connellan. He said :

"Too many organizations will seize upon the four-day workweek as the cure for such problems as absenteeism and turnover[5].

"While it is possible that such a novel work schedule will have a short-term effect —perhaps even for as long as several years—it should be remembered that absenteeism is not the basic problem but rather a symptom."

As Mr Connellan sees it, that problem is "that many people have little or no interest in their jobs" and that most jobs "do not challenge the ability of individuals" holding them.

Evidence was cited from psychological testing that the average person uses only about 10 per cent of his ability. Mr Connellan said that the typical business organization demands only a small part of that productivity. [...]

From *U.S. News and World Report*
May 3, 1971

Business.

Virginia O. Hayes, company president, [...] says : "A mandatory[6] 35-hour week would only cripple[7] profitable concerns. Fixed employee costs—insurance, disability payments, taxes—would increase because more employees would be needed to produce the same amount of goods. Probably, increased prices would begin to reduce the demand for goods, and the vicious recession cycle would start all over again"
[...]

"Cutting the workweek," says William Cosulas, president of a Beverage Company, [...], "would encourage workers to seek additional part-time work for added income and could well keep some of the unemployed from getting jobs," [...]
Robert E. Adams, general manager of an oil company, [...] is also against shortening the workweek. "With the already existing coffee breaks, extra holidays on long weekends, sick leave, extended vacations, and many other fringe benefits, it appears to me that we are lucky to get 35 hours of production now," he says.

Thomas R. Henderson company president, [...] feels that "we have enough leisure time now. Quality of life can deteriorate with too little gainful work and too much leisure time."

From *Nations's Business*
March 1976

---

schedules   /'skedʒʊls/ /'skedʒəls/   argues   /'ɑrgjuːz/
psychological   /ˌsaɪkə'lɑdʒɪkəl/   mandatory   /'mændətori/

---

1. schedules *(Am.)* : timetables *(Eng.)*   2. shift : change.   3. wreak havoc : cause chaos.   4. contended : argued.   5. turnover : *ici, rotation du personnel.*   6. mandatory : compulsory.   7. to cripple : to handicap.

A UNDERSTANDING THE TEXT

1. What group is in favor of the shorter workweek ? 2. What are the different definitions of a "shorter workweek" ? 3. Why is Joseph Cointin against the shorter workweek ? 4. According to Thomas Connellan, what problems will the shorter work-week not solve ? Why not ? 5. How does Virginia Hayes describe the "vicious recession cycle" ? 6. Do you agree with William Cosulas ? Justify your answer. 7. Is Robert Adams sympathetic to the worker's situation ? Explain. 8. How does Thomas Henderson agree/disagree with Adams ? 9. Who do you think should decide how long the workweek will be ? 10. To what extent did you expect the people here to react the way they did ?

B LANGUAGE AT WORK

Evaluation

Using too much/too many *or* enough, quite enough/not enough, *say what the position of the different people quoted is or may be on*

the number of hours per day	productivity
fringe benefits	absenteeism
interest in the job	turnover
part-time work	unions
coffee-breaks	leisure time
etc.	

Consequences

- **Phrases :**

as a consequence	and so
in consequence of	so that
consequently	that's why
accordingly	

- **Verbs :**

to bring about	to lead to
to give rise to	to result in
to give birth to	

Using as many of these expressions as you can, describe the possible or likely consequences of a shorter workweek.

Example :
As a consequence of a shorter workweek, people would actually work longer each day.
A shorter workweek would bring about all sorts of problems.

C FOLLOW UP WORK

1. Compare the various tables of p. 137 and comment them.
2. What are the pros and cons of a 32-hour workweek ?
3. Robert Adams says sick leave is a "fringe benefit". In your opinion what are basic worker rights and what are "extras" ?
4. Thomas R. Henderson, company president, feels that workers have enough leisure time now. *"Quality of life can deteriorate with too little gainful work and too much leisure time."* Do you think the workers in his company would agree with him ? How about the workers' wives ? How about you ?

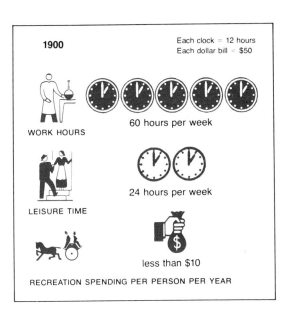

1900

Each clock = 12 hours
Each dollar bill = $50

WORK HOURS — 60 hours per week

LEISURE TIME — 24 hours per week

RECREATION SPENDING PER PERSON PER YEAR — less than $10

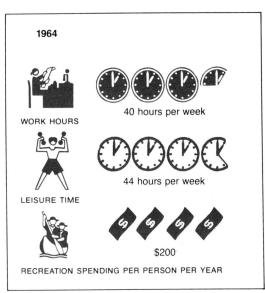

1964

WORK HOURS — 40 hours per week

LEISURE TIME — 44 hours per week

RECREATION SPENDING PER PERSON PER YEAR — $200

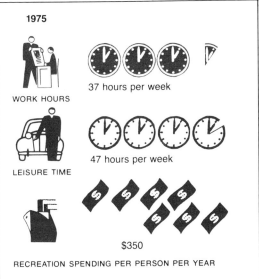

1975

WORK HOURS — 37 hours per week

LEISURE TIME — 47 hours per week

RECREATION SPENDING PER PERSON PER YEAR — $350

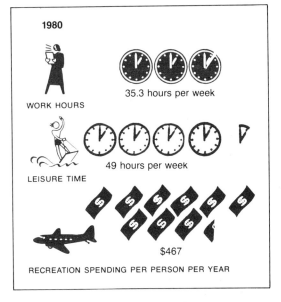

1980

WORK HOURS — 35.3 hours per week

LEISURE TIME — 49 hours per week

RECREATION SPENDING PER PERSON PER YEAR — $467

Source: U.S. Department of Commerce publication
July 1981 Survey of Current Business

$106,414 million dollars per year in recreation spending
227.7 million persons

GROWING UP ON T.V.

In the typical American household a TV set is turned on for six and a half hours a day. While each member of the household is not glued to the screen for all that time some viewers are more persistent than others. Generally the heaviest viewing groups are women, blacks, the elderly and children.

5   By the time children enter kindergarten most are averaging more than 30 hours a week of TV viewing and see 400 commercials in that time. Kids of all ages watch not only by day but also by night ; 18 million children are still in the viewing audience between 8 and 9 P.M. and no fewer than 1 million are still watching at midnight. By the time the child finishes high school, he will have spent 18,000 hours with the
10   "T.V. curriculum" and only 12,000 with the school curriculum.

Meanwhile people in all age groups tend to watch more and more television each year—no matter what the programs are ! And now a second explosion of T.V. technology that is likely to increase viewing time dramatically is upon us.

Home-video tapes recording and playback devices[1] are increasingly popular. The
15   home recorder can tape[2] off the air for future viewing while the viewer is asleep away or watching another channel. If the video recorder's growth parallels that of the T.V. set, within a decade most of us will own one. The attractions of T.V. will be virtually boundless[3].

So, as we are about to be "liberated" from the networks' schedules, we may be
20   addicted more thoroughly and blindly than ever to the viewing habit. It is therefore now more imperative than ever that we understand the cumulative effects of television watching, particularly upon young children. In fact, we now have evidence, that habitual viewing can affect a young persons basic outlook and sensibilities, predisposition to violence and hyperactivity, I.Q., reading ability,
25   imagination, play, language patterns, critical thinking, self-image, perception of others, and values in general. Further, habitual T.V. viewing can affect the physical self as it can alter brain waves, reduce critical eye movements, immobilize the hands and body and undermine nutrition and eating habits.

As the cumulative pattern of influences flows from television, we begin to see
30   radical cultural effects ; we see them in the United States, and I believe they will be seen increasingly in other parts of the world as the experience of television becomes more and more pervasive[4]. Ritual and structure are disappearing from the home. When families use television routinely, the social structure and rituals of the group tend to be regulated by its viewing patterns.

35   It seems that as traditional institutions have crumbled (under pressure of divorce, mobility, absence of extended family[6]) television has filled in the spaces. As a

result, the transmission of culture to children does not come so much through the family as it comes from outside-mainly via television.

A major difference between the family and school of the past and those of today lies in their sources of information, entertainment, and learning. Before television, family members were more available[7] to each other : wisdom came from elders close at hand and from the direct experience of growing up. School was also a major source of information, and play was the child's entertainment. For these, the community offered contact or structure. Inside this structure, parents raised their children in the way they had learned from their own parents. Children developed their senses through play, discovering along the way how to use their hands, imaginations, and social skills[8] while experiencing lots of human contacts in learning. This life met many of the child's basic needs, and eventually most children learned to trust, to care, to think, to communicate, and to value what their elders valued. Through the rituals of family life, culture was handed down.

Now culture is handed up. Packaged in rock music, situation comedies[9] and T.V. advertisements, mass media deliver culture to the young who hand it up to adults. Since the 1950's and 1960's, American radio and T.V. have teased youth into new tastes and values and then played to these in large and profitable dimensions. Mass media were responsible for the time in the 1950's when the young began calling the tunes[10] and the youth culture was born. Now, from the cities of the Soviet Union to the farmlands of Argentina, rock music, jeans and the "Pepsi generation"—transported by media—are reorganizing not only our own families but families everywhere.

Kate Moody, *Growing up on Television,* 1980

---

1. device : *(ici) système.* 2. to tape off the air : to record a T.V. programme. 3. boundless : unlimited. 4. pervasive : widespread. 5. the cumulative pattern of influences : *cet ensemble d'influences accumulées.* 6. extended family (including grandparents and relatives) ≠ nuclear family. 7. available : accessible. 8. social skills : ability to establish relationships with others. 9. situation comedies : humorous T.V. programmes. 10. calling the tunes : being in a position to command.

A UNDERSTANDING THE TEXT

1. Compare viewing time in the United States, as described. In what ways is viewing as illustrated in the text different from or similar to viewing in France ? 2. Can you imagine why women, blacks, the elderly and children are heavy TV viewers ? 3. What does the writer mean by "a second explosion of TV technology" ? 4. Why does this imply a liberation from the network schedules ? 5. What do the quotation marks in "liberated" reveal about the writer's attitude ? 6. To what is TV viewing compared in the sentence : "We may be *addicted* more blindly to the viewing *habit*." What is the image meant to suggest ? 7. What has television become a substitute for in our society ? 8. How can you explain the widespread influence of TV in our society ? 9. When was the Youth culture born ? 10. What is symbolical of the Youth culture ? 11. How far can its impact be felt ? 12. What was responsible for the explosion of the Youth Culture ?

Expressing imperative requirements

Examples :

- It is imperative that we understand the cumulative effects of T.V on children.
- It is imperative for us to understand the cumulative effects of T.V. on children.
- It is imperative that we should understand the cumulative effects of T.V. on children.

Make sentences using :

it is necessary/indispensable/all important/imperative/essential/vital/crucial

and :

to exert pressure on the media/monitor the viewing behavior of children/control the use of violence on T.V./take charge of the T.V. revolution/realize what our responsibilities are/acknowledge that T.V. is an integral part of childhood/learn to use T.V. wisely/etc.

Speculating about the future

To express future meaning, the present tense is used in preference to the auxiliary WILL/SHALL In temporal clauses.

Example :

- *"By the time* the child *finishes* high school he will have spent 18,000 hours with the T.V. curriculum."

On the same model, complete :

a) By the time a child...   he will have watched 18.000 T.V. murders according to figures on T.V. viewing. (to reach age 18)
b) By the time pay-cable...   an almost infinite library of entertainment will be available to consumers. (to hit the mass market)
c) By the time most of us...   we shall have become hopelessly addicted to the viewing habit. (to own a video-recorder)
d) By the time...
e) When... ...
f) Once... ...
g) As soon as... ...

C FOLLOW UP WORK

1. Comment on the contrast : "Through the rituals of family life, culture was handed *down*." "Now culture is handed *up*." What differences in social attitudes does this imply ?
2. The writer claims that children play less since they've become heavy TV viewers. Explain.
3. Will the advent of television change the way children use T.V. ?
4. We cannot live without television.

FOR YOUR EYES ONLY
(HBO)

24 HOUR SPORTS
(ESPN)

CULTURE
(CBS CABLE)

TURN YOUR TV INTO AN ENTERTAINMENT CENTER
WITH MANHATTAN EYES...

SEE 27 CHANNELS WITH MORE CHOICES THAN EVER BEFORE! ...ALL WITH SUPERIOR RECEPTION

BIG SAVINGS, TOO!
50% OFF
YOUR CABLE
CONNECTION!

SEE INSIDE FOR MORE INFORMATION

24 HOUR NEWS
(CNN)

SPECIALTY
(USA NETWORK)

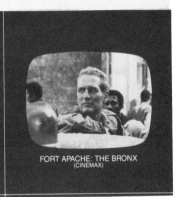

FORT APACHE: THE BRONX
(CINEMAX)

15 REASONS FOR NOT WATCHING TV

1) "I feel hypnotized when I watch television."
2) "Television sucks my energy."
3) "I feel like it's brainwashing me."
4) "I feel like a vegetable when I'm stuck there at the tube."
5) "Television spaces me out."
6) "Television is an addiction and I'm an addict."
7) "My kids look like zombies when they're watching."
8) "TV is destroying my mind."
9) "My kids walk around like they're in a dream because of it."
10) "Television is making people stupid."
11) "Television is turning my mind to mush."
12) "If a television is on, I just can't keep my eyes off it."
13) "I feel mesmerized by it."
14) "TV is colonizing my brain."
15) "How can I get my kids off it and back into life ?"

Can you find the play on words?

WHAT IS PROGRESS ?

Albert Einstein once told the students at the California Institute of Technology that he doubted whether present-day Americans were any happier than the Indians who were inhabiting the continent when the white man first came. Not many are likely to agree with so extreme a statement but quite a few, I think, would admit
5 that, leaving the Indians out of it, we are not *as much* happier than our grandfathers as it would seem our gains in health, security, comfort, convenience, as well as our release from physical pain, ought to make us. Does this failure to pay /rɪ'liːs/ off have something to do with a misjudgment concerning what man really wants most or, at least, a failure to take into account certain of the things he wants besides
10 comfort, wealth and the rest ?

Only more of the same is promised him by even the most optimistic utopians. The /'prɑmə̦st/ more intellectual among them talk in general terms of greater per capita wealth, of less poverty and less manual work, and of faster means of communication. Those who write the popular articles published over and over again in those periodicals
15 which exist chiefly to make readers dissatisfied with their current refrigerator or automobile usually go into more detail. By 1980, they say, you will be broiling[1] steaks in electronic stoves, owning a two-helicopter garage and, of course, looking at television in full color. These assurances are supposed to make it easier for the housewife to put up with mere electric ovens, ninety-mile-an hour automobiles and
20 soap operas[2] in black and white. From such makeshifts[3] they are supposed to lift sparkling eyes toward a happier future. And perhaps that is precisely what they do do. But will they be as much happier as they now think they inevitably must be ? Is it really what they want ? Is the lack of these things soon to become chiefly responsible for the irritations, frustrations and discontents they now feel ?
25 Suppose they were promised instead that by 1980 the world in which they live will be less crowded, less noisy, less hurried and, even, less complicated. Suppose they were told that they will have more opportunities to see the beauties and to taste the pleasures of sea and mountain and stream, to have more contact with the wonders of trees and flowers, the abounding life of animal creatures other than human.
30 Would the prospect look even brighter ? Perhaps not. But that does not convince me that such a world would not, in actual fact, make for more happiness than the one they are promised.

Joseph Wood Krutch, *Grand Canyon*

---

1. broiling : cooking.   **2.** soap opera : melodramatic program on radio or T.V. originally paid for by soap companies.   **3.** makeshifts : temporary substitutes.

A UNDERSTANDING THE TEXT

1. What did Einstein think about modern America ?
2. How does the author feel about what Einstein said ? 3. How does the author explain the fact that Americans do not seem to be as happy as their grandfathers thought they would be ? 4. What do ''optimistic utopians'' predict for America in the future ? 5. How does the author feel about all the publicity given to new and better products for consumers ? 6. What questions does he ask ? 7. What alternative to the present idea of ''progress'' does the author offer ? Does he feel this alternative would make the future better ? 8. What are some new products you would like to have ? Explain why you want them. 9. Do you think you are happier than your father or grandfather was at the same age ? Justify your answer. 10. Why do you think the American system assumes that a greater quantity of consumer goods will increase the quality of people's lives ?

B LANGUAGE AT WORK

Passives

Examples :

> • More and more things *are promised* him/to man.
> • People *are supposed* to lift sparkling eyes toward a happy future.

Using passives as in the examples above, imagine some of the things that are promised to man by optimistic utopians and pessimistic observers. Use as many verbs as you can.

Expressing doubts and certainties

Phrases you will need :

> • It seems to me that...
> • I am (almost) certain that/(quite)sure that...
> • My impression is that...
> • I have the conviction/the firm belief that...
> • I have doubts about...
> • I feel suspicious about...
> • It's improbable that...

Read the text again. Then, using as many of the above phrases as you can, point out what seems to be certain and what is uncertain about the future.

C FOLLOW UP WORK

1. What does progress mean to you ?
2. If you could choose, what period of history would you prefer to live in ?
3. Progress is an illusion.

What Video Games Are Doing to Kids

"They increase the child's skills, competency and self-awareness, and they should be encouraged rather than deplored."
Interview with Mitchell W. Robin, professor of psychology and data processing, New York City Technical College :

Q : Why do you believe video games are valuable for children ?
A : Video games tend to increase eye-hand coordination and improve reflexes. Also, they're skill-oriented games.

Q : How do you answer critics who say that playing video games a is solitary, anti-social activity ?
A : Many of these games require solitary practice, as do swimming, golf and many other sports. But once you've mastered the skill, you wish to compete with other humans.

Q : Parents charge that children spend their lunch money, borrow and even steal money to pay for these games. Is the video-games industry exploiting children's lack of judgment ?
A : It's the job of the parents to provide the child with basic integrity, a definition of right and wrong, self-control and the ability to realistically appraise a situation. So when the child goes into a video arcade he learns that if he spends his lunch money on games, that day he goes without lunch.

Q : Aren't these games addictive ?
A : I don't call them addictive ; I call them rewarding. The game is structured so you get the results of your actions immediately. This is referred to as "reinforcement".

Q : Parents say that these games are diverting children from reading, homework and sports. How can that be beneficial ?
A : I don't know if it's beneficial, but it seems very similar to the kinds of activities adults engage in all the time. There are thousands of adult males who think nothing of spending a Saturday in front of the TV set watching football... there are equally as many housewives glued to the TV set, watching soap operas. I know of no studies that indicate that being glued to soaps or football games have made them less responsible, less loving, less mature.

Q : Why hasn't the industry popularized those games that enhance spelling and math skills ?
A : Who says they haven't ? They're not in the arcades ; they're in the homes. They're not in the arcades because arcades are amusement centers. I don't know of any other game that has been required to be instructive as well as amusing.

"Watch a teenager dumping quarters into a machine, see the zombified look in that child's eyes. Is this what we want for our future generations ?"
Interview with Ronnie Lamm, president, Middle Country School District PTA Council, Brookhaven, N.Y.

Q : Why do you object to video games ?
A : We have not taken a stand against video games, but against the massive proliferation of these games throughout our community.
Suddenly, we parents are finding a tremendous increase in "lost" lunch money. Elsewhere police report an increase in vandalism of vending machines and parking meters.

Q : A few children may be addicted, but for the majority, aren't video games simply an occasional diversion ?
A : Any single activity that encompasses a child's entire thoughts and time is a disservice to parents. Psychologists have used words like "mesmerizing", "narcotizing", "addictive", to describe what happens when a child interacts with a video game. There's also a lack of quality of supervision in video game rooms and arcades. Where are our children hanging out ? Is it any better than a public street corner ?
Give parents some help. Throughout history society has aided parents. Society has determined that minors should not drink, gamble or be exposed to certain dangers.

by Sue Mittenthal,
San Francisco Chronicle,
August 3, 1982.

Youngsters trying their skills at one of the many video games : A learning aid or a time waster ?

SURVEYING THE SCENE

1. Which of the texts in this chapter give you an image of the United States which you already had ? Which ones give you a new insight into Americans ?
2. In what ways do you think the American way of life differs from that of the French ?
3. Compare and contrast Steinbeck's views in *Plastic World* with Einstein's in *What is Progress* ?
4. Read *Garden City* p. 80. How far do you think O'Keefe, ''the praying businessman'' might like to live in Garden City ? What be his social position there ?
5. To what extent does the scene described in *Golden Ulcers* explain Ross Pelletier's and Charlie Landesfahr's positions in *Selling America* ?
6. What other aspects of life in the United States would you like to read about in this chapter and why ?

Some books you might like to read : *The Loved One (Le Cher Disparu)* by E. Waugh.
Babbitt and *Elmer Gantry* by Sinclair Lewis.

Some films you might like to see : *American Graffiti* by G. Lucas.
In the Heat of the Night (Dans la chaleur de la nuit) by N. Jewison.

VI. CONFLICTING VALUES

A WELFARE MOTHER

An interview with Janice Jones, a divorced mother with two children.

INTERVIEWER : *How long have you been on welfare[1] ?*
MRS JONES : For the last three years, and let me tell you, it's been a nightmare. I'm nervous, uptight[2] and thinking all the time.

I. : *What is it that bothers you ?*
5 **MRS J.** : I'm just not used to the whole idea of welfare. There's no money, no way to plan. I'm just not used to it.

I. : *Has it always been this way or was it worse ?*
MRS J. : Well, I can still remember the first time I had an appointment to go to the welfare office to apply[3]. I didn't go. I felt so guilty because I had to get on it, but I didn't have anywhere else to turn to
10 at the time.

I. : *Is your life easier now ? At least you know you will receive a certain amount of money each month.*
MRS J. : Are you kidding ? We can't eat properly on $50 worth of food stamps[4] a month. I don't know how people manage with older children, especially with teenagers. I have to stretch every dollar.
15 I'm always looking for bargains. We eat a lot of soup and beans.

I. : *Do your children know you are on welfare ?*
MRS J. : Of course, little kids sense there is something wrong. When I buy used clothing, I try to get things that look new. But kids talk about where they get their clothes. If you can't go to the movies or ice skating then you're obviously a deprived person.

20 **I.** : *But certainly you are not the only people in this neighborhood in this situation.*
MRS J. : I'm sure we're not, but you never tell anybody that you're on welfare. A lot of people with food stamps don't shop close to home for that reason. You feel so terrible that you don't want anybody to know what you're going through.

I. : *Don't you talk over your problem with anyone ?*
25 **MRS J.** : My sisters are the only ones who know we're on welfare. I just try not to let the neighbors know. I would have liked to keep it from my children. But it's hard to keep anything from kids.

I. : *Have your ideas about welfare changed since you've been receiving benefits ?*
MRS J. : Now, I know why people cheat on welfare. You have to in order to make ends meet. The welfare program forces you to be a thief or a liar. For example, if welfare finds out that you got an
30 extra $30 by selling a table, they deduct it from your relief check. So you learn quickly not to tell.

I. : *Have you ever looked for a job ?*
MRS J. : Sure, lots of them. A few months ago I wanted to work but all I could find were jobs as a waitress, cook or housekeeper. As a housekeeper I got $325 per month, which was less than I got on welfare. It was impossible to live, so I gave it up after 6 months.

35 **I.** : *Do you think you'll be able to get off welfare ?*
MRS J. : Lord knows how. As long as you need help real bad, welfare is the only place to go. I only hope to God that my children won't ever need it.

---

1. on welfare : receiving government money. **2.** uptight : extremely nervous. **3.** to apply : to ask for. **4.** food stamps : stamps given by the Federal government to be used as payment when buying food.

Should welfare just keep their bellies full, or help keep them from getting a bellyful of welfare?

A   TRUE OR FALSE ?

1. Living on welfare was a nightmare for Mrs Jones.
2. She didn't feel guilty about applying for welfare.
3. Her life became easier once she got on welfare.
4. She buys cheaper food and shops for bargains to save money. 5. Her children don't know that the family receives welfare payments. 6. By not using food stamps in stores near their homes, some people hide the fact that they are on welfare.
7. People cheat on welfare because they are basically dishonest. 8. Mrs Jones would prefer to live on welfare rather than work. 9. She hopes that her children will never need to go on welfare.

B   ANSWER THESE QUESTIONS :

1. How long has Mrs Jones been on welfare ?
2. What bothers her about being on welfare ?
3. What happened the first time she had to get welfare ? Why ? 4. Why hasn't welfare made her life easier ? 5. How did her children find out that the family is on welfare ? 6. Who knows that Mrs Jones is on welfare and who doesn't ? 7. How can the welfare program force people to be dishonest ?
8. Why did Mrs Jones gives up her job as a housekeeper ?

C   EXPLAIN IN YOUR OWN WORDS :

1. I'm nervous and uptight.
2. I have to stretch every dollar.
3. I'm always looking for bargains.
4. If you can't go to the movies you're obviously a deprived person.
5. It's hard to keep anything from kids.
6. To make ends meet.

D   DISCUSSION

The welfare system is wrong if is encourages people to cheat.

A SHOOTING AT A LIQUOR STORE

— "Hear about the shooting in Newton Street ?"

— "No," said Gus.

— "They got a policeman on the fire for shooting a guy that works in a liquor store on Olympic[1]. Officer rolls up to the store answering a silent alarm, and just as he's
5 getting ready to peek in[2] the window to see if it's for real or phony[3], the proprietor comes running out and starts screaming and pointing toward the alley[4] across the street. One officer runs in the alley and the other circles the block and picks a spot where he thinks anybody back there would come out, and in a few minutes he hears running footsteps and hides behind the corner of an apartment house with his gun
10 out and ready, and in a few seconds a guy comes busting around the corner with a Mauser in his hand and the officer yells freeze and the guy whirls around and the officer naturally lets go and puts five right in the ten ring[5]." Rantlee placed his clenched fist against his chest to indicate the tight pattern of the bullets.

— "So what's wrong with the shooting ?" asked Gus.

15 — "The guy was an employee in the store who was chasing the suspect with the boss's gun."

— "The officer couldn't have known. I don't see any real problem. It's unfortunate, but..."

— "The guy was black and some of the black newspapers are playing it up, you
20 know, how innocent people are killed every day by the storm troops in occupied south central Los Angeles. And how the Jew proprietor in the ghetto sends his black lackeys to do the jobs he hasn't got the guts to do. Odd how the Jews can support the blacks who hate them so much."

— "I guess they haven't forgotten how they suffered themselves," said Gus.

25 — "That's a kind thought," said Rantlee. "But I think it's because they make so goddamn much money off these poor ignorant black people from their stores and rents. They sure as hell don't live among them. Jesus Christ, now I'm a Jew hater. I tell you, Plebesly, I'm transferring to the valley[6] or West L.A. or somewhere. These niggers[7] are driving me crazy."

Joseph Wambaugh, *The New Centurions*

---

1. on Olympic : on Olympic Avenue. **2.** to peek in : to look in furtively. **3.** phony : false. **4.** alley : passageway between buildings. **5.** puts five right in the ten ring : *fait mouche cinq fois.* **6.** the valley : the San Fernando valley. **7.** niggers : pejorative for blacks unless said by another black.

He might have been the man who discovered a cure for cancer.

Dropouts become losers.

They lose.

And we lose.

Today's dropouts might have been tomorrow's scientists. Or doctors. Or teachers.

But what might have been will never be.

For one out of three high school students doesn't stick around to graduate.

The dropout is ten times as likely to become a juvenile delinquent.

And the juvenile delinquent is perhaps a thousand times more likely to become a criminal.

It doesn't have to happen.

Good schools with good teachers and good facilities can produce good citizens. And that can make our world a better place in which to live.

Which is why money spent on education represents the best investment we can make.

An investment in the future of America.

This message is sponsored by the Copier Duplicator and VariTyper division of the Addressograph Multigraph Corporation.

A   UNDERSTANDING THE TEXT

1. Who was shot and how did it happen ?
2. Besides the fact that the dead man was innocent, what complicated the situation ? 3. What was the position of the newspapers ? Why did they publicize the incident ? 4. According to Officer Rantlee and Officer Plebesly, why do Jewish people continue to operate businesses in the black ghettoes ? 5. Why was Officer Rantlee so upset ? 6. What was the economic and social relationship between the Jewish proprietor and his Black clientele ? 7. Why do you think the liquor store owner sent his assistant to catch the thief ? What do you think the owner did in the meantime ? 8. Do you think the policeman and/or the owner should be prosecuted ? Support your answer. 9. What are some forms of racism indicated in the text ? 10. In the United States both Jewish people and Blacks are minority groups. What, then, is the irony in the text ?

B   LANGUAGE AT WORK

Giving definite or speculative information

You witnessed the robbery described in the text and the police are questioning you about the robber — what he looked like, how he acted, and so on. You may say things such as :

- **He had a black beard. (Definite information)**
- **He looked nervous. (Speculative information)**

On the same models use verbs such as had, was, seemed, sounded, appeared, looked,... *to make statements to the police giving both definite and speculative information.*

Now you are looking at five suspects the police picked up after the robbery. Through a process of elimination by logical deduction you are able to indicate the real thief. You will say for example :

> • **It can't have been Suspect Number One because he doesn't have a black beard.**

Using the same model make sentences using expressions such as can't have been/must have been, because/therefore, *to show your reasoning.*

C FOLLOW UP WORK

1. You are a reporter for one of the black newspapers mentioned in the text. Write an article, including the headline, describing the robbery and killing. Now, write an editorial commenting upon the incident.

2. Do you think the incident in the text is an example of police brutality ? Support your answer.

3. The law is too lenient. Support your argument.

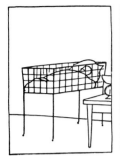

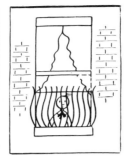

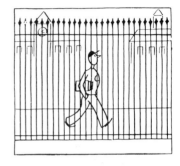

FRANKIE RODRIGUEZ,

Why should I worry about the world ?
I figure it this way : Who's gonna take
care of you ? Nobody ! [...] and you
ain't got no education, what're you
gonna do ? [...] So I figure like this :
If I can't make money the right way,
I'm sure gonna make it the wrong
way. [...] And if you rob and get away
with it, you're lucky. But you can't be
robbin' all your life, an' don't get
caught. So you figure like this : You're
gonna spend a couple of times in jail.
But you ain't got no education, so
that's it. It don't bother me. 'Cause I
don't really care about the world, and
the world don't care about me.

Studs Terkel, *Division Street*

1. What did Frankie think about education ?
2. Do you think he was angry ? At what or whom ?
3. What did he want to do ?
4. What did he think would happen to himself ?
5. What do you think will happen to him ?

What do you think these women mean by the American Dream ?
Do you agree that it is for men only ?

CAROL

By the time Carol was twenty-six she was making a lot of money for a girl her   /'kærəl/
age, and she had quit her job to write full time. [...] All her friends from high
school had married and she had been a bridesmaid[1] several times. Her college
friends had married too, but she did not see them anymore because the ones she
5 liked did not live in New York. She now had her name on magazine covers
occasionally, and she had a certain following and received fan letters, some of them
from men proposing marriage. She wrote a piece on lonely people who wrote love
letters to strangers. It was the first piece she had written with heart, and afterward
she had to have her telephone number unlisted.

10 Her mother and her mother's friends viewed her rising career with dismay[2]. Her
mother said, "Boys don't want to marry girls who are too independent."

Because everyone she met at parties talked about their analysis, Carol treated
herself to a year of analysis to find out why she had never married. [...] The doctor
was just a man to her, she couldn't think of him as a doctor or an authority,
15 although once when she had a sore throat she asked him to look at it since she was
paying him anyway, and he prescribed some pills. She was aware that he thought
she was funny and interesting because he laughed a lot at the things she said. She

also became aware after a few months that he didn't think she was sick, or at least what he considered her sickness was that she did not fit into the role he saw for her
20 as a young woman.

— "You are lonely," he said. "I would like to see you married. You would be a wonderful mother."

— "But I really don't feel I'm ready for that. There are so many things I haven't done yet."

25 — "You're lucky you can write. You can stay at home with the children and write."

— "Only if they're zombies[3]", she said.

— "You could marry a rich man. You could have a nurse for the children."

— "Then why have them ? If I had kids I'd want to enjoy being with them."

30 — "Your parents must have made you feel very unwanted," he said sadly.

— "Unwanted ? They never let me out of their sight."

— "You must understand you are rejecting being feminine."

— "If being feminine means washing some guy's socks, then how come every Chinese laundryman down on the corner doesn't feel his masculinity threatened ?"

35 — "You retreat into words," he said.

— "That's how I express myself."

— "You could express yourself as a woman if you had a man to take care of you."

— "Then how come I don't fall in love ?" Carol asked. [...] "I'd get married if I could find somebody I really loved."

40 — "There have been cases where love came afterward."

— "You mean a marriage of convenience ?" she said, horrified.

— "It has worked."

— Not for me, she thought. "Do you think I'm really neurotic[4] ?" she asked. /nʊˈrɑtɪk/

— "The only area in which you function perfectly is your work. In the human area
45 you need more work here."

She could see herself trotting obediently off to the analyst twice a week until she got married, and then still "more work" at the analyst until she produced two children, a number the doctor found ideal for mental health, and then more sessions of "work" until she was safely living in the suburbs. It could take years !

Rona Jaffe, *The Other Woman*

----

1. bridesmaid : *demoiselle d'honneur.* 2. dismay : consternation. 3. zombies : lifeless creatures. 4. neurotic : *névrosé.*

A UNDERSTANDING THE TEXT

1. What kind of work does Carol do ? Do you think she is successful ? Justify your answer. 2. Why was Carol's mother upset ? Do you agree with what she said ? Justify your opinion. 3. Why did Carol decide to go and see an analyst ? 4. Did the analyst find anything wrong with her ? 5. Why did Carol not want to have children ? 6. Do you think Carol had an unhappy chidhood ? Justify your answer. 7. How do Carol and the analyst differ on the meaning of the word "feminine" ? 8. What is a "marriage of convenience" ? What did Carol think of the idea ? 9. Do you agree with the analyst's conclusions ? Justify your opinion. 10. If Carol wanted to "get better" what would she have to do ? 11. Do you think you would like to know someone like Carol ? Justify your answer. 12. In what way do you think Carol reflects the American Dream ?

Making a choice

Phrases you will need :

- on the one hand... on the other hand...
- either... or...
- ..., but also...
- *Modals :* may/might

Read the text again. Then, using the above, show the alternatives that are open to Carol at this stage of her life.

Conditions

Example :

• If		would
• In case		could
	she got married, she	
• Supposing		might
• On the supposition that		should

Using the above elements, describe Carol's life in its positive and negative aspects if she got married now.

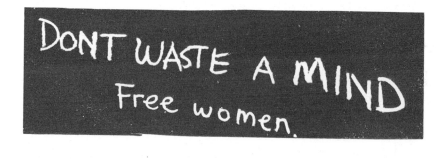

C   FOLLOW UP WORK

1.   Here is a list of the qualities that are generally accepted as masculine and feminine.
Masculine : hard, tough, brutal, cold, brave, assertive, strong, unemotional.
Feminine : soft, gentle, kind, affectionate, timid, quiet, weak, emotional.
Critize these lists and give your own views.
2.   Carol should get married. It would solve all her problems.

D DEBATE

These are accurate descriptions of men and women.

THE FINISHED PRODUCT

Mr Media

Tall, dark, handsome
working model
Guaranteed
indefinitely
improves with age
Power-driven

Where would you be
without him ?
An essential item

A life-long
investment

Mrs Media

36-25-36
Blonde model

Approximately 25-year
guarantee

Runs
Cheaply
on Love
Every home should have one !

An attractive
decoration
A bargain at any
price

" *Welcome aboard. This is your captain, Margaret Williamson, speaking.* "

"STRICTLY CONFIDENTIAL"

Much of the surveillance of individuals by trained investigators has been made easier by the proliferation of record-keeping in our increasingly bureaucratic society. I found it startling to learn how much information about one's private life is readily available to any skilled investigator who knows where to check accessible records and make a few routine inquiries. Detectives told me some of the presumably private information about myself—or just about any adult who is not a hermit—that any investigator could readily produce in most areas of the United States. They were referring just to an "easy" kind of checkout. An investigator in the New York State area could produce for a curious client most of the facts about you or me listed below, and it could be done within a few days. Here are the facts :

— Whether there are any significant blemishes[1] on your record where you have worked.

— How much money you have in your checking account at the bank (roughly), whether you borrow money often and for what, whether you have been delinquent[2] in paying bank loans, and whether you have any outstanding[3] loans.

— Whether you are a poor credit risk.

— Whether you have ever suffered from mental illness for which you were confined[4], been treated for a heart ailment, or been a victim of convulsive disorders. (This information can often be found in a public document—one's original application for a driver's licence.)

— Whether you are a known sexual deviate.

— Whether you actually received that college degree, if you claim one.

— Whether you have ever been arrested, or had any lawsuits filed against you[5].

— A good surmise[6] as to whether you were legitimately born, when and where, and the occupation of your parents at the time.

— Your net worth (provided you have a sizeable unsecured bank loan), the value of your home, its layout[7] and construction, its furnishings and upkeep, and what kind of locks there are on your doors.

— Whether you have been involved in an automobile accident in recent years.

— Whether your loyalty has ever been questioned by any of the better-known investigative bodies, public or private.

— Whether you are a registered Democrat, Republican, or have failed to register a party preference.

When I expressed curiosity about my own credit rating one detective said, "Give me a couple of hours." Within that period he called and gave me data from a credit report on me. It contained a fairly thorough[8] summary of my life, employers, agents, abodes, and offspring[9] for the past two decades[10], and the precise assessed value of my home in Connecticut. He chuckled[11] and added : "They say that, though you pay your bills, you occasionally take your time about it." He added that such reports often will provide a guess as to the person's annual income but that apparently my income was too erratic for a guess to be made.

Vance Packard, *The Naked Society*, 1964

/sɜr'veɪləns/
/ˌɪndʒ'vɪdʒuəls/
/ˌbjuərə'krætɪk/

/dɪ'lɪŋkwənt/

/diːveɪt/

/'θʌrəʊ/
/kə'netɪkət/

---

1. blemishes : bad marks. **2.** delinquent : here, late. **3.** outstanding : here, not paid yet. **4.** confined : imprisoned. **5.** had any lawsuits filed against you : *fait l'objet de poursuites.* **6.** a surmise : a guess. **7.** layouts : plans. **8.** thorough : complete. **9.** offspring : children. **10.** decades : *décennies.* **11.** chuckled : laughed.

A UNDERSTANDING THE TEXT

1. What has made it easier for trained investigators to get private information on individual citizens ? **2.** What are some examples of private information that is easily available to an investigator ? **3.** What information did the investigators get on the credit rating of the author ? How long did it take them ? **4.** What is the author's attitude toward record-keeping in a bureaucratic society ? Use evidence from the text to support your answer. **5.** In line 30 what does the author mean by "loyalty" ? What are some examples of "investigative bodies" ? **6.** Why do you think information about a person's private life is easier to obtain in a bureaucratic society ? **7.** Who do you think would be interested in knowing whether or not a person has been treated for a heart ailment ? **8.** What are some ways in which public knowledge of this private information could be used to help and to hurt both the individual and society ? **9.** How often is a census taken in France ? Explain why you think it is/it is not an invasion of privacy.

B LANGUAGE AT WORK

Active and passive participles

Examples :

- I found it startl*ing* to learn how much private information is readily available.
  I was startl*ed* to learn it.
- I was shock*ed*.
  The information was shock*ing*.

Using the same models make two sentences with each of the following elements, using verbs such as startle, shock, surprise, irritate, interest, horrify, fascinate, amuse... :

surveillance of individuals — record keeping — private information — work record — checking account — bank loans — mental illness — education — police record — locks — political loyalty — credit rating.

Asking questions

Read the text again. Then, using it as a basis, ask the questions an investigator might ask about a bank customer applying for credit.

C FOLLOW UP WORK

1. You have just learned that your bank released extensive "private" information about your financial situation to an automobile dealer you wanted to buy a new car from. The automobile dealer then released the information to a loan company, which has since begun to pester you with offers for loans. You are upset at both the indiscretion of the bank and the unethical practices of the automobile dealer. Write an angry letter to each company, expressing what obligations you feel they have to private citizens.
2. What do you think of computer dating ?
3. The enormous amount of data stored and made available by computers enables governments to serve their citizens better.

INTERRACIAL DATING*

Mariana sat with her legs tucked under, knees pointed toward Stiver, as they drove. She watched him and the road ahead, noticing his nervousness while fighting the heavy traffic in East Los Angeles. She knew the Anglos[1] unfamiliar with this section were always ill at ease here. Stiver seemed to relax as he took the freeway[2]
5   on-ramp[3] and let the powerful auto surge ahead.

She liked him, she decided, but she was honest, and would not allow herself to think of him as a ticket to the other world so soon. (...)

She looked at him earnestly[4] for a full minute, deciding something. "Tell me the truth," she said. "Are you really interested in finding out about us ? The Mexicans
10   in East L.A. ?"

"Why, of course," he said with too much sincerity. "And... I'd also like to get to know you better. You're a very attractive woman."

"Take me where they'll serve us drinks," she said suddenly. He slowed and took an off-ramp, turned onto a boulevard and soon pulled into the parking lot of a
15   cocktail lounge.

Dave knew many places where they served college students on the legal age borderline. They were usually nice, quiet places where there was never trouble, and it was usually dark inside.

When they were seated, drinks in front of them, she looked at him evenly[5],
20   "Well, ask away. What do you want to know about us ?"

"I sense that you're very upset for some reason. You want to blow off steam[6]."

"Not upset, no more than usual. It's just that... do you know you're the first Anglo that's ever taken me outside East L.A. ?"

"You've gone with... Anglos... before ?" He was surprised.

25   "They come to our parties and dances. They use our slang and mingle, but they have just one thing on their minds. Why is it that, I wonder—why the white guys think darker people's women are easier to get into bed with. Can you tell me ?"

She could tell he was surprised by her conversation, and perhaps a little embarrassed. She knew her conservative, demure[7] exterior was deceptive[8] and
30   everyone to whom she spoke naturally was surprised not to find a naive prudish maiden[9] inside.

"Well... no... I guess it's true, what you say. Maybe it's because throughout history, primarily by coincidence, lighter-skinned people have generally been in a position to take advantage of others." He was adlibbing[10] to the best of his ability.

35   "No," she said thoughtfully, "I don't think that has much to do with it."

He blinked. She went on : "Look, why does a guy like you come over to East L.A. and think he can make out with a girl[11] he hardly knows ?" Stiver thought a moment. He almost said something he didn't want to.

40 "Put it this way, then. Why don't you go to some white girl you hardly know and proposition her ? Aren't there plenty of girls at college ?" (...)

"I would never go up to a girl I hardly knew and proposition her. Because I'm not that kind of... I mean, a decent guy doesn't..."

"A decent guy doesn't try," she cut in.

"No ! I mean, you don't walk up to a decent girl and..."

45 "Aha ! And you reached the answer all by yourself, didn't you ? I don't know what kind of grades you're getting in sociology, David, but I give you an 'A' tonight."

Stiver's first reaction at being graded by Mariana was anger. Then he forced himself to examine what she said. (...)

50 They sat saying nothing, listening to the music coming from the dining room.

He was watching her in the dim light, very aware of her rare, unspoiled beauty. Her bold talk, her direct manner when she spoke of things important had somewhat suprised him at first, but he was beginning to see she was a direct person, direct without being forward. (...)

55 She looked at him evenly. "I'm a Mexican, David. It's not a dirty word. Let me hear you say it." He hesitated. "Go on. Say. 'You're a Mexican.' I want to hear you say it."

Richard Vasquez, *Chicano,* 1970

---

* dating a girl/a boy : *sortir avec une fille/un garçon.* **1.** Anglos : Chicano slang for White Americans. **2.** freeway : *autoroute (sans péage).* **3.** on-ramp/off-ramp ; *bretelle d'accès/de sortie.* **4.** earnestly : *avec sérieux.* **5.** evenly : unemotionally. **6.** blow off steam : relieve emotional tension. **7.** demure : quiet and serious. **8.** deceptive : cf. to deceive : *tromper.* **9.** maiden : girl (obsolete). **10.** adlibbing : improvising. **11.** to make out with a girl : *"sortir" avec une fille.*

A   UNDERSTANDING THE TEXT

1. What was Stiver's professed motive for dating Mariana ? **2.** Why did he feel ill at ease while driving away with Mariana from her parents' home in East Los Angeles ? **3.** Why don't Anglos usually take Mexican girls outiside East L. A. ? **4.** What is meant by "she would not allow herself to think of him as a ticket to the other world so soon" ? **5.** How long did it take Mariana to realise what Stiver's real motive was ? **6.** How can we tell Mariana was still quite young ? **7.** What was deceptive about her "conservative, demure exterior" ? Had Stiver been taken in as well as others ? **8.** Why was Stiver surprised by her conversation ? **9.** If you were to grade Stiver's and Mariana's honesty which of them would get an "A" ? **10.** What was the most embarrassing question she put to him ? **11.** Although this was a very personal question, does it bear any relation to racial prejudice in general ? **12.** "Say 'You're a Mexican.'" Why was Mariana's request so very important to her ?

Poujade — Let´s go on!... terminale — 6

B LANGUAGE AT WORK

Expressing reactions and feelings

Example :

> • **Mariana's parents** *approved of* **Stiver** *interviewing* **their daughter.**
> • **Mariana's parents** *approved of* **his** *interviewing* **their daughter.**
> • **Mariana's parents** *approved of* **Stiver***'s interviewing* **their daughter.**

1 *On the same model, complete the following sentences :*

    a) They did not object to Stiver...
    b) They weren't opposed to Mariana and Stiver...
    c) Mariana did not mind Stiver...
    d) She was intrigued by her date...
    e) He was puzzled at the girl...
    f) He was intrigued by his date...
    g) He was taken aback by her...
    h) She did not approve of Anglos...
    i) She hated Anglos...
    j) She resented Stiver...
    k) At one point he was irritated by Mariana...

2 *Using the same phrases say how you personally react to racialist attitudes.*

C FOLLOW UP WORK

1. What new light does the text throw on the matter of racism ?
2. Are racial prejudices restricted to Blacks
    a) in the U.S.
    b) in France ?
3. Is racial prejudice a factor in dating between young people ?
4. Imagine what happened to these two young people later on.

Numbering 10 million, Hispanics are the second largest minority group in the United States, with 70 percent living in three states : California, Texas and New York. Fifty percent are under age 20.

Mexican-Americans in particular face special problems. Many of them enter the country illegally along the open 2,000 mile U.S.-Mexican border, crossing the Rio Grande River. They are called "wetbacks" (a racial insult).

Seeking better jobs and living conditions, both legal and illegal aliens have often suffered from discrimination and loss of identity. Conditions have been improving, however, as these immigrants form effective organizations to protect their rights and proclaim their cultural heritage.

Called "Spanish Harlem" this part of New York City is inhabited by Blacks and Puerto Ricans. It is on these streets that the pushers of drugs make their living from the 100,000 addicts in the city.

SATURDAY NIGHT IN HARLEM

Saturday night. I suppose there's a Saturday night in every Negro community throughout the nation just like Saturday night in Harlem. The bars will jump[1]. The precinct station[2] will have a busy night. The hospital's emergency ward will jump.

Cats[3] who have been working all their lives, who've never been in any trouble before, good-doing righteous[4] cats, self-respecting, law-abiding[5] citizens, they'll all come out. Perhaps it'll be their night in the bar, their night in the police station, maybe their night in the emergency ward.

/ˈraɪtʃəs/

They tell me that young doctors really try hard for a chance to do their internship in Harlem Hospital. It offers such a wide variety of experiences. They say it's the best place in the city where a surgeon can train. They say you get all kinds of experience just working there on Saturday nights.

It's usually the older folks who practice this Saturday night thing, or some of the younger cats who haven't come out of the woods yet, young cats who drink a lot of liquor, who didn't quite finish junior high school, who still have most of the Southern ways [...], the young cats who carry knives, the young cats who want to be bad niggers. It's usually the guys around eighteen to twenty-five, guys who haven't separated themselves from the older generation yet or who just haven't become critical of the older generation. They follow the pattern[6] that has been set by the older generation, the Saturday night pattern of getting drunk, getting a new piece of ass, and getting real bad—carrying a knife in your pocket and ready to use it, ready to curse, ready to become a Harlem Saturday night statistic, in the hospital, the police station, or the morgue.

/lɪkəʳ/
/ˈsʌðərn/

The intern who comes to Harlem and starts his internship around April will be ready to go into surgery by June. He's probably already tried to close up windpipes for people who've had their throat slit. Or tried to put intestines back in a stomach. Or somebody has hit somebody in the head with a hatchet. Or somebody has come into his house at the wrong time and caught somebody else going out the window. That's quite a job too, putting a person back together after a four or five-story fall.

/ɪn'testɪnz/

I suppose any policeman who's been in Harlem for a month of Saturday nights has had all the experience he'll ever need, as far as handling violence goes. Some of them will have more experience than they'll ever be able to use.

To me, it always seemed as though Saturday night was the down-home night. In the tales I'd heard about down-home—how so-and-so got bad and killed Cousin Joe or knocked out Cousin Willie's eye—everything violent happened on Saturday night. It was the only night for anything to really happen, because people were too tired working all week from sunup to sundown to raise but so much hell[7] on the week night. Then comes Saturday, and they take it kind of easy during the day, resting up for another Saturday night.

Down-home, when they went to town, all the niggers[8] would just break bad, so it seemed. Everybody just seemed to let out all their hostility on everybody else. Maybe they were hoping that they could get their throat cut. Perhaps if a person was lucky enough to get his throat cut, he'd be free from the fields. On the other hand, if someone was lucky enough to cut somebody else's throat, he'd done the guy a favor, because he'd freed him.

Claude Brown, *Manchild in the Promised Land*, 1965

---

1. jump : be busy.   **2.** precinct station : police station.   **3.** cats : men (black slang).   **4.** righteous : respectful of moral laws.   **5.** law-abiding : respectful of civil laws.   **6.** pattern : example, habit.   **7.** to raise hell : to have a good time.   **8.** niggers : pejorative for blacks unless said by another black.

A UNDERSTANDING THE TEXT

1. What is the general atmosphere like in Harlem on a Saturday night ? 2. What kind of people end up in the bars, hospitals, and police stations ? 3. Why do young doctors want to work in Harlem hospital ? 4. What pattern of behavior has the "older generation" set in Harlem ? 5. Who tries to follow this pattern ? What do you think they all have in common ?   What are some examples of what an intern learns to do in Harlem Hospital ? What does the author think of those "accidents" ? Why do people describe them that way to the doctors and to the police ? 7. How much experience does a policeman get while working in Harlem ? 8. Why do people often get violent on Saturday night and not during the week ? 9. What are some of these people hoping will happen on Saturday night ? What is the irony of this situation ?   10. To what extent is this pattern of Saturday night violence, a general social phenomenon or a characteristic of black communities only ? 11. Why does the author not mention women in this text ? What do you think they do on a Saturday night in Harlem ? Why ?

B LANGUAGE AT WORK

Expressing impressions

Examples :

> • It *looks as if/as though* Harlem is a dangerous place on Saturday nights.
> • It *seems as if/as though* the emergency ward was jumping last Saturday.
> • It *sounds as if/as though* Saturday night is a very special night.

Using one of the above constructions, express your impressions of Harlem after reading the text.

Expressing probability

Examples :

> • *Perhaps* it'll be their night in the bar, *maybe* their night in the emergency ward.
> • He's *probably* tried to close up windpipes, or tried to...
> • Anything *may* happen in Harlem on a Saturday night.

Using the above constructions, explore the possible reasons which account for the behavior of the Harlem blacks on Saturday nights.

C FOLLOW UP WORK

1. Write a newspaper article describing a fight in a local bar on a Saturday night. Be sure to answer the questions Who ? When ? Where ? Why ? Give your article a headline.

2. Describe the different social pressures people are forced to live with during the work week.

3. Violence is increasing in large cities because modern society tends to put more presure on people. Discuss.

MAKING A FUTURE

Biff and Happy, the two sons of a traveling salesman, are home again together on a visit, and exchange reflections before going to sleep in the old room they shared while they were living with their parents.

HAPPY

But I think if you just got started—I mean—is there any future for you out there ?

BIFF

I tell ya, Hap, I don't know what the future is. I don't know—what I'm supposed to want.

HAPPY

5 What do you mean ?

BIFF

Well, I spent six or seven years after high school trying to work myself up. Shipping clerk, salesman, business of one kind or another. And it's a   /klɜrk/
measly manner of existence. To get on that subway on the hot mornings in summer. To devote your whole life to keeping stock, or making phone
10 calls, or selling or buying. To suffer fifty weeks of the year for the sake of a two-week vacation, when all you really desire is to be outdoors, with your shirt off. And always to have to get ahead of the next fella. And still—that's how you build a future.

HAPPY

Well, you really enjoy it on a farm ? Are you content out there ?

BIFF *(with rising agitation)*

15 Hap, I've had twenty or thirty different kinds of jobs since I left home before the war, and it always turns out the same. I just realized it lately. In Nebraska when I herded cattle, and the Dakotas, and Arizona, and now in Texas. It's why I came home now, I guess, because I realized it. This farm I work on, it's spring there now, see ? And they've got about fifteen new
20 colts. There's nothing more inspiring or—beautiful—than the sight of a mare and a new colt. And it's cool there now, see ? Texas is cool now, and it's spring. And whenever spring comes to where I am, I suddenly get the feeling, my God, I'm not getting anywhere ! What the hell am I doing, playing around with horses, twenty-eight dollars a week ! I'm thirty-four
25 years old, I oughta be makin' my future. That's when I come running home. And now, I get here, and I don't know what to do with myself. *(After a pause)* I've always made a point of not wasting my life, and every time I come back here I know that all I've done is to waste my life.

/nə'bræskə/
/də'kotəz/
/ˌærə'zonə/

HAPPY

You're a poet, you know that, Biff ? You're a—you're an idealist !

/aɪ'dɪəlɪst/

BIFF

30 No, I'm mixed up very bad.

Arthur Miller, *Death of a Salesman*, 1949

A   UNDERSTANDING THE TEXT

1. What is Biff sad about ?   2. What sort of jobs has he had since he left school ?   3. How, according to him, does one build a future ?   4. Why does he consider it to be ''a measly manner of existence'' ? 5. What does his present job consist in ? 6. How does he feel about it ?   7. What is it that he likes in his present job ? What is it that he does not like ? 8. Why has he come home ? 9. What makes Biff come home from time to time ? What does home mean to him ? 10. What does spring have to do with it all ? 11. What is it that makes Happy call his brother a poet, an idealist ? 12. Why does Happy not succeed in cheering up his brother ? 13. What forces is Biff caught between ? 14. To what extent do you agree that Biff has wasted his life ? 15. What makes this scene dramatic ?

B   LANGUAGE AT WORK

Expressing helplessness

Examples :

- I don't know... I'm mixed up...
- What am I to do ? How can I... ?

Using the above constructions, express Biff's helplessness as he might express it himself.

Stating amount or quantity

Examples :

> • It's spring there now, and they've got *many* new colts to look after. They've not got *much* time to themselves.
> • Biff has *few* friends, and *little* money in the bank.

Using much/many, little/few, *ask and answer questions corresponding to the following situations :*

a) Biff has only one or two friends in Texas.
b) He earns only $28 a week.
c) He has had twenty or thirty different kinds of jobs.
d) He has to look after more than a dozen mares every day.
e) He spent six or seven years after high school trying to work his way up.
f) In his last job, he was sometimes making forty phone calls in a day.
g) He only had a two-week vacation.

Past and perfect

Examples :

> • I've had twenty or thirty different jobs since I left home.
> • All I've done is to waste my life.
> • I realized it when I herded cattle in Nebraska.

Using pasts and present perfects, give an account of Biff's life from the moment he left home up to now (you may invent episodes, of course, but also use the text).

C FOLLOW UP WORK

1. Comment upon Biff's remark : *"I'm thirty-four years old, I oughta be makin' my future."*
2. Would you prefer to be a traveling salesman or a ranch hand ?
3. How do you imagine your own future ? What are you doing to "make it" ?
4. Do you think Biff was being influenced by his parents and society when he said : *"Every time I come back here I know all I've done is to waste my life"* ?
5. It is better to live in the present and enjoy it than to build a future. Support your argument.

SUBVERTED DEMOCRACY ?

In Arthur Hailey's novel, Overload, *Nim Goldman is vice-president with GSP&L (Golden State[1] Power and Light), the public utility providing California with electricity. As such he has had to cope with environmentalists opposed to some of his company's projects. He is here addressing a convention of the National Electric Institute and counter-attacking his critics.*

"Most of us here—probably all of us," he said, "share two important beliefs. One belief concerns environment.

"The environment we live in should be cleaner than it is. Therefore those who work responsibly towards that objective deserve our support.

5 "The second belief concerns the democratic process. I believe in democracy, always have, though lately with some reservations. Which brings me back to the environment.

"Some of those who call themselves environmentalists have ceased to be reasonable believers in a reasonable cause and have become fanatics. They are a

10 minority. But by noisy, rigid, uncompromising, often uninformed fanaticism, they are managing to impose their will on the majority.

"In doing so, such people have prostituted the democratic process, have used it ruthlessly[2]—as it was never intended to be used—to thwart[3] everything but their own aims. What they cannot defeat by reason and argument they obstruct by delay

15 and legalistic guile[4]. Such people do not even pretend to accept majority rule because they are convinced they know *better* than the majority. Furthermore, they recognize only those aspects of democracy which can be subverted to their own advantage."

The last words produced a burst of handclapping. Nim put up a hand for silence,

20 and went on.

"This breed of environmentalist opposes *everything*. There is nothing, absolutely nothing, we of the power industry[5] can propose which does not arouse their ire[6], their condemnation, their fervent and self-righteous[7] opposition.

"But the fanatics among environmentalists are not alone. They have allies. (...)

25 "The allies I spoke of," he declared, "are the growing number of appointees[8] on regulatory boards, put there for political reasons only."

Nim sensed[9], among his audience, rapt[10] and immediate interest.

"There was a time, in this state and elsewhere, when the boards and commissions[11] regulating our industry were few in number and could be relied on

30 for reasonably fair, impartial judgements. But not any more. Not only have such boards proliferated (...), but a majority of board members receive their appointments as blatant political rewards. Seldom, if ever, do they get where they are through merit or experience. As a result, such commissioners and board members have little or no business knowledge—indeed, some openly display an

35 anti-business prejudice—and all have political ambitions which govern their every action and decision.

"That is precisely why and how our extremist critics and opponents find themselves with allies. For it is the militant, so-called populist points of view[12], the anti-power-company stances[13], which nowadays make news and gain attention.
40 The quiet, balanced, thoughtfully-arrived-at decisions do not, and the commissioners and board members whom I speak of know that lesson very well indeed.

"Expressed another way : what ought to be positions of impartial public trust are being abused and turned against the public interest.

45 "I have no easy remedy to suggest for these two formidable problems nor, I suspect, have any of you. The best we can do is to let the public know, whenever possible, that their reasonable interests are being undermined by a minority—an insidious alliance of fanatics and self-serving politicians."

Nim decided to leave it here.

Arthur Hailey, *Overload,* 1979

---

1. Golden State : California. 2. ruthlessly : mercilessly. 3. to thwart : to frustrate. 4. guile : duplicity. 5. the power industry : *secteur de l'énergie électrique.* 6. ire : anger. 7. self-righteous : moralistic and intolerant. 8. appointee : person appointed. 9. sensed : became conscious of. 10. rapt : absorbed, intent. 11. commissions, boards : federal agencies, regulatory agencies, government agencies. 11. rapt : absorbed, intent. 12. populist point of view : *point de vue gauchisant.* 13. stance : position.

A UNDERSTANDING THE TEXT

1. What part of the community does Nim Goldman represent (labor force, big business, etc.) ? 2. In what type of society is the majority rule observed ? 3. What is the issue under discussion ? 4. What does Nim Goldman profess to believe in ? 5. What reservations does he have about the democratic process ? 6. What are his accusations against the environmentalists he calls *"fanatics"* ? In what way, according to him, do they *"subvert democracy"* ? 7. How does he suggest they are against democracy ? 8. How does he undercut their arguments ? 9. What is the alliance denounced by Nim Goldman ? 10. What is the normal task of the boards and commissions ? 11. Why, according to Nim Goldman, were regulating boards formerly *"fair and impartial"* ? 12. How do you account for the *"proliferation"* of such boards ? 13. In what ways can the appointees' political ambitions conflict with public interested ? 14. How does Nim Goldman manipulate his audience ?

PUBLIC UTILITY : a privately owned and operated business supplying the public with a commodity or service such as electricity, gas, water, transportation or telephone. The service is subject to public regulation.
REGULATORY BOARD : federal or government agency which regulates an industry or economic activity. Typical of American institutions, it is placed halfway between the executive and legislative branches of government and often adopts a judicial role.

B LANGUAGE AT WORK

Influencing people

In his speech Nim Goldman states :

- "The environment in which we live *should* be cleaner than it is."

What should be done/ought to be done about it ? Respond to the following statements on the above model :

a) Rivers are fouled up by chemicals.
b) Water pollution is a menace to us all.
c) Trash and litter pile up.
d) Forests are set afire and destroyed.
e) Wild life is endangered.
f) Fertilizers and pesticides can be a health hazard.
g) Oilslicks destroy marine life and pollute the coastline.
h) The level of noise in big cities has been proved to cause stress.
i) Exhaust fumes poison the air we breathe in cities.
j) Atomic wastes are sunk at sea or buried deep in the earth.

Suggestions : to put an end to - stop - clean up - forbid - restrict - deter from - control - warn - regulate - inform - tolerate - allow - be aware of - realize - rescue - save from - find other means of - get involved in - be committed to - devote time and energy to.

C FOLLOW UP WORK

1. Do you think that protecting the environment rates higher than industrial growth and new jobs ?

2. Explain : *"They have prostituted the democratic process."*

SURVEYING THE SCENE

1. This chapter takes a look at some conflicting values in the United States. Make a list of the different conflicts which arise in each of the texts in the chapter.
2. Look at the list you have just made. Which of these conflicts exist in France ? Do they exist for the same reasons ? Which conflicts could be eliminated according to you, and how ?
3. How do you think Officers Plebesly and Rantlee *(A Shooting at a Liquor Store)* would have liked to have been transferred from the Los Angeles Police Department to the New York City Police Department *(Saturday Night in Harlem)* ?
4. What other problems exist in the United States and France as a result of other conflicting values ?

A book you might like to read : *Future Shock (Le choc du futur)* by A. Toffler.

Some films you might like to see : *Rebel Without a Cause (La fureur de vivre)* by N. Ray.
East of Eden (A l'est d'Eden) by E. Kazan.
West Side Story by Robert Wise and Jerome Robbins.

VII. SOCIAL SCENES

A TEENAGER LOOKS FOR WORK

An interview with Berri Brown, 18, living in St Louis, Missouri.

INTERVIEWER : *Do you think it is easy for a teenager to find work ?*
BERRI : No. You don't have experience and usually companies want people with experience. A lot of times you're not old enough for the job, mature enough. Then there's the problem of transportation. They always ask for transportation. They want to make sure that you can get to work on time and
5 consistently[1]. And also, that you don't have to rely on your parents to drive you to work.

I. : *Do you think it is important for a teenager to work ?*
B. : Yes. There's lots of reasons why. For me, I think young people should work at a variety of jobs.

I. : *To get money ?*
B. : No, for experience. Say, if you have worked waiting on people then you know how to treat people
10 who are waiting on you.

I. : *What else do you mean by experience ?*
B. : Well, you can get a better job afterwards.

I. : *Were you able to get a better job once you started working ?*
B. : No, there aren't so many jobs available.

15 **I. :** *How old were you when you first started working ?*
B. : About 13 to 14. I worked in the Poppycock Restaurant when my cousin, who owned it, was pregnant. But I didn't get paid.

I. : *What did you do ?*
B. : I was a waitress, dishwasher. It was a counter type job and I did almost everything.

20 **I. :** *Did you like it ?*
B. : It was work, but I enjoyed serving people. You get to meet a lot of different people.

I. : *What other jobs have you had ?*
B. : I was a lab technician and a salesgirl.

I. : *Do you think these jobs will help you in what you want to do later on in life ?*
25 **B. :** Yes and no. Yes, in that I feel I have more understanding of other people's jobs. No, in that my jobs were not really involved in what I wanted to do. I wanted to do saleswork because I wanted to learn about fashion, but I never got to sell clothes. I never seem to get the right kind of job. Yet my girlfriend, Debbie, could always get a job even if she was fired[2], the next day she could get something else.

30 **I. :** *Why do you think she was different ?*
B. : Well, for one thing she has the clothes to wear for a sales job and the looks. There's a lot of discrimination, not only in color, just sheer looks. If you look elegant you can get an elegant job.

I. : *But can't you always look elegant, even if it is just for the interview ?*
B. : Not if you don't have the clothes or the know-how.

35 **I. :** *What do you mean ?*
B. : If no one around you dresses elegantly then you have no model and you have only magazines to look at. And in magazines you just see models and most people aren't. You see jeans outfits that cost $100 just to put together.

I. : *Do you worry about going on interviews ?*
40 **B. :** Yeah ! I hate interviews. They are not really interested in what you know ; it's your age, your looks, your dress, and like I said who you know ; also luck.

"I like your looks, Ramsey.
You're hired."

I. : *How do you feel after your interviews, if you didn't get the job ?*
B. : Well, the first time it's O.K., the second time you feel bad and then you start getting down. It's degrading and negative to be turned down.

45 **I. :** *What would your parents say ?*
B. : That's also what used to get me down. Everytime I'd come home Dad would ask me : How did it go ? What did they say ? Do you think you'll get it ?

I. : *Wasn't he just trying to be interested and helpful ?*
B. : Yes, and he's right. But when you've finished a day full of interviews and he's questioning you
50 too, it makes you insecure. You start wondering, did I really do my best, did I show enough self-confidence. Sometimes I'd just get so frustrated that I'd start crying.

---

1. consistently : here, every day. 2. fired : sacked.

A TRUE OR FALSE ?

1. Companies are not interested in whether prospective employees have cars or not. 2. Berri was able to get a better job once she had work experience. 3. Berri didn't get paid for the first job she had. 4. She didn't enjoy serving people in the restaurant. 5. Berri's friend always finds jobs, even after she has been fired. 6. Berri thinks that looks and clothes don't play a part in getting a job. 7. Dressing elegantly without money is not so difficult, according to Berri. 8. Berri thinks that luck is necessary in finding a job. 9. She is at once depressed after being turned down for a job. 10. Her father's interest makes her question her self-confidence.

B ANSWER THESE QUESTIONS :

1. What do most companies want to know about a future employee ? 2. What was the first job Berri had ? 3. How old was she then ? 4. Why did she enjoy this job ? 5. What other jobs has she had ? 6. In what ways does she think these jobs will help her later ? 7. Why did she want to do saleswork ? 8. What did Berri's father ask her whenever she came home from an interview ? 9. Why did she start crying ?

C EXPLAIN IN YOUR OWN WORDS :

1. A counter type job.
2. Not if you don't have the know-how.
3. It's degrading and negative to be turned down.
4. That's what used to get me down.
5. It makes you insecure.

D DISCUSSION

Young people should work even if they don't need the money because it is a good experience.

KID'S COUNTRY

Children are a relatively modern invention. Until a few hundred years ago they did not exist. In medieval and Renaissance painting you see pint-sized[1] men and women, wearing grown-up clothes and grown-up expressions, performing grown-up tasks. Children did not exist because the family as we know it had not evolved.

Children today not only exist ; they have taken over, in no place more than in America, and at no time more than now. It is always Kids' Country here. Our civilization is child-centered, child-obsessed. A kid's body is our physical ideal. Plastic surgeons scissor and tuck up[2]. New hair sprouts, transplanted, on wisdom's brow. One way or another we are determined to "keep in shape", and invariably this means keeping a kid's shape. In Kids' Country we do not permit middle-age. Thirty is promoted over 50, but 30 knows that soon his time to be overtaken will come.

We are the first society in which parents expect to learn from their children. Such a topsy-turvy[3] situation has come about at least in part because, unlike the rest of the world, ours is an immigrant society, and for immigrants the only hope is in the kids. In the Old Country[4], hope was in the father, and how much wealth he could accumulate and pass along to his children. In the growth pattern[5] of America and its ever-expanding frontier, the young man was ever advised to GO WEST ; the father was ever inheriting from his son.

Kids' Country may be the inevitable result.

Kids' Country is not all bad. America is the greatest country in the world to grow up in *because* it is Kids' Country. We not only wear kids' clothes and eat kids' food ; we dream kids' dreams and make them come true. It was, after all, a boys' game to go to the moon.

But what we are experiencing now seems in many ways the exact opposite of medieval and Renaissance life. If in the old days children did not exist, it seems equally true today that adults, as a class, have begun to disappear, condemning all of us to remain boys and girls forever, jogging[6] and doing push-ups[7] against eternity.

Shana Alexander, *Newsweek, Dec. 1972*

---

1. pint-sized : small.   2. to tuck up : here, to hide excess skin.   3. topsy-turvy : upside down.   4. Old Country : Europe.   5. growth pattern : *schéma de croissance.*   6. jogging : running for exercise.   7. push-ups : *pompes.*

A UNDERSTANDING THE TEXT

1. What does the writer mean when she says that children are a "modern invention" and "did not exist" in medieval and Renaissance times ? 2. How does she describe America ? 3. What are some examples of methods used to make people look younger ? 4. What does the writer want to suggest when she says, "New hair sprouts, transplanted, on wisdom's dome" ? 5. How does American family structure differ from that in the Old Country ? Why or why not is this difference inevitable ?   6. What are some of the advantages and disadvantages of the fact that America is "kids' country" ? 7. According to the writer, what is the American trip to the moon an example of ? Explain why you agree or disagree. 8. What will become of adults in "kids' country" ?

B LANGUAGE AT WORK

Expressing aim

> • in order to   in order that
> + *infinitif*   + *modal*
> • so as to   so that
> • for the purpose of
>   + verb + *ing*
> • for (= *rare*)

Using the above patterns, explain what people have in mind, what their aim is when they

— undergo plastic surgery
— get themselves a facelift
— do aerobics
— have hair transplants
— wear kids' clothes

— use kids' lingo
— eat kids' foods
— do some jogging
— do push ups and exercises.

C FOLLOW UP WORK

1. Explain the advantages America possibly draws from its emphasis on youth ?

2. How far do you think France is also "Kids' Country" ? Support your argument.

3. The falling birth rate suggests that before the end of the century there should be a definite 'greying of America''. In what ways do you think this could change the face of things ?

4. The older you get, the wiser you are.

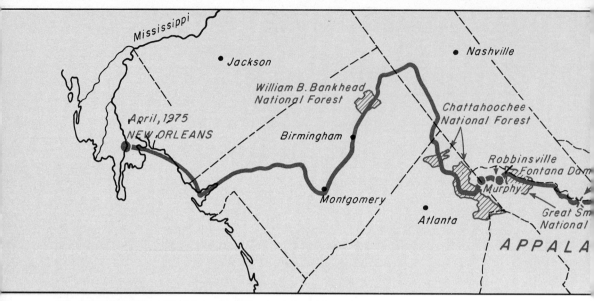

A WALK ACROSS AMERICA

*Confused by our turbulent times, a young Connecticut Yankee sets out to span the
continent in search of his country and himself.*

I finally reached Robbinsville, North Carolina (pop. 587), the next morning.
Since there were no jobs in Robbinsville, I headed toward the bigger town of
Murphy (pop. 2,035), where I'd heard there were some construction jobs to be had.

I had $15 left when, after a 36-mile hike in cold, damp[1] weather, Cooper (my
5 dog) and I walked into Murphy on a Friday evening. I passed some lighted
basketball courts where a bunch[2] of black teenagers were playing. They came over
when they saw me and Cooper, asked the usual questions, then invited me to play. I
couldn't resist.

Later, exhausted, we camped out for the night in their neighborhood across the
10 railroad tracks. Two of the teenagers, Eric and Bruce, invited me to their home for
a southern meal next day. And that's how I met my second mother, Mary Elisabeth
Lloyd.

She was standing there in the door of the house trailer[3] where the Lloyd family
makes its home in the leafy depths of Smokey Hollow. She told me later that when
15 she first saw my scraggly[4] red beard, she thought, "Oh-oh, what have the boys
brought home to dinner this time ?". But when she saw how Cooper liked me, she
figured I must be worth her trust. Dogs don't lie. Soon we were immersed in a
dinner of cake-rich corn bread, forever-simmered turnip[5] greens, ham chunks[6],
freshly caught perch, bream[7], and catfish, and rivers of Kool-Aid[8].

20 In the middle of the meal, Mary Elizabeth rose and announced that she believed
God had sent me to test their faith and henceforth[9] I was one of the family. Bruce,
15, immediately volunteered his bedroom, saying he would sleep on the spring-
protruding couch in the living-room.

In that loving family everybody had a nickname. Mary Elizabeth was Red. Her
25 husband, Frank Lloyd Jr., was Grumpy, Bruce's nickname was Onion, Eric's was
Bubba, and so on. Mine was Al—shortened from Albino.

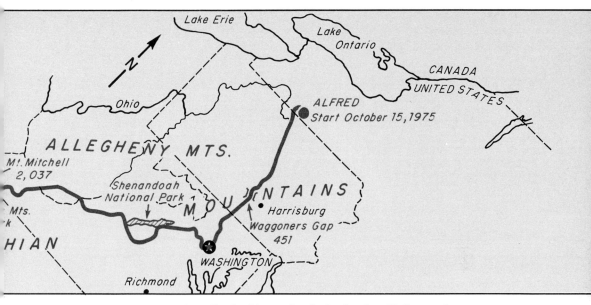

For the next several months I lived with my family in Smokey Hollow and
worked sawing logs[10] at a veneer mill. When Frank Lloyd Jr. lost his job, my
weekly wages of about $75 helped buoy[11] a family economy sustained otherwise /buːi/ /bɔɪ/
30 only by the $2.80 an hour Mary Elizabeth received at a local yarn mill.

Weekends I would usually go wandering with Cooper through the mountain
wilds, coming back Sunday morning to attend Mount Zion Baptist Church where /ˈzaɪən/
Mary Elizabeth's 73-year-old Father, Pau Pau, was a deacon[12]. He would put me in
the front pew, and there I would sit, the only grain of salt in a shaker of black
35 pepper.

I would get carried along by all that gospel singing and rhythmic shouting and
finger-snapping counterpoint between preacher and congregation. No rock concert
I'd ever been to, even Woodstock, could surpass Little Mount Zion Baptist Church
for sheer electric excitement.

40 For a time my stay in Smokey Hollow became problematical. A whiskey still[13]
had been busted by Government agents, and a rumor got out that I was an
undercover agent sent to that dry county to look for more "leaks"—that is stills.
When Frank Jr. heard that some bootleggers were talking about doing me and
Cooper harm, Mary Elizabeth and the family rose to my defence. A small arsenal
45 was kept at the ready. Sharp eyes were peeled. The boys let it be known that any
raiding party in these parts would be met head-on[14]. People saw that I worked hard
at the veneer mill and that I did not go snooping[15] around, and soon the rumors
were forgotten—drowned you might say—as local stills started to flow again and
life returned to normal.

Peter G. Jenkins, *National Geographic Magazine,* 1977

---

1. damp : humid. **2.** a bunch : a group. **3.** a house trailer : *une maison mobile.* **4.** scraggly : *ébouriffée.* **5.**
turnips : *rutabagas.* **6.** chunks : pieces. **7.** a bream : *une brême.* **8.** Kool-Aid : a drink made with fruit-
flavored powder. **9.** henceforth : from that moment on. **10.** logs : *des bûches.* **11.** to buoy : to keep
floating. **12.** a deacon : *un bedeau.* **13.** a still : *un alambic (clandestin ici).* **14.** would be met head-on : would
meet with a resistance. **15.** to snoop : to spy.

A UNDERSTANDING THE TEXT

1. How did the author eventually wind up with the Lloyds in Murphy ? 2. What do you think are the "usual questions" that the black teenagers asked the narrator ? 3. How do you explain that the black teenagers lived "across the railroad tracks" ? 4. Why did Mary Elizabeth welcome him although she was put off by his outlook at first ? 5. What shows that the Lloyds are typical Southern Baptists ? 6. Why does the author say that when he was in church he was "the only grain of salt in a shaker of black pepper" ? 7. What do you think made the services at Mount Zion Baptist Church so exciting for the author ? 8. What exactly was the incident at Smokey Hollow all about ? 9. What is a "dry" county ? 10. How did the Lloyds react in the circumstances ? 11. What is interesting in this episode ? 12. What is suggested by the last remark that "local stills started to flow again and life returned to normal" ?

B LANGUAGE AT WORK

Sequence of tenses

1. *Examples :*

> • He has been back home for quite a while now.
> • He had been on the road for a few weeks when he reached Robbinsville.

Using the same constructions, imagine the possible narrative of the author's adventures and itinerary Mary Elisabeth may have made to Pau Pau the week after the Connecticut boy arrived in her family.

2. *Examples :*

> • Bruce said : "I'll sleep on the couch in the living-room."
> • He said he would sleep on the couch in the living-room.

A few days after the author's arrival, Bruce and Eric made plans with their new friend, pointed out the things he should see, etc. Using the above constructions, imagine what they said.

C FOLLOW UP WORK

1. In what ways is or is not this text in keeping with the usual images one has of America ? Support your argument.

2. In what ways do you think an experience such as the one the author had in Smokey Hollow enabled him to "find himself" ?

The City of New Orleans

Chicago-Champaign
Carbondale-Memphis
Jackson-New Orleans

Trains in the USA have in many cases been superseded by buses or planes that are often cheaper and faster, to the point that some big cities are no longer connected by train to the rest of the country. The recent consolidation of heavily indebted private railroad companies into a national network, Amtrak, does not seem to have stopped the decline. In this song, Steve Goodman recaptures all the nostalgia attached to the progressive disappearance of the train, "America's native son".

59			Train Number			58
The City Of New Orleans			Train Name			The City Of New Orleans
Daily			Frequency of Operation			Daily
Ⓡ 🍴 Ⓧ			Type of Service			Ⓡ 🍴 Ⓧ
🛏						🛏
	Km	Mi	*(Illinois Central Gulf)*			
6 10 P	0	0	Dp	**Chicago, IL** *-Union Sta. (CT)*	Ar	9 00 A
㉔ 6 52 P	40	25		Homewood, IL	D	7 55 A
7 22 P	92	57		Kankakee, IL		7 14 A
8 12 P	185	115		Rantoul, IL		6 22 A
8 38 P	208	129		**Champaign-Urbana, IL**		6 06 A
9 18 P	280	174		Mattoon, IL		5 11 A,
9 45 P	323	201		Effingham, IL ⊕		4 47 A
10 36 P	408	254		Centralia, IL ⊕		4 03 A
11 32 P	498	310	Ar	**Carbondale, IL**	Dp	3 07 A
11 47 P	498	310	Dp	🚌 *(St. Louis)*	Ar	2 52 A
12 52 A	584	363		Cairo, IL ●		1 49 A
1 49 A	653	406		Fulton, KY ●		12 52 A
2 42 A	725	451		Dyersburg, TN ●		11 53 P
4 25 A	850	528	Ar	**Memphis, TN**	Dp	10 16 P
4 40 A	850	528	Dp		Ar	10 01 P
5 50 A	947	589		Batesville, MS ●		8 43 P
6 37 A	1012	629		Grenada, MS		7 59 P
7 00 A	1049	652		Winona, MS ●		7 37 P
7 29 A	1097	682		Durant, MS		7 09 P
8 05 A	1154	717		Canton, MS		6 36 P
8 41 A	1191	740		**Jackson, MS**		6 06 P
9 12 A	1245	774		Hazlehurst, MS ● ⊠		5 26 P
9 34 A	1278	794		Brookhaven, MS ●		5 06 P
10 02 A	1316	818		McComb, MS		4 44 P
10 53 A	1400	870		Hammond, LA		3 53 P
12 15 P	1486	923	Ar	**New Orleans, LA** *(CT)*	Dp	2 55 P

Riding on the City of New Orleans,
Illinois Central, Monday morning rail,
Fifteen cars, fifteen restless riders,
Three conductors, twenty-five sacks of mail.
Along the southbound Odyssey
The train pulls out of Kentucky,
Rolls along past houses, farms and fields,
Passing trains that have no name,
Freightyards full of old black men,
The graveyards of the rusted automobiles.

Good morning, America, how are you ?
Don't you know me ? I'm your native son.
I'm the train they call the City of New Orleans.
I'll be gone five hundred miles when the day is done.

Dealing cards with the old men in the club car,
Penny a point and no one keeping score,
Pass the paper bag that holds the bottle,
Feel the wheels a-rumbling neath[1] the floor.
And the sons of Pullman porters,
The sons of engineers,
Ride their fathers' magic carpet made of steel.
Mothers with their babes asleep
Are rocking to the gentle beat ;
The rhythm of the rails is all they feel.

Good morning, America, how are you ?
Don't you know me ? I'm your native son.
I'm the train they call the City of New Orleans.
I'll be gone five hundred miles when the day is done.

Night time on the City of New Orleans,
Changing cars in Memphis, Tennessee.
Half way home and we'll be there by morning,
With the Mississippi darkness rolling down to the sea.
And all the towns and people seem
To fade into a bad dream,
The steel rails, they still ain't heard[2] the news.
Conductor, sing this song again,
The passengers will please refrain :
This train's got the disappearing railroad blues.

Good night, America, how are you ?
Don't you know me ? I'm your native son.
I'm the train they call the City of New Orleans.
I'll be gone five hundred miles when the day is done.

Steve Goodman

1. a-rumbling neath : rumbling beneath.   2. ain't heard : haven't heard.

A UNDERSTANDING THE TEXT

1. What is the route followed by the 'City of New Orleans' ?   2. What are the fifteen restless riders ? Why do you think they are "restless" ?   3. Why does the 'City of New Orleans' claim to be America's "native son" ? Isn't the railroad a British invention ?   4. What elements suggest the public's disaffection with the train and its lessened economic importance ?   5. How does the text suggest that the persons traveling on the train are not "fast", dynamic people ?   6. Why is the bottle in a paper bag ? Could this be a trace of puritanism ?   7. Why do you think the sons of Pullman porters, the sons of engineers, ride on the train ? What do you think is their image of the train and why ?   8. Why does the author call it "their fathers' magic carpet" ?   9. How is the theme of death suggested and progressively imposed before the end of the song ?   10. To what· extent is this song "a blues" ?

B FOLLOW UP WORK

Explain in your own words why the train is fighting a losing battle against the bus, the car or the plane in America as opposed to France for instance. Give examples.

THE NEW LEARNING

Suppose you buy a computer that can play chess[1] with you. You can punch in your move and it will indicate a countermove. (...)

While you're having fun and while you're playing a game, what you're really doing is learning how to play chess better. It is impossible to engage in any activity
5 with an intellectual content[2], in an interested and concentrated manner, without learning. When a computer makes it possible for you to engage in such activities on your terms—in your good time, in your way, in an interested and concentrated manner—then how can you help but learn ?

The computer is the most efficient educational device[3] ever invented, because it
10 makes it impossible for you not to learn. Teachers can be insensitive, books can be dull, but computers produce a system in which only you count. And you cannot be insensitive or dull to yourself. (...)

You will be learning without even knowing you are learning, because we don't call it learning when we are doing something we want to do, anymore than we call it
15 work. (...)

If it becomes possible for youngsters to satisfy their curiosity by making use of the world's accumulated knowledge through a device that culls that knowledge and retrieves specific items on command, why should it be only youngsters who will use the device ? (...)

20 People who enjoy golf, or tennis, or fishing, or sex, when they are young do not willingly stop because they reach the age of 35, or 40, or 50, or any age. They continue with undiminished enthusiasm for as long as they are physically able to do so.

So it will be with learning.

25 It may seem strange to place learning in the class of pursuits[4] which we associate with fun and pleasure, but learning is fun. For those who, even in our own inefficient educational system, find themselves enjoying it, learning is the greatest pleasure in the world and outlasts all the others.

How much more so would it be when education is completely under one's own
30 control, when one can learn what one wants, and how one wants ; when one can learn something today and another thing tomorrow at will ; when one can follow the track of curiosity at one's own speed and choice, wherever it might lead ? (...)

The result ?

There will be greater intellectual depth and variety to humanity than the world
35 has ever seen. It will be an exciting world, a bubbling and effervescent world in which hosts of interests will compete with each other, and human beings will race each other to be the first with a new discovery, a novel idea, a better book, a more illuminating truth, a cleverer device.

They will look back on everything that existed before the age of the personal
40 computer as a time that belonged to the infancy of the human species ; and they will
consider the personal computer the path to adulthood for humanity.

Isaac Asimov, *Apple Magazine,* 1981

---

1. chess : *échecs.*   2. content : *contenu.*   3. device : *technique.*   4. pursuits : an activity that going : *complet, intégral.*

A UNDERSTANDING THE TEXT

1. What makes it impossible for you not to learn when using a computer, according to Asimov ?
2. What kind of information may be retrieved through a home computer ?   3. In the opening lines what are the different things the writer states which he considers as essential to the learning process ?
4. What is the author's attitude toward age and the New Learning ? To what extent can adults benefit from this kind of learning ?   5. What seems especially attractive about this computerized system of education ? 6. Do you consider the new freedom given to the individual learner an asset or a drawback in relation to the learning process ?
7. What are the various reasons for the writer's enthusiasm about the "new learning" ? Does this fit with the rest of the picture he presents ?   8. What is the only reservation in his optimistic predictions ?
9. At the present date, education researchers stress the importance of group-work in the learning process. Does computer learning ignore that aspect ?   10. Does the idea of communicating with a screen and learning on your own appeal to you ? Justify your answer.   11. Can information flashed on a screen be as thorough and rewarding as reading books and learning at the same time ?
12. What do you think are the drawbacks and limitations of the "new learning". You can make use of the interviews on p. **144** *(What video games...)* as well.

Computer Assisted Learning.

B LANGUAGE AT WORK

Expressing inevitability

Example :

- "When a computer makes it possible, how can you help but learn ?"

One might also have said :

- ...you cannot but learn.
- ...it is impossible for you not to learn.
- ...you can't help learning.
- ...the only thing left is to learn.

Using the above models, complete the following sentences :

a) This new educational device is so very efficient...
b) He has been studying computer science for so long...
c) She has spent so many years in California...
d) Diana has been working so hard for her exam...
e) He is so keen on video games...

and these too (be careful with the verb tenses) :

f) He started playing electronic chess three years ago...
g) The game was such fun...
h) The girl in the video store was so persuasive...
i) After buying this videogram...
j) Since all my friends had bought high-tech gadgets...

C FOLLOW UP WORK

1. "Learning is fun." How do you react to this statement ?
2. The writer's views are utopian !
3. To what extent was Asimov influenced by traditional attitudes when he wrote this article ? Remember that "Faith in God, faith in Man, faith in Work" are fundamental to the Puritan doctrine.

THE TERRIBLE PEOPLE

People who have what they want are very fond of telling people who haven't what
    they want that they really don't want it.
And I wish I could afford to gather all such people into a gloomy castle on the
    Danube and hire half a dozen capable Draculas to haunt it.
5 I don't mind their having a lot of money, and I don't care how they employ it.
But I do think that they damn well ought to admit they enjoy it.
But no, they insist on being stealthy
About the pleasures of being wealthy,
And the possession of a handsome annuity   /əˈnuːᵻti/
10 Makes them think that to say how hard it is to make both ends meet is their bounden
    duity[1].
You cannot conceive of an occasion
Which will find them without some subtle evasion.
Yes indeed, with arguments they are very fecund ;
15 Their first point is that money isn't everything, and that they have no money anyhow
    is their second.
Some people's money is merited,
And other peoples is inherited.
But wherever it comes from,
20 They talk about it as if it were something you got pink gums from[2].
This may well be,
But if so, why do they not relieve themselves of the burden by transferring it to the
    deserving poor or to me ?
Perhaps indeed the possession of wealth is constantly distressing,
25 But I should be quite willing to assume every curse of wealth if I could at the same
    time assume every blessing.
The only incurable troubles of the rich are the troubles that money can't cure,
Which is a kind of trouble that is even more troublesome if you are poor.
Certainly there are lots of things in life that money won't buy, but it's very funny—
30 Have you ever tried to buy them without money ?

Ogden Nash, *The Terrible People*, **1933**

---

1. duity : duty (to rhyme with "annuity"). **2.** something you got pink gums from = something that should give
you an allergy.

A UNDERSTANDING THE TEXT

1. Who are the "terrible people" ? **2.** What would the poet like to do with them ? Why would it be a punishment ? **3.** What are some arguments the "terrible people" use to conceal the fact that they are rich and enjoy it ? **4.** What does the poet suggest the "terrible people" should do with their money ? What is humorous about his suggestions ? **5.** Under what conditions would the poet accept to be rich ? **6.** What kind of troubles do rich people have ? What kind do poor people have ? **7.** What is the poet trying to say in the last three lines ? **8.** What is the tone of the poem ?

B LANGUAGE AT WORK

Prepositions + -ing form

Examples :

> • *After saying* they have no money, they buy a new car.
> • They are fond *of telling* other people that money isn't everything.
> • They like to complain about the problems *of being* wealthy.

Using the same models make more sentences to describe the "terrible people" and the author's opinion of them. Use expressions such as before/after/by, *and* to insist on, to listen to, to be fond of, to be interested in, to be tired of, to think about, to complain about.

Expressing wishes

Examples :

> • I wish I were rich ; If only I were rich
> • I wish I had money/If I had money I would buy a yacht
> • I wish I could afford a yacht

Using the above constructions, express your own immediate wishes. Then ask your neighbors what they would do "if they were rich..."

C FOLLOW UP WORK

1. The poem suggests that wealthy people do not like to admit they enjoy being rich. Do you agree ?
2. How much money would you like to have ? What are some things that money can/cannot buy ?
3. Some people argue that world peace depends upon a redistribution of the world's wealth. What is your opinion ?
4. Money is the root of all evil.

A modern sculpture in Texas.

CAR CULTURE

Motivational researcher Ernest Dichter [...] is shrewdly insightful when he suggests that the auto is the "most powerful tool for mastery" available to the ordinary Western man. "The automobile has become the modern symbol of initiation. The licence of the sixteen-year-old is a valid admission to adult society." /'ɔːtəməʊbil/

5 In the affluent nations, he writes, "most people have enough to eat and are reasonably well housed. Having achieved this thousand-year-old dream of humanity, they now reach out for further satisfactions. They want to travel, discover, be at least physically independent. The automobile is the modern symbol of mobility..." In fact, the last thing that any family wishes to surrender, when
10 hardpressed by financial hardship, is the automobile, and the worst punishment an American parent can mete out to a teenager is to "ground" him—*i.e.* to deprive him of the use of an automobile.

Young girls in the United States, when asked what they regard as important about a boy, immediately list a car. Sixty-seven percent of those interviewed in a
15 recent survey said a car is "essential", and a nineteen-year-old boy, Alfred Uranga of Albuquerque, N.M.[1], confirmed gloomily that "If a guy doesn't have a car, he doesn't have a girl." Just how deep this passion for automobility runs among the youth is tragically illustrated by the suicide of a seventeen-year-old Wisconsin boy, William Nebel, who was "grounded" by his father after his driver's licence was
20 suspended for speeding. Before putting a .22 caliber rifle bullet in his brain, the boy penned a note that ended, "Without a licence, I don't have my car, job or social life. So I think that it is better to end it all right now." It is clear that millions of young people all over the technological world agree with the poet Marinetti who, more than half a century ago, shouted : "A roaring racing car [...] is more
25 beautiful than the Winged Victory[2]."

/'ælbə,keki/

Alvin Toffler, *Future Shock*, 1970

---

1. N.M. : New Mexico. **2.** the Winged Victory : *la Victoire de Samothrace.*

A UNDERSTANDING THE TEXT

1. How does Dichter describe the car ?   2. What do you think Western man "masters" with a car ?   3. What is the social importance of a driving licence in America ?   4. How does Dichter describe the lifestyle of people in affluent nations and the importance of the car to these people ?   5. What is the worst punishment American parents can give to their children ?   6. What do girls and boys in America think about the car ? Explain why you agree or disagree.   7. Why did William Nebel commit suicide ? Do you think there was another reason ? Explain.   8. In what way does the poet Marinetti compare a racing car and the Winged Victory ? Do you agree or disagree ?

B LANGUAGE AT WORK

Expressing necessity

Examples :

- • A car is a must.
- • It is necessary/indispensable/compulsory for a teenager to have a car nowadays.
- • A teenager needs/has got to have/must have a car.
- • If he doesn't have a car, he can't have a girl.
- • Unless he has a car, he can't have a girl.

Using the above patterns, give the reasons why a car is regarded as a must by American teenagers.
Then, using the same constructions again, say why a car is a must for the following people :

- — a doctor
- — a journalist
- — a pizza-delivering service
- — a traveling salesman
- — a suburbanite

- — an elevator-repairman
- — a rich businessman
- — a career girl
  etc.

C FOLLOW UP WORK

1. What are some positive and negative aspects of the car ? What is the future of the car ? Will it replace mass transit systems ? Will environmentalists force its use to be limited ?
2. Can you think of other objects in everyday life that are also status symbols ? Why are they considered as such ?
3. Cars are also a necessary part of life in France.

THE UNICORN IN THE GARDEN

Once upon a sunny morning, a man who sat at his breakfast table looked from his scrambled eggs to see a white unicorn with a gold horn quietly cropping the roses in the garden. The man went up to the bedroom where is wife was still asleep and woke her. "There's a unicorn in the garden," he said. "Eating
5 roses." She opened one unfriendly eye and looked at him. "The unicorn is a mythical beast," she said, and turned her back on him. The man walked slowly downstairs and out into the garden. The unicorn was still there ; he was now browsing among the tulips. "Here, unicorn," said the man, and he pulled up a lily and gave it to him. The unicorn ate it gravely. With a high heart, because
10 there was a unicorn in his garden, the man went upstairs and roused his wife again. "The unicorn," he said, "ate a lily". His wife sat up in bed and looked

/tuːlɪps/

190

at him, coldly. "You are a booby[1]," she said, "and I am going to have you put
in the booby-hatch[2]." The man, who had never liked the words "booby" and
"booby-hatch," and who liked them even less on a shining morning when there
15 was a unicorn in the garden, thought for a moment. "We'll see about that," he
said. He walked over to the door. "He has a golden horn in the middle of his
forehead," he told her. Then he went back to the garden to watch the unicorn ;   /'fɔrɪd/
but the unicorn had gone away. The man sat down among the roses and went to
sleep.

20 As soon as the husband had gone out of the house, the wife got up and dressed
as fast as she could. She was very excited and there was a gloat in her eye. She
telephoned the police and she telephoned a psychiatrist ; she told them to hurry   /sə'kaɪətrɪst/
to her house and bring a straight-jacket[3]. When the police and the psychiatrist
arrived, they sat down in chairs and looked at her, with great interest. "My
25 husband," she said, "saw a unicorn this morning." The police looked at the
psychiatrist and the psychiatrist looked at the police. "He told me he ate a lily,"
she said. The psychiatrist looked at the police and the police looked at the
psychiatrist. "He told me he had a golden horn in the middle of his forehead,"
she said. At a solemn signal from the psychiatrist, the police leaped from their
30 chairs and seized the wife. They had a hard time subduing her, for she put up a   /siːzd/
terrific struggle, but they finally subdued her. Just as they got her into the
straight-jacket, the husband came back into the house.

"Did you tell your wife you saw a unicorn ?" asked the police. "Of course
not," said the husband. "The unicorn is a mythical beast." "That's all I wanted
35 to know," said the psychiatrist. "Take her away. I'm sorry, sir, but your wife is
as crazy as a jaybird[4]." So they took her away, cursing, and screaming, and
shut her up in an institution. The husband lived happily ever after.

Don't count your boobies before they are hatched.

James Thurber : The Thurber Carnival

---

1. a booby : here, a madman. **2.** a booby-hatch : (colloq.) a mental institution. **3.** a straight-jacket : *une camisole de force.* **4.** as crazy as a jaybird : totally insane.

A UNDERSTANDING THE TEXT

1. How does the author begin and end his story ? In what type of stories do you find this ? **2.** What happened when the man was having breakfast ? **3.** How did his wife react to his story ? **4.** What does the woman's attitude toward her husband suggest about their relationship ? **5.** Why does she use words like "booby" and "booby hatch" ? **6.** What does the man mean when he says : "We'll see about that" ? **7.** Why was the woman so excited when she called the police and the psychiatrist ? **8.** What did the policeman and the psychiatrist do when they arrived ? Why did they look at the woman with great interest ? **9.** Why did she put up such a terrific struggle ? **10.** How do you explain that at the end the man says that the unicorn is a "mythical beast" ? **11.** Do you think that the author prefers the husband or the wife ? Justify your answer. **12.** What do you think the husband and the wife look like ? **13.** How do you understand the last line ?

Register modulations in reporting events

1. *The woman is giving an emotional report of the incident to the police. Complete her report. She begins like this :*

   "It was terrible ! My husband woke me and said there was a unicorn in the garden, eating roses ! He's obviously crazy ! I told him...".

2. *The psychiatrist is giving an objective report of the incident to another doctor. Complete his report. He begins like this :*

   "Apparently, doctor, the woman under observation is deranged. When I arrived she told me her husband was crazy...".

3. *The policeman is giving a humorous account of the incident to a fellow officer. Complete his account. He begins like this :*

   "It was hilarious ! This crazy lady called us and said...".

C FOLLOW UP WORK

1. What makes us laugh or smile in this famous story ? What is pathetic ?

2. Here are some possible explanations of the story :

a) the man tricked his wife into believing he was crazy ;

b) the man was dreaming and sleep walking, and after he awoke he remembered nothing of what had happened before ;

c) the wife was crazy and imagined the whole incident.

First, choose one of the explanations and say why you think it is the correct one. Then, explain why you think the other two are not correct.

THE FORGOTTEN WARRIORS

Americans have always been good at homecoming ceremonies, the public splashes[1] with which victors are cleansed :

/klenzd/

> "Then men will cheer,
> Boys will shout,
> 5   The ladies they will all turn out,
> And we'll all feel gay
> When Johnny comes marching home."

After Kilroy[2] crushed Tojo[3] and Hitler and sailed home en masse, all the nation came down to the docks to wave the flag, to weep, to gather its own back into the
10 American embrace.

Nothing was too good for those wonderful guys. The mere uniform made a man a hero. He could hardly pay for his drinks. Congress stuffed his pockets with benefits. The awful memories of combat and carnage were bathed away in the great national wash of relief and welcome. Hardly any Americans thought much then, or
15 even afterward, about Dresden blasted[4], Hamburg gone, Hiroshima and Nagasaki reduced to radioactive powder. All of those American firestorms had, of course, consumed innocent civilians. But, the ceremonies said, never mind. *Ego te absolvo*[5]. You boys did what you had to do.

The troops who went to Korea got a muted[6] version of the welcome. But then
20 came America's longest, strangest war. From that one, in Viet Nam, the boys came home alone, mostly one by one. Sometimes they would arrive in the middle of the night, almost as if they were sneaking back[7]. It was an abrupt, surreal transition—36 hours earlier, they had been in Nam, humping[8] though that alien place with too much firepower and confusion and moral responsibility on their
25 backs. Then they were plucked out of their bizarre yearlong excursion, set down in commercial jetliners ; the stewardesses passing among them like sweet American hallucinations, Hefner[9] visions, and dropped out of the sky back into an America that had turned ugly.

A trooper would head for the bar and order a beer. "You got an ID[10]" the
30 bartender would demand. Well, it was the nation's first teen-aged war. An adolescent might be old enough to look upon (even to perform) horrors that would make Goya[11] turn away. But back home, he was not old enough to drink. And in a day or two, if the soldier stayed in uniform, a fellow American would ask some stunning[12], stopping version of : "How many babies did you kill ?" For many Viet
35 Nam veterans, the moment of return, that bleak[13] homecoming was the beginning of a long rage. Well, everyone is getting older now. A child who was born during the Tet offensive of early 1968 is already a teen-ager. The last helicopter went whumping ignominiously off the U.S. embassy roof in Saigon more than six years ago. And the Viet Nam veterans are not kids any more. Why is it that so many of
40 them, so many of those Americans who fought the war, still return to it with sharp, deep, sometimes obsessive memories. Why can't they let it go ? Some 2.9 million Americans served in Indochina. The majority of them managed to put their lives together after the war and proceed calmly enough. They have their careers, their children, some memories—not always unpleasant—of Indochina.

45 But nearly 100,000 vets came back with severe physical disabilities : fast evacuation by helicopter and excellent medical care saved thousands of men—many without arms and legs—who might otherwise have died. Another 50,000 fear that they may have cancer from the blitzing[14] American herbicide Agent Orange. But

Viet-Nam veterans demonstrating in Washington D.C. on Memorial Day.

the real devils of the war work in the mind. Something like a quarter of those who
50 served may still be suffering from substantial psychological problems.

The nation energetically repressed the whole experience of Viet Nam for much of
the '70s. All the logic of the ME Generation[15] was actually a headlong[16] flight from
the lethal[17] surprises found in obscure Cochin China.

Now, the war in Viet Nam is re-emerging as an item[18] of profoundly unfinished
55 moral and psychological business. It is not so much a nasty secret as a subject that
Americans tactfully agreed not to discuss for a time.

The men (and as many as 7,500 women) who served in the war brought back with
them pain and problems—rage and guilt, sorrows and confusion—that have gone
ignored[19] and unattended for years. Now, at last, they seem to be commanding
60 some attention. Over the July Fourth weekend some vets[20] planned a
demonstration on the site in Washington where a Viet Nam memorial will be built-
a dark, somberly graceful V of granite bearing the names of the 57,692 Americans
who died in the war. It took the best part of a decade to get America to *want* that
memorial.

Lance Morrow, *Time Cover Story,* 1981

---

1. splash : ostentatious display.   **2.** Kilroy : symbolic name of the G.I. in the Second World War.   **3.** Tojo :
Japanese general in the Second World War.   **4.** blasted : destroyed.   **5.** *Ego te absolvo :* traditional absolution
formula after confession.   **6.** muted : more discreet.   **7.** sneaking back : coming back furtively.   **8.** humping :
crapahutant.   **9.** Hefner : a Chicago businessman who was at the head of the Playboy Empire (*Playboy*
magazine, clubs, Bunny girls,...).   **10.** ID : identification papers.   **11.** Goya : Spanish painter (1746-1828) who
produced a series of engravings called *The Disasters of War.*   **12.** stunning : causing shock.   **13.** bleak :
cheerless, depressing.   **14.** blitzing : devastating.   **15.** the ME generation : a phrase used in the '70s to describe
the collective attitude of young people.   **16.** headlong flight : *fuite en avant.*   **17.** lethal : deadly.   **18.** an item of
business : *une affaire.*   **19.** to ignore : to refuse to take notice of.   **20.** vets or veterans : *anciens combattants.*

A UNDERSTANDING THE TEXT

1. How were the homecoming GI's welcomed after the First World War ? 2. How were the troops treated on their return from Korea ? 3. What was different about the return of the Viet Nam veterans ? What kind of experiences turned their homecoming into "an unsettling, surreal experience" ? 4. How long did most servicemen stay in Viet Nam ? 5. Was is paradoxical about the bartender's question ? 6. What there a general consensus about America's participation in the Viet Nam war ? 7. What were the veterans accused of ?

8. Why did most Viet Nam veterans feel anger and frustration at the attacks against them ? 9. Why did the nation try to repress the whole Viet Nam experience after the war ? 10. Could those who actually served in Viet Nam, and especially those whose "psyche was scarred" by what they had gone through, forget about the war ? Explain. 11. How many veterans were permanently disabled by the war ? 12. Comment on the sentence : "All the logic of the Me Generation... Cochin China." (lines 51-52). 13. Why is the verb "want" stressed in the last sentence ?

B LANGUAGE AT WORK

Phrasal verbs

Examples :

- **The awful memories of combat and carnage were** *bathed away* **in the great national wash of relief and welcome.**
- **They were** *plucked out* **of their bizarre yearlong excursion.**

Using the above models complete the following sentences.

a) They came in furtively.
They ..... .   (sneak .....)
b) They came back furtively.
They ..... .   (sneak .....)
c) They came back furtively.
They ..... .   (sneak .....)
d) The sight of the corpses made him look in another direction.
The sight of the corpses made him ..... .   (look .....)
e) The village was totally destroyed by napalm.
The village ..... by napalm.   (burn .....)
f) The men's hopes and illusions disappeared.
The men's hopes and illusions ..... .   (fade .....)
g) He got out of camp as silently as possible so as to escape notice.
He ..... of camp.   (creep .....)
h) The boy read the book from beginning to end. It was not easy to read it through.
The boy ..... the book.   (struggle .....)
i) The men went through the jungle with the utmost difficulty.
The men ..... the jungle.   (struggle .....)
j) He left the airbase. He was driving a car.
He ..... the airbase.   (drive .....)
k) He walked out of camp without anybody seeing him.
He ..... camp.   (steal .....)
l) They had no ammunition left.
They ..... ammunition.   (run .....)
m) The village was bombed. The villagers' homes were destroyed.
The villagers ..... homes.   (bomb .....)

1. In your opinion were the Viet Nam veterans treated fairly when they returned ?
2. The Viet Nam veterans were scapegoats for America's guilt for the Viet Nam war.

3. Why at the time did Americans give little or no thought to the thousands of casualties suffered by the Germans in Hamburg and Dresden or by the Japanese in Hiroshima and Nagasaki ?

The Portable War Memorial

The soldiers in this sculpture by Edward Kienholz are a parody of a famous American statue — the Iwo Jima Memorial — which depicts U.S. marines planting the American flag on the island of Iwo Jima in the Pacific after a bloody battle at the end of World War Two. Where are Kienholz's soldiers trying to plant the American flag ? Why do you think he includes a Coca-Cola bottle, a hot dog stand, and an "Uncle Sam" conscription poster in his sculpture ? What is the significance of the *Portable War Memorial* with its changeable dates ? What do you think Kienholz is trying to say ?

SURVEYING THE SCENE

1. Look at the titles of the texts in this chapter.
   a) What particular aspect(s) of American society is (are) considered in each of the texts ?
   b) Which groups and/or classes of Americans are seen ? Which are not ?
2. What do you think Biff *(Making a Future)* would have thought of the ideas expressed in *Car Culture* and *The Terrible People* ?
3. In what ways may the fact of ''growing up on TV'' explain some of the characteristics described in *Kids' Country* ?
4. How far do you think ''the new learning'' may be ''a kid's dream'' ?
5. What do Berri *(A Teenager Looks for Work)* and the young people mentioned in *Car Culture* have in common ?
6. Judging from the texts in this chapter, what are some characteristics of American society which you like/don't like ? Support your argument.

Some books you might like to read : *The Ballad of the Sad Café (La Ballade du café triste)* by C. McCullers.
Love Story by E. Segal.
The Naked and the Dead by Norman Mailer
Catch 22 by Joseph Heller.

Some films you might like to see : *The Salt of the Earth (Le sel de la terre)* by H. Biberman and M. Wilson.
Midnight Cowboy (Macadam Cowboy) by J. Schlesinger.
Taxi Driver, by M. Scorsese.

The U.N. general assembly in New York City.
Inset : the space shuttle.

VIII. AMERICA AND THE WORLD

WHAT IS FRANCE FOR YOU ?

An interview with the Mayor of Palos Heights, a Chicago suburb with a blue-collar population.

MAYOR : Oh... Lafayette, Statue of Liberty, the French Revolution, Mme Lafarge[1] and her knitting needles... World War I, and the taxicabs leaving Paris and going to the front...

INTERVIEWER : *Were you there, or ... ?*

M. : No, I'm just a history buff[2]. Uh... the French underground during World War II, the resistance,
5 De Gaulle...

I. : *What did you think of De Gaulle ?*

M. : I liked him—he was all for France, and he was a Frenchman, therefore he should have been all for France, and I think if some of our leaders in this country had been more his way, we wouldn't be in the mess we're in today, really... He knew where his priorities were...

10 **I.** : *You weren't bothered by his anti-American...*

M. : Offended by him ? No, that didn't offend me a bit, I used to sit back and say : good for you ; it's about time somebody started telling us where to go. We have no business telling those people what to do. We have no business telling anybody what to do. But France—I have no problem with France... I don't even have any real big problem with Britain or anybody else, I ... you know, their country...
15 they live, and we live and we have mutual interests and we have divergent interests and where they're mutual we should cooperate and where they're divergent, we just forget about it and, you know, just live and let live. I'm not even mad at the Russians—till they push the button, then I get mad[3], then I get mad...

I. : *Do you have any image of French people ?*

20 **M.** : Yeah -uh-uh... I find it very difficult in my mind to imagine a French businessman. My imagination or my image of the French is romanticists, musicians, singers... passionate people... of course that's the image you get in the movies we've seen, things like that... you don't... very nationalistic, extremely nationalistic people. We could certainly learn something from them. When they sing the *Marseillaise*, believe it or not, I get a bigger lump in my throat[4] than when they play the
25 *Star Spangled Banner*, only because of the passion with which it's sung or played. They play the American anthem, or the national anthem here, the *Star Spangled Banner,* at a ball game for instance, before it starts, you see guys[5] drinking beer, eating hot dogs, talking, lighting a cigarette, walking back or forth, staring at the pretty girls or whatever they're doing, nobody pays any damned attention to it. Does that mean that we're less patriotic than the French. Possibly not. Less demonstrative,
30 certainly.

I. : *What about French women ? I think there's a lot of stereotypes here about French women...*

M. : Yes, I think there is... but I don't really pay any attention to that, I don't really think it's true, I think it's a myth that the movies produced, just... well I... You know... we fought two wars over there in 19... so we had two literally ... the father of the son was there in 1917, the son was there in 1942-43
35 '44, '45 really, and I ... as Americans go, they will... you know, talk about crossing the street, they'll say they flew over it, I mean that's how it'll come back, they exaggerate quite a bit. Then the stories

Walt Disney's Epcot's "view" of France.

coming home and all that business, added to the myth a little bit... I know some French girls who've moved to this country and I don't find them a great deal different than American girls, although they're... I will say one thing, they can sure handle a man a lot better than an American woman can...
40 oh yeah. Psychologically, they can twist you around their fingers[6], *that* I've noticed. Whether it's a national trait or whether it's something they were taught while they were little girls, I don't know, but whatever it is, *Vive la France* !

1. Mme Lafarge : a French woman accused of poisoning her husband in the mid 19th century, whose trial was a *cause célèbre.*   **2.** a (history) buff : a person who is very interested in (history).   **3.** mad : angry.   **4.** I get a lump in my throat : *j'ai la gorge qui se serre.*   **5.** guys : men.   **6.** they can twist you around their (little) finger : *elles vous mènent par le bout du nez.*

A   TRUE OR FALSE ?
1. This man is very keen on history.   **2.** He does not appreciate De Gaulle's position on foreign affairs.   **3.** He supports American intervention in the world.   **4.** He isn't prejudiced against the French.   **5.** He has a romanticized view about French people singing the Marseillaise.   **6.** "God bless America" is the American national anthem.   **7.** He claims that the Americans are more demonstrative than the French.   **8.** French women are often pictured as vain and superficial in the U.S.   **9.** The Mayor shares these stereotyped views about French women.

B   ANSWER THESE QUESTIONS
1. How do *you* picture a typical American business-man ?   **2.** What stereotypes about American women can commonly be heard in France ?   **3.** Would you say this man's views are on the whole chauvinistic and bigoted or easy-going and tolerant ? Justify your answer.   **4.** What is remarkable about this interview, taking into account that Palos Heights is a blue—collar suburb South west of Chicago in the American heartland.

C   EXPLAIN IN YOUR OWN WORDS :
1. The mess we're in today.
2. I'm not even mad at the Russians.
3. It is very difficult to imagine a French businessman.

D   DISCUSSION
Movies produce myths.

201

You Have a New Brother

[...] As South Viet Nam collapsed and the long war came to a sudden end, over 2,000 Vietnamese children were airlifted from their country to the United States. [...]

Late-afternoon sun gilded the airport waiting room. Sun glanced from the sides of the jet as it screamed to a stop. Slowly, children began to emerge from the corridor of the jetway[1]; some were infants, some as old as ten. Names were called, and families and children came together shyly, curiously. Adults took children in their arms or held out hands to be taken. From now on, for better or worse, their lives would never be the same.

The plane seemed to have nearly emptied when a young man emerged, carrying a little boy with braces[2]. The child seemed to be about five years old, perhaps 30 pounds. Heavy braces were locked around his tiny legs from waist to foot. And he was screaming, his face twisted with unhappiness. [...] Jean and Bill Bello had been waiting for this moment. Jean took Nguyen Van Hai in her arms. She cradled him; he sobbed without stopping. On the airplane trip he had asked excitedly about hamburgers and New York City; the volunteer who carried him from the plane said he was a "gallant[3] and charming boy". But the floodlights[4] of a television crew had terrified him, and now he had been abruptly awakened and thrust into the arms of strangers. His new parents sat with him, held him, trying to ignore the confusion around them. Finally they started to carry him out to where the other Bello children waited.

"Suddenly, I think every flashbulb in New York went off," Bill Bello says. "And then there was *real* screaming. Our caseworker grabbed a blanket and wrapped it around Van Hai's legs, and we pushed our way through the reporters and out into the parking lot. It was a bad moment—we just wanted to get away."

When the family reached their Volkswagen bus, new faces pressed forward in an excited cluster—two small white ones, two small brown ones. In broken school French, Jean told the boy that these were his brothers and sisters. Nguyen Van Hai stopped, surveyed the group, sniffed loudly—and started to sob again. And then seven-year-old Mark Bello held out a toy. The little boy took it. The sobbing stopped. "He's happy now!" three-year-old Tanya said. Her caramel-color face dimpled. "He's happy now!" [...]

The Bellos' experience began years before. [...] Bill and Jean Bello are in their early 30s. Bill's work is in computer programming; Jean is a physical therapist[5]. Their son, Mark, was born in 1968; their daughter, Stephanie, the year after that. Their family made them happy, and they wanted more children.

[...] They adopted a black baby [...] Eric.

Their experience was successful, and the next year they adopted a little girl, also black, named Tanya. All the kids got along fine [...] and their predominantly white community of Yorktown Heights barely blinked[6]. "I can't say what we would have done if we had gotten a very violent or negative reaction," Bill Bello says. "The fact is that we didn't—and our church was always there bolstering[7] us through it all." After the six-month trial period with each baby, the entire family met with the judge to make the adoptions final. [...]

On Sunday, March 30, 1975, the Bellos heard the news: South Viet Nam was falling, and the television report announced that a number of Vietnamese orphans would be airlifted out of the country. [...]

"Bill and I looked at each other and said, "Why not?" Jean says. "We called the agency that had handled Eric's and Tanya's adoptions and asked if there was anything we could do to help. We said we could take a handicapped child."

Because of the success of the Bellos' previous adoptions and Jean's background in physical therapy, the child would be immediately available if they wanted him in their home. And he would be coming that Sunday evening. In 48 hours. [...]

From *McCall's*, May 1976

Volkswagen /'volkswægən/   therapist /'θerəpɪst/   vietnamese /ˌvɪetnə'mɪz/

---

1. jetway: telescopic corridor to get on and off airplanes. 2. braces: *attelles*. 3. gallant: lively. 4. foodlights: spotlights. 5. physical therapist: reeducation specialist. 6. blinked: looked with surprise. 7. bolstering: supporting.

A UNDERSTANDING THE TEXT

1. Who were the children being brought to the United States ? Why were they being brought there ? 2. What does the writer mean when she says : "Their lives will never be the same". 3. Describe Nguyen Van Hai as he emerged from the plane. 4. What frightened the little boy ? 5. Why did Jean speak to him in French ? 6. Who were the other Bello children ? 7. Are Jean and Bill Bello exceptionally qualified to adopt children ? Justify your answer. 8. How did the community react to a mixed-race family ? 9. Why did the agency accept the Bellos' offer to take a handicapped child ? 10. What do you think of Jean and Bill Bello ? 11. What is the time sequence of this passage ? Do you think the order is effective ? Justify your answer. ·

B LANGUAGE AT WORK

Assuming things

Vietnamese children boarding a U.S. helicopter just before Saigon's fall.

Examples :

- **Nguyen Van Hai is screaming loudly.** → **He must be frightened.**
- **Jean and Bill Bello have a large family.** → **They must love children.**
- **Jean is comforting the little boy.** → **She seems to understand.**

On the same models make sentences using **must** *or* **seem.**

a) The plane from Vietnam was due at 4 o'clock. It is now 4.30.
b) Many people keep checking at the desk and looking at their watches.
c) On the airplane trip Nguyen Van Hai is asking about hamburgers and New York City.
d) A group of men with cameras is clustered around one of the doors.
e) Two women are getting off the plane. They are wearing white uniforms.
f) The four little children are pressing their noses against the window of the Volkswagen bus.
g) Tanya is giving her new brother one of her toys.
h) Nguyen Van Hai is taking the toy. He stops crying.
i) Everybody likes Jean and Bill Bello.

C FOLLOW UP WORK

1. Suppose you were a social worker in the adoption agency which is handling the cases of the Vietnamese orphans. What questions would you ask prospective parents and why ?

2. What do you think of adoption, and of people like the Bellos ? Support your argument.
3. Adoption gives children opportunities they might not otherwise have. Discuss.

Fill out this coupon and save a child

Just by completing this simple questionnaire, you can befriend a needy child through Save the Children Federation. For only fifty-two cents a day, your money, combined with that of other sponsors, can breathe new life into an impoverished village...help hard-working people in their fight for dignity...turn despair into hope for a child who has known only disaster. Fifty-two cents may not buy much where you live. But for the poorest of the poor where the need is so desperate, it can work miracles.

Q 3/7

My Name is:_____

Address_____

City_____State_____Zip_____

Tell us how you want to help, by answering these questions:

1. What geographical area are you interested in?

Urgent need exists in all the areas listed below. Select an area, or let us assign a child where the need is greatest.

☐ **Where the need is greatest**
☐ Appalachia (U.S.)
☐ Bangladesh
☐ Chicano (U.S.)
☐ Colombia
☐ Dominican Republic
☐ Honduras
☐ Indian (Latin America)
☐ Indian (U.S.)
☐ Indonesia
☐ Inner Cities (U.S.)
☐ Israel
☐ Korea
☐ Lebanon
☐ Mexico
☐ Rural South (U.S.)

2. Any sex or age preference?

If so, our personnel who are familiar with conditions in the area you have chosen will select a child in accordance with your wishes.

☐ Boy   ☐ Girl   ☐ No preference

Age ☐ 4 to 7   ☐ 8 to 12   ☐ No preference

3. Would you like a picture of your sponsored child?

Shortly after assignment is made, we can send you a photograph and brief personal history, if you desire.

☐ Yes   ☐ No

4. Would you like to correspond with your sponsored child?

If desired, correspondence can help build a meaningful one-to-one relationship. Translations, where necessary, are supplied by Save the Children Federation.

☐ Yes   ☐ No

5. Would you like information about the child's community?

Several times a year you can receive detailed reports on the activities and projects being undertaken in the community to benefit your sponsored child. Would you like to receive such information?

☐ Yes   ☐ No

6. How do you wish to send your payment?

☐ Monthly, $16
☐ Quarterly, $48
☐ Semi-annually, $96
☐ Annually, $192
Enclosed is my first payment: $_____

7. Do you wish verification of Save the Children Federation credentials?

Save the Children is indeed proud of the handling of its funds. An exceptionally large percentage (78.1%) of each tax deductible dollar you donate is used for direct aid and supporting program services. Due to volunteered time, labor and materials, your donation provides your sponsored child with benefits worth many times your total gift. An informative annual report and audit statement are available upon request.

☐ Yes   ☐ No

8. Would you rather make a contribution than become a sponsor of an individual child at this time?

☐ Yes, enclosed is my contribution of $_____.
☐ Check here for general information about our unique programs for aiding impoverished children.

YOUR SPONSORSHIP PAYMENTS AND CONTRIBUTIONS ARE INCOME TAX DEDUCTIBLE.

Mail to:
SAVE THE CHILDREN FEDERATION®
48 Wilton Road, Westport, Connecticut 06880
God bless you for caring enough!

Member of the International Union for Child Welfare and the American Council of Voluntary Agencies for Foreign Service.

In the future will there be a computer in every home?
Does this make you feel secure?

INTERNATIONAL BUSINESS MACHINES

A multi-nation-*al company is one which operates in more than one country.
Athough the company itself is "multinational", its headquarters are generally in
the country of origin. There are French multinationals, as well as Dutch, German,
and English—to name only a few. But the country which is the headquarters of the
most multinationals is the United States. And I.B.M. is probably one of the best-
known American multinationals. The following extract describes one aspect of its
global operations.*

I.B.M., as it is commonly called, is one of the world's great companies. It has
over 70 percent of the general purpose computer market in the U.S., and has
produced at least half of all the computers now installed in Western Europe. Its
share of the non-Communist world is between sixty-five and seventy percent.
5 Britain is one of the few countries where it is not a market leader. I.B.M. employs
people from all over the world in its many activities.

A computer company must invest a lot of time and money in research and
development. And so, I.B.M. has laboratories throughout the world. It does not
concentrate its research in the U.S. because it is particularly sensitive to some of the
10 problems which could arise due to its dominant position in any country where it
operates. If all its laboratories were in the U.S. this would probably encourage a
massive "brain drain"[1] of researchers from the rest of the world. Furthermore,
I.B.M. tries to help the countries where it operates by enabling them to participate
in its technological advance through work done in local laboratories.

15 But there is a political price to pay for the scientific and social benefits. All
I.B.M.'s subsidiaries[2] are controlled and coordinated from its headquarters in the
U.S. And so they have to do whatever headquarters tells them to do. The various
I.B.M. laboratories in different countries and their research programes are
connected to one another. They could no more live apart from each other than a
20 man's arm could live apart from his body. To talk of nationalization or the
subordination of a laboratory's work to national ends is quite simply impractical.

How does I.B.M. decide where it is going to build a laboratory? There are
several things to consider. One of the most important is the educational level of the
local population, especially in technical and scientific subjects. It is much easier to
25 recruit staff with the necessary qualifications and skills in, say, Germany or Britain,
than in Spain or Greece.

A laboratory is one of the best ways in which a company can identify itself with a
country, and obtain the approval of the local government. By building one it can
show that it is willing to contribute something to the country as well as to make

/ˈaɪˈbɪˈem/
/ˈpɜrpəs/
/ˈjuərəp/

/ˈlæbrətɔrɪz/

/rɪˈsɜrtʃərz/

/ˌteknəˈlɑdʒɪkəl/

/səbˈsɪdieriz/

30 profits there. But it is difficult to know whether I.B.M. responds better to harsh or gentle treatment from the authorities. One of I.B.M.'s biggest European research facilities was built up at La Gaude near Nice during the period when de Gaulle was in power, and there was greater official hostility to foreign companies than anywhere else in Europe.

35 I.B.M.'s position in the countries where it operates carries enormous political implications. In the past, nations have always considered advanced technological research as a top secret matter. This has been equally true of projects handled directly by government agencies and those carried out by private companies. Computers are a branch of this sort of research, on vital and strategic as well as

40 economic and industrial grounds. Yet all the countries which rely on I.B.M. are dependent on each other in this field. The company headquarters knows everything that is going on, and coordinates all the programes. Apart from the U.S., they can have no secrets. In fact, it is just the opposite. Their interdependence means that there must be a free exchange of information. In many ways, then, national secrets

45 are more of an idea than a reality.

Adapted from Christopher Tugendhat, *The Multinationals*

---

1. brain drain : *la fuite des cerveaux.*   2. subsidiaries : *filiales.*

A   UNDERSTANDING THE TEXT

1. What makes I.B.M. one of the world's great companies ? **2.** Why does I.B.M. have its laboratories all over the world ? **3.** Do you think scientists should remain in their own countries ? **4.** What do you think causes a "brain drain" ? What are the consequences ? **5.** How are I.B.M.'s subsidiaries coordinated ? **6.** Why would nationalizations be "impractical" ? **7.** What is one of the most important things I.B.M. must consider when deciding upon a site for a new laboratory ? Why do you think this is so ? **8.** Why is a foreign laboratory a good thing for the company ? **9.** What is significant about I.B.M.'s installation at La Gaude ? **10.** What are the enormous political implications resulting from I.B.M.'s position in the countries where it operates ? **11.** What does the expression "national secret" mean ?

B LANGUAGE AT WORK

Asking for definite information

Examples :

> • **What's a multinational ?**
> • **Do you know/Can you tell me what a multinational is ?**

On the same models use both these structures with interrogatives such as where, how, who, *etc., to ask questions about I.B.M.*
You want to know about :

a) the size of I.B.M. ;
b) I.B.M.'s share of the U.S. market ;
c) the number of I.B.M. computers now installed in Western Europe ;
d) the strength of I.B.M. in Britain ;
e) the people who work for I.B.M. ;
f) I.B.M.'s investments in research and development ;
g) the position of I.B.M.'s subsidiaries with regard to head office ;
h) choosing a site for a lab ;
i) I.B.M.'s relations with local government ;
j) the type of people who work for I.B.M.

C FOLLOW UP WORK

1. Above is a list of the twenty biggest companies in the world. What are some of the products associated with these companies ? Why do you think some countries have more multinationals than others ?

2. Would you prefer to work for a French or a multinational company ? Support your argument.

THE BIGGEST MULTINATIONALS

By one definition, a multinational company is one with sales above $ 100 million, operating in at least six countries and overseas subsidiaries accounting for at least 20 per cent of its assets. Some 4,000 companies qualify, accounting for 15 per cent of the gross world product. The twenty biggest are listed below.

	Company	Base	World Sales*		Company	Base	World Sales*
1	Exxon	U.S.	$ 108.1	11	International Business Machines	U.S.	$ 29.1
2	Royal Dutch/Schell	Britain/ Netherlands	$ 82.3	12	Gulf Oil	U.S.	$ 28.2
3	Mobil	U.S.	$ 64.5	13	Atlantic Richfield	U.S.	$ 27.8
4	General Motors	U.S.	$ 62.7	14	General Electric	U.S.	$ 27.2
5	Texaco	U.S.	$ 57.6	15	Unilever	Britain/ Netherlands	$ 24.1
6	British Petroleum	Britain	$ 52.2				
7	Standard Oil of California	U.S.	$ 44.2	16	E.I. du Pont de Nemours	U.S.	$ 22.8
8	Ford Motor	U.S.	$ 38.2	17	Française des Pétroles	France	$ 22.8
9	Standard Oil (Indiana)	U.S.	$ 29.9	18	Shell Oil	U.S.	$ 21.6
10	ENI	Italy	$ 29.4	19	Kuwait Petroleum	Kuwait	$ 20.6
				20	Elf-Aquitaine	France	$ 19.7

* In billions

THE H-BOMB

We're told that H-Bombs today can destroy the world. Does it ever bother you ?

Yes, because in August of this year we went to South Dakota. We were lucky enough to tour Ellsworth Air Force Base. We saw these terrific bombers, these tremendous B-52's. We went through the bomber. It amazed us, all the equipment that is in this plane. The plane is so loaded down, if I'm not mistaken it can carry
5 only two bombs. This multimillion-dollar thing. Then we drove up the country of South Dakota. We saw these, they're called silos. They're the missiles, I think they're called. They're out in the middle of wheat fields. Evidently at a moment's notice a button can be pushed and these things will be shot off.

/ɪˈkwɪpmənt/

/saɪləʊz/
/ˈmɪsəls/

It makes you feel, oh, aren't we lucky to have such an organization as S.A.C.[1].
10 And then you, see these young kids, these eighteen-year-olds, and they're responsible for your safety. But they are put through rigid training. So you feel, gee, aren't we lucky ? That we have this.

You feel so insignificant when you see this tremendous B-52 plane, with eight engines, four on each wing. And the wingspan[2] of the plane we were under. We
15 went out and saw the launching, and they take off on their practices within fifteen seconds of each other, and if you think that isn't a sight ! To see these tremendous big planes come at you. The first plane you can see, the second one, in the fifteen-second time that it takes, is completely blacked out because of this take-off from those eight engines. You see it come up out of this black mess, and when the third
20 plane comes up, it is wavering because of the air current. But they all get off and they're gone, but you're so glad that they're for our side.

Studs Terkel, *Division Street*

---

1. S.A.C. : Strategic Air Command.   **2.** wingspan : the maximum width of an aircraft.

A data bank.

C FOLLOW UP WORK

1. Why does the micro-chip present such an interest for foreign spies ? Support your argument.

2. In what way can it be said that the United States is the victim of its belief in free enterprise and the free circulation of men and ideas ? Support your argument.

3. The West is showing appalling naivety in its relationship with the U.S.S.R. Discuss.

The Policeman. Paul Newman.

HOLLYWOOD   HOLLYWOOD

By the end of the thirties, Hollywood had tested, refined and codified the money-making formula on the basis of which most of its successful films have since been made. All the different types of films associated with Hollywood had emerged : the back-stage musical, the screwball[1] comedy, the gangster story, the costume drama,
5 the Western, the tearjerker[2], the suspense-thriller, the confessional tale, the knockabout farce[3], the semi-historical biography, the pseudo-classic and the Walt Disney animated cartoon. These were the staple[4] items on the Hollywood menu, and by and large they have remained so to the present day. The most solidly satisfying and the most truly American of these is the Western. [...]

    There has never been a period when the Western was totally out. Its popularity
10 seems to be constant. There are several possible explanations of why this should be so : nostalgia for a way of life that was free and unhampered[5] by the ties and restrictions of "civilised" behavior, the pride of a sedentary American society in the physical prowess, capacity for endurance and sheer guts[6] of their forebears. [...]

/'mənju:/

Charlton Heston and Ava Gardner in *55 Days at Peking* by Samuel Bronston.

15 And, of course, the Western enjoys the advantage of being able to crystallise its
moral [and other] conflicts in a simple and exciting situation : two men facing each
other with guns in their hands. In no other kind of drama can latent feelings be so
easily made over. [...].

Next to the Western, the film most readily associated with Hollywood is the
20 musical. At its best it owes little to the operetta or the musical comedy from which it
has evolved. [...] As the musical became established as a sure-fire[7] box-office
attraction, it resorted increasingly to the most banal plot of all : the back-stage
story of the rise to fame and wealth of a simple chorus girl. There were innumerable
and indistinguishable variations [...] on this theme and they made the Hollywood
25 musical a pejorative term for many years. [...] Vincente Minelli [and others] freed
the musical from the too-familiar back-stage milieu, from the need to contrive
"natural" opportunities for the characters to burst into song, and from show biz[8]
sentimentality. Instead [...] directors permitted their characters to sing in the streets
of New York [...], on the Empire State building, in subways ; song and music
30 became an integral part of the story, advancing the action and the development of
the characters. [...]

The animated cartoon film is also very much a product of Hollywood. As a
popular way of story-telling, the cartoon owes its existence entirely to Walt Disney

/ˈvɪnˌsənt
ˌmɪˈneli/

who, on this score, must be regarded as one of the great innovators of the cinema.
35 The first Mickey Mouse adventure appeared in 1928 and was an immediate success. /'mɪkɪ maʊs/
In the next three years, Disney turned out ninety of these short features[9] and in
them his inventiveness, his ingenuity and his sense of fantasy grew and developed
amazingly. With his first full length feature, *Snow White and the Seven Dwarfs*
(1938), it seemed that the cinema might have found its purest artist : all the
40 grotesque characters of the story were magnificently realised by Disney's /grəʊ'tesk/
draughtsmen under the supervision of the maestro : and the story was unfolded /'drɑːftsmən/
with much imagination and many inspired touches. But the most daring use of the
medium was *Fantasia* (1940), an abstract film in which Disney sought to provide the
visual equivalent to classical music. Up to this stage, Disney was still developing :
45 and though he did not actually do any of the drawing in his films, they were his
conceptions. [...]

   The achievements of the commercial cinema came to a climax in 1939 when
David O. Selznick produced *Gone With the Wind*, which might be described as the
apotheosis of the Hollywood film. It was the longest novelette[10] ever made (running /ˌæpə'θiəs s/
50 three hours and forty minutes) and had, as they say, "everything" : a beautiful
self-centered heroine (Vivian Leigh) who suffered the whole range of emotional /'vɪˌviːən̪li:/
upheavals[11] ; a roguish[12] hero (Clark Gable), rough in manner but strong and
resourceful in moments of crisis ; a gentle and gentlemanly second-lead[13] (Leslie
Howard) ; a good woman (Olivia de Havilland) who nearly dies in childbirth ; the
55 American Civil War ; attempted rape ; marital strife ; crimson[14] sunsets ; a doctor
who has to operate without chloroform ; a hero who carries his struggling wife up
the grand-staircase ; a pregnant heroine who falls down the grand-staircase ; the
decline and decay of the South ; the prostitute with a heart of gold ; the scoundrel[12]
who becomes a millionaire. What more could anyone conceivably be given ? It
60 made a fortune. Some years later, on being reissued again and despite our present
familiarity with the epic, it was still highly successful.

Thomas Wiseman, *Cinema*

---

1. screwball : *loufoque.* **2.** tearjerker : melodrama. **3.** knockabout farce : *bouffonnerie.* **4.** staple : basic. **5.** unhampered : unrestricted. **6.** guts (fig.) : courage. **7.** sure-fire : certain. **8.** show biz : show business. **9.** short feature : *court métrage.* **10.** novelette : popular romantic story. **11.** upheavals : trauma. **12.** roguish scoundrel : ruffian. **13.** second-lead : *second rôle.* **14.** crimson : bright red.

A UNDERSTANDING THE TEXT

1. How long ago did Hollywood find the secret of successful movie making ? **2.** What are some of the types of films associated with Hollywood ? Give a few examples. **3.** What are the reasons for the Western's constant popularity ? Do you like Westerns ? Why ? Justify your answer. **4.** How has the musical changed over the years ? **5.** How have movies in general changed ? **6.** Why was Walt Disney regarded as one of the great innovators of the cinema ? **7.** What has made *Gone With The Wind* endure ? **8.** According to you, what is the "formula" for a successful film today ? **9.** What kind of films do you prefer ? Why ?

"Now in this scene,
Franz Schubert, the
composer,
falls asleep and dreams
his melody while the girls
dance it out on
the piano keys. Get it ?"

B LANGUAGE AT WORK

Superlatives

Example :

> • **It was the longest novelette ever made, the most famous
> in the world.**

On the model of the above, describe such films as the Jazz Singer *(First "talking" film)*,
L'arroseur arrosé *(first ever)*, Fantasia by *Walt Disney*, Cleopatra *(expensive)*, Hellzapoppin *(crazy) or whatever film that you may feel to be particularly*

— boring
— stupid
— a hit
— amusing
— funny

— interesting
— complex
— moving
— a flop
  etc.

Dustin Hoffman in *Kramer vs. Kramer.*

Giving opinions

Examples :

> • According to me/in my opinion/as for me/I think that/in my mind what makes a good film is...

Using the above phrases, say the things which for you make

— a good western
— a good horror film
— a good comedy
— a good dramatic film
— a good musical

— a good science fiction film
— a good cartoon
— a good thriller
— a good cloak and dagger film
etc.

C FOLLOW UP WORK

1. You have to write a column for the local paper about a movie you have seen recently. Summarize the plot, and give your opinion of the film. Remember not to give away the entire story !

2. What is the best film you have ever seen ? Support your argument.

3. Look at the movie page of today's paper. Which of the films do you think will be the most successful ? Why ?

Blue Jeans Culture

The idea that he might one day be hailed as a world fashion leader would surely have given old Levi Strauss a hearty laugh. His famous pants had started out as a roll of tent canvas which he hoped to peddle[1] to prospectors on his arrival in California in 1850. Company legend has it that a miner greeted young Strauss with the news that he should have brought pants instead of tent material on the long trip from New York. "Pants don't hold up worth a hoot[2] in the diggings," the miner said, at which point Strauss beat a path to the nearest tailor and ordered more cloth from his brothers in New York. They sent him the now-familiar tough cotton fabric from France, and the miners started pouring into Strauss's store to plop down[3] a dollar for a pair of "Levi's pants."

Last year, denim[4] enthusiasts the world over paid $405 million for assorted Levi products, including 75 million pairs of pants, a figure which makes Levi Strauss the world's No 1 pants-maker. American students have been known to finance their entire summer European travels by selling off extra Levi's, and in Russia a pair with the leather logo patch[5] intact can fetch $90 in the black market. Levi's have been ensconced[6] in the Smithsonian[7] and presented a special Coty Award as America's most significant contribution to international fashion.

As a measure of flattery, Levi's have been imitated and copied—illegally—more than any other piece of clothing. They are shipped through Europe in plain brown boxes to avoid theft. Despite trademark registration in more than 50 countries, the company uncovered at least 50 counterfeit "Levi" models last year. The official Levi tag now goes on more than 2,000 items ranging from plush corduroy[8] pants to handbags, notebooks and theater seats. But the keystone of the company's operations is still the basic blue-denim jeans, which have remained virtually unchanged for 122 years. The only alterations in design have been a slight modification of the copper rivets on seams, changing the rear patch from real leather to one of synthetic material (a decision which required a board of directors' meeting) and removing the crotch[9] rivet, an instant decision made when a former company president, Walter Haas, once stood too long near a blazing campfire.

From *Life Magazine*,
Nov 24, 1972

Levi Strauss /'li:vaɪ 'straʊs/   laugh /læf/   tough /tʌf/
enthusiasts /ɪn'θu:ziæsts/   finance /fə'næns/ /'faɪnæns/
Smithsonian /smɪθ'sonɪən/   corduroy /'kɔrdərɔɪ/   synthetic /sɪn'θetɪk/

---

1. to peddle : to sell.   **2.** hold up worth a hoot : last at all ; (it is not worth a hoot = it is no good at all).   **3.** to plop down : to drop.   **4.** denim (originally French : *serge de Nîmes*) : blue jean material.   **5.** logo patch : trademark.   **6.** ensconced : here, exhibited.   **7.** the Smithsonian (Institute) : the national museum of science and industry in Washington.   **8.** corduroy : *velours côtelé*.   **9.** the crotch : *l'entre-jambes*.

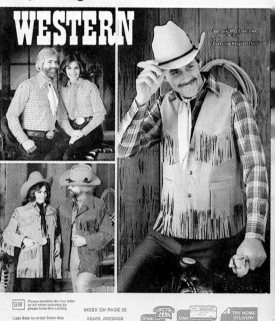

A   UNDERSTANDING THE TEXT

1. Why did Levi Strauss go to California ?   2. What made him start manufacturing men's pants ? 3. Where did the cloth come from ?   4. Are Levi's popular ? Justify your answer.   5. How have some American students financed their summer European travels ? 6. Do you agree that Levi's are "America's most significant contribution to international fashion" ? Justifiy your answer. 7. How are blue jeans shipped through Europe ? Why is this so ? 8. What is one of the problems the Levi Strauss Company has ? 9. What are some of the other Levi Strauss products ? What is still the most popular ? 10. What minor alterations in design have been made ? How were the modifications decided in each case ? 11. Why do you think so many people wear blue jeans ?

B LANGUAGE AT WORK

Equivalents of French *en* + participe présent

Examples :

- *On arriving* in California, young Levi Strauss didn't expect to have such a success with his canvas.
- Students have financed their travels *by selling* extra Levi's. Other brands became successful *by copying* Levi Strauss.

Using the above patterns, give an account of the history of blue jeans and of their success as mentioned in the text or as you may imagine.

Passives

Examples :

- Students *have been known to* finance their travels by selling off extra blue jeans.
- Levi Strauss *is said to* have started with just a roll of tent canvas.

Using the above constructions, report all the things that you have heard about the golden legend of blue jeans.

C FOLLOW UP WORK

1. If you could dress as you liked, how would you dress ? Support your argument.
2. In so far as everyone sings the praise of blue jeans, what could be said *against* them ?
3. To follow fashion is to be a slave !
4. Blue jeans are popular because they are sexless and classless. Discuss.

A revival of the Past : Boston Common.

WHO SPEAKS FOR EARTH ?

A few million years ago there were no humans. Who will be here a few million years hence ? In all the 4.6-billion-year history of our planet, nothing much ever left it. But now, tiny unmanned[1] exploratory spacecraft from Earth are moving, glistening and elegant, through the solar system. We have made a preliminary
5 reconnaissance of twenty worlds, among them all the planets visible to the naked eye, all those wandering nocturnal lights that stirred our ancestors toward understanding an ecstasy. If we survive, our time will be famous for two reasons : that at this dangerous moment of technological adolescence we managed to avoid self-destruction ; and because this is the epoch in which we began our journey to the
10 stars.

The choice is stark[2] and ironic. The same rocket boosters[3] used to launch probes[4] to the planets are poised to send nuclear warheads[5] to the nations. The radioactive power sources on Viking and Voyager derive from the same technology that makes nuclear weapons. The radio and radar techniques employed to track and guide
15 ballistic missiles and defend against attack are also used to monitor and command the spacecraft on the planets and to listen for signals from civilizations near other stars. If we use these technologies to destroy ourselves, we surely will venture no more to the planets and the stars, our chauvinisms will be shaken further. We will gain a cosmic perspective. We will recognize that our explorations can be carried
20 out only on behalf of all the people of the planet Earth. We will invest our energies in an enterprise devoted not to death but to life : the expansion of our understanding of the Earth and its inhabitants and the search for life elsewhere. Space exploration—unmanned and manned—uses many of the same technological and organizational skills and demands the same commitment[6] to valor[7] and daring
25 as does the enterprise of war. Should a time of real disarmament arrive before nuclear war, such exploration would enable the military-industrial establishments of the major powers to engage at long last in an untainted[8] enterprise. Interest vested[9] in preparations for war can relatively easily be reinvested in the exploration of the Cosmos. (...)

Tomorrow's metropolis.

Some 3.6 million years ago, in what is now northern Tanzania, a volcano erupted, the resulting cloud of ash covering the surrounding savannahs. In 1979, the paleoanthropologist Mary Leakey found in that ash footprints—the footprints, she believes, of an early hominid, perhaps an ancestor of all the people on the Earth today. And 380,000 kilometers away, in a flat dry plain that humans have in a moment of optimism called the Sea of Tranquility, there is another footprint, left by the first human to walk another world. We have come far in 3.6 million years, and in 4.6 billion and in 15 billion.

For we are the local embodiment of a Cosmos grown to self-awareness[10]. We have begun to contemplate our origins : starstuff pondering[11] the stars ; organized assemblages of ten billion billion billion atoms considering the evolution of atoms ; tracing the long journey by which, here at least, consciousness arose. Our loyalties are to the species and the planet. We speak for Earth. Our obligation to survive is owed not just to ourselves but also to that Cosmos, ancient and vast, from which we spring.

Carl Sagan, *Cosmos*

---

1. manned ≠ unmanned ; manned (spacecraft) : *habité.* **2.** stark : harsh. **3.** a rocket booster : *le premier étage d'une fusée.* **4.** probes : *sondes.* **5.** warheads : *ogives.* **6.** commitment : *engagement.* **7.** valor : courage. **8.** untainted : uncorrupted. **9.** vested interests : *investissements (financiers, scientifiques,* etc.). **10.** self-awareness : *prise de conscience.* **11.** pondering : meditating over.

A UNDERSTANDING THE TEXT

1. Throughout the ages what was man's attitude to "those wandering, nocturnal lights" in the sky above ? **2.** In the course of the last decades what have been our major achievements in the field of space exploration ? Choose examples from the text. **3.** Why does the writer describe our era as "this dangerous moment of technological adolescence" ? **4.** What choice are we now confronted with ? **5.** What is ironic about such a choice ?

6. What does Carl Sagan mean by "an untainted enterprise" ? **7.** What is paradoxical about the situation ? **8.** What gains can the people of our planet obtain from new technologies ? **9.** What is the symbolic value of those two human footprints mentioned in the text ? **10.** What is the writer's message ? **11.** To what extent is it relevant to "the American Dream" ?

B LANGUAGE AT WORK

Expressing a hypothesis, a remote possibility

The auxiliary SHOULD may insist on hypothetical conditions.

> • **If a time of real disarmament should arrive...**
> • *(in somewhat literary style)*
>   **Should a time of real disarmament arrive...**

Using the above models complete and transform the following sentences :

a) If governments invested more money in the exploration of the Cosmos...
b) If space travel became available to all...
c) If evidence of life on a distant planet were discovered...
d) If extraterrestrial aliens landed on our planet before we reached theirs...
e) If extraterrestrial powers interfered with our space programs...
f) If we bore in mind that the human species is an endangered species...
g) If we realized that our loyalties are not restricted to our immediate environment...
h) If we avoided the notion that a person or a society that is different from us is to be distrusted or hated...

C FOLLOW UP WORK

Is the writer's optimism justified when he says :
"We will invest our energies in an enterprise
devoted not to death but to life" ?

SURVEYING THE SCENE

1. In what way do the Bellos in *You Have a New Brother* typify the American goodwill apparent in other texts throughout the book ?
2. What is the importance of American products in our life ? In what ways does this represent an economic problem ? How far does this represent a cultural threat ?
3. What is terrifying in the power of the U.S. as suggested by *The H-Bomb* ?
4. How far do you think the Mayor of Palos Heights typify a certain American difficulty in understanding other cultures ?
5. In what ways you think *Who Speaks for Earth ?* is typical of American idealism as suggested by many texts in this book ?

Some books you might like to read : *The Last Tycoon (Le dernier Nabab)* by F.S. Fitzgerald.
Three Days of the Condor (Les trois jours du Condor) by J. Grady.
The Fifth Horseman (Le Cinquième Cavalier) by D. Lapierre et L. Collins.

Some films you might like to see : *Horse Feathers (Plumes de cheval)* by N. McLeod and Marx Brothers.
Hellzapoppin by H.C. Potter.
That's Entertainment ! (Il était une fois Hollywood) by J. Haley Jr.
Some Like it Hot (Certains l'aiment chaud) by B. Wilder.
E.T. by Steven Spielberg.

SHORT STORIES

DÉSIRÉE'S BABY

As the day was pleasant, Madame Valmondé drove over to L'Abri to see Désirée and the baby.

It made her laugh to think of Désirée with a baby. Why, it seemed but yesterday that Désirée was little more than a baby herself ; when Monsieur in riding through the gateway of Valmondé had found her lying asleep in the shadow of the big stone pillar.

The little one awoke in his arms and began to cry for "Dada". That was as much as she could do or say. Some people thought she might have strayed there of her own accord, for she was of the toddling age. The prevailing belief was that she had been purposely left by a party of Texans, whose canvas-covered wagon, late in the day, had crossed the ferry that Coton Maïs kept, just below the plantation. In time Madame Valmondé abandoned every speculation but the one that Désirée had been sent to her by a beneficent Providence to be the child of her affection, seeing that she was without child of the flesh. For the girl grew to be beautiful and gentle, affectionate and sincere,—the idol of Valmondé.

It was no wonder, when she stood one day against the stone pillar in whose shadow she had lain asleep, eighteen years before, that Armand Aubigny riding by and seeing her there, had fallen in love with her. That was the way all the Aubignys fell in love, as if struck by a pistol shot. The wonder was that he had not loved her before ; for he had known her since his father brought him home from Paris, a boy of eight, after his mother died there. The passion that awoke in him that day, when he saw her at the gate, swept along like an avalanche, or like a prairie fire, or like anything that drives headlong over all obstacles.

Monsieur Valmondé grew practical and wanted things well considered : that is, the girl's obscure origin. Armand looked into her eyes and did not care. He was reminded that she was nameless. What did it matter about a name when he could give her one of the oldest and proudest in Louisiana ? He ordered the *corbeille* from Paris, and contained himself with what patience he could until it arrived ; then they were married.

Madame Valmondé had not seen Désirée and the baby for four weeks. When she reached L'Abri she shuddered at the first sight of it, as she always did. It was a sad looking place, which for many years had not known the gentle presence of a mistress, old

225

Monsieur Aubigny having married and buried his wife in France, and she having loved her own land too well ever to leave it. The roof came down steep and black like a cowl, reaching out beyond the wide galleries that encircled the yellow stuccoed house. Big, solemn oaks grew close to it, and their thick-leaved, far-reaching branches shadowed it like a pall. Young Aubigny's rule was a strict one, too, and under it his negroes had forgotten how to be gay, as they had been during the old master's easy-going and indulgent lifetime.

The young mother was recovering slowly, and lay full length, in her soft white muslins and laces, upon a couch. The baby was beside her, upon her arm, where he had fallen asleep, at her breast. The yellow nurse woman sat beside a window fanning herself.

Madame Valmondé bent her portly figure over Désirée and kissed her, holding her an instant tenderly in her arms. Then she turned to the child.

"This is not the baby !" she exclaimed ; in startled tones. French was the language spoken at Valmondé in those days.

"I knew you would be astonished", laughed Désirée, "at the way he has grown. The little *cochon de lait* ! Look at his legs, mamma, and his hands and finger-nails, —real finger-nails. Zandrine had to cut them this morning. Isn't it true, Zandrine ?"

The woman bowed her turbaned head majestically, "Mais si, Madame."

"And the way he cries," went on Désirée, "is deafening. Armand heard him the other day as far away as La Blanche's cabin."

Madame Valmondé had never removed her eyes from the child. She lifted it and walked with it over to the window that was lightest. She scanned the baby narrowly, then looked as searchingly at Zandrine, whose face was turned to gaze across the fields.

"Yes, the child has grown, has changed," said Madame Valmondé, slowly, as she replaced it beside its mother. "What does Armand say ?"

Désirée's face became suffused with a glow that was happiness itself.

"Oh, Armand is the proudest father in the parish, I believe, chiefly because it is a boy, to bear his name ; though he says not,—that he would have loved a girl as well. But I know it isn't true. I know he says that to please me. And mamma," she added, drawing Madame Valmondé's head down to her, and speaking in a whisper, "he hasn't

punished one of them—not one of them—since baby is born. Even Négrillon, who pretended to have burnt his leg that he might rest from work—he only laughed, and said Négrillon was a great scamp. Oh, mamma, I'm so happy ; it frightens me."

What Désirée said was true. Marriage, and later the birth of his son, had softened Armand Aubigny's imperious and exacting nature greatly. This was what made the gentle Désirée so happy, for she loved him desperately. When he frowned she trembled, but loved him. When he smiled, she asked no greater blessing of God. But Armand's dark, handsome face had not often been disfigured by frowns since the day he fell in love with her.

When the baby was about three months old, Désirée awoke one day to the conviction that there was something in the air menacing her peace. It was at first too subtle to grasp. It had only been a disquieting suggestion ; an air of mystery among the blacks ; unexpected visits from far-off neighbors who could hardly account for their coming. Then a strange, an awful change in her husband's manner, which she dared not ask him to explain. When he spoke to her, it was with averted eyes, from which the old love-light seemed to have gone out. He absented himself from home ; and when there, avoided her presence and that of her child, without excuse. And the very spirit of Satan seemed suddenly to take hold of him in his dealings with the slaves. Désirée was miserable enough to die.

She sat in her room, one hot afternoon, in her *peignoir*, listlessly drawing through her fingers the strands of her long, silky brown hair that hung about her shoulders. The baby, half naked, lay asleep upon her own great mahogany bed, that was like a sumptuous throne, with its satin-lined half-canopy. One of La Blanche's little quadroon boys—half naked too—stood fanning the child slowly with a fan of peacock feathers. Désirée's eyes had been fixed absently and sadly upon the baby, while she was striving to penetrate the threatening mist that she felt closing about her. She looked from her child to the boy who stood beside him, and back again ; over and over. "Ah !" It was a cry that she could not help ; which she was not conscious of having uttered. The blood turned like ice in her veins, and a clammy moisture gathered upon her face.

She tried to speak to the little quadroon boy ; but no sound would come, at first. When he heard his name uttered, he looked up, and his mistress was pointing to the door. He laid aside the great, soft fan, and obediently stole away, over the polished floor, on his bare tiptoes.

She stayed motionless, with gaze riveted upon her child, and her face the picture of fright.

Presently her husband entered the room, and without noticing her went to a table and began to search among some papers which covered it.

"Armand," she called to him, in a voice which must have stabbed him. if he was human. But he did not notice. "Armand," she said again. Then she rose and tottered towards him. "Armand," she panted once more, clutching his arm, "look at our child. What does it mean ? tell me."

He coldly but gently loosened her fingers from about his arm and thrust the hand away from him. "Tell me what it means !" she cried despairingly.

"It means," he answered lightly, "that the child is not white : it means that you are not white."

A quick conception of all that this accusation meant for her nerved her with unwonted courage to deny it. "It is a lie ; it is not true ; I am white ! Look at my hair, it is brown ; and my eyes are gray, Armand, you know they are gray. And my skin is fair," seizing his wrist. "Look at my hand ; whiter than yours, Armand," she laughed hysterically.

"As white as La Blanche's," he returned cruelly ; and went away leaving her alone with their child.

When she could hold a pen in her hand, she sent a despairing letter to Madame Valmondé.

"My mother, they tell me I am not white. Armand has told me I am not white. For God's sake tell them it is not true. You must know it is not true. I shall die, I must die. I cannot be so unhappy, and live."

The answer that came was as brief :

"My own Désirée : Come home to Valmondé ; back to your mother who loves you. Come with your child."

When the letter reached Désirée she went with it to her husband's study, and laid it open upon the desk before which he sat. She was like a stone image : silent, white, motionless after she placed it there.

In silence he ran his cold eyes over the written words. He said nothing. "Shall I go, Armand ?" she asked in tones sharp and agonized suspense.

"Yes, go."

"Do you want me to go ?"

"Yes, I want you to go."

He thought Almighty God had dealt cruelly and unjustly with him : and felt, somehow, that he was paying Him back in kind when he stabbed thus into his wife's soul. Moreover he no longer loved her, because of the unconscious injury she had brought upon his home and his name.

She turned away like one stunned by a blow, and walked slowly towards the door, hoping he would call her back.

"Good-by, Armand," she moaned.

He did not answer her. That was his last blow at fate.

Désirée went in search of her child. Zandrine was pacing the sombre gallery with it. She took the little one from the nurse's arms with no word of explanation, and descending the steps, walked away, under the liveoak branches.

It was an October afternoon ; the sun was just sinking. Out in the still fields the negroes were picking cotton.

Désirée had not changed the thin white garment nor the slippers which she wore. Her hair was uncovered and the sun's rays brought a golden gleam from its brown meshes. She did not take the broad, beaten road which led to the far-off plantation of Valmondé. She walked across a deserted field, where the stubble bruised her tender feet, so delicately shod, and tore her thin gown to shreds.

She disappeared among the reeds and willows that grew thick along the banks of the deep, sluggish bayou ; and she did not come back again. (...)

Some weeks later there was a curious scene enacted at L'Abri. In the centre of the smoothly swept back yard was a great bonfire. Armand Aubigny sat in the wide hallway that commanded a view of the spectacle ; and it was he who dealt out to a half dozen negroes the material which kept this fire ablaze.

A graceful cradle of willow, with all its dainty furbishings, was laid upon the pyre, which had already been fed with the richness of a priceless *layette*. Then there were silk gowns, and velvet and satin ones added to these ; laces, too, and embroideries ; bonnets and gloves ; for the *corbeille* had been of rare quality.

The last thing to go was a tiny bundle of letters ; innocent little scribblings that Désirée had sent to him during the days of their espousal. There was the remnant of one back in the drawer from which he took them. But it was not Désirée's ; it was part of an old letter from his mother to his father.

He read it. She was thanking God for the blessing of her husband's love :

"But, above all," she wrote, "night and day, I thank the good God for having so arranged our lives that our dear Armand will never know that his mother, who adores him, belongs to the race that is cursed with the brand of slavery."

Kate Chopin

Good Moments in Bad Timing

My car broke down, and I wonder if you would be kind enough to let me use your phone . . .

THE BRIDE

COMES TO YELLOW SKY

I

THE great Pullman was whirling onward with such dignity of motion that a glance from the window seemed simply to prove that the plains of Texas were pouring eastward. Vast flats of green grass, dull-hued spaces of mesquit and cactus, little groups of frame houses, woods of light and tender trees, all were sweeping into the east, sweeping over the horizon, a precipice.

A newly married pair had boarded this coach at San Antonio. The man's face was reddened from many days in the wind and sun, and a direct result of his new black clothes was that his brick-colored hands were constantly performing in a most conscious fashion. From time to time he looked down respectfully at his attire. He sat with a hand on each knee, like a man waiting in a barber's shop. The glances he devoted to other passengers were furtive and shy.

The bride was not pretty, nor was she very young. She wore a dress of blue cashmere, with small reservations of velvet here and there, and with steel buttons abounding. She continually twisted her head to regard her puff sleeves, very stiff, straight, and high. They embarrassed her. It was quite apparent that she had cooked, and that she expected to cook, dutifully. The blushes caused by the careless scrutiny of some passengers as she had entered the car were strange to see upon this plain, under-class countenance, which was drawn in placid, almost emotionless lines.

They were evidently very happy. "Ever been in a parlor-car before?" he asked, smiling with delight.

"No," she answered; "I never was. It's fine, ain't it?"

"Great! And then after a while we'll go forward to the dinner, and get a big lay-out. Finest meal in the world. Charge a dollar."

"Oh, do they?" cried the bride. "Charge a dollar? Why, that's too much—for us—ain't it, Jack?"

"Not this trip, anyhow," he answered bravely. "We're going to go the whole thing."

Later he explained to her about the trains. "You see, it's a thousand miles from one end of Texas to the other; and this train runs right across it, and never stops but four times." He had the pride of an owner. He pointed out to her the dazzling fittings of the coach; and in truth her eyes opened wider as she contemplated the sea-green figured velvet, the shining brass, silver, and glass, the wood that gleamed as darkly brilliant as the surface of a pool of oil. At one end a bronze figure sturdily held a support for a separated chamber, and at convenient places on the ceiling were frescos in olive and silver.

To the minds of the pair, their surroundings reflected the glory of their marriage that morning in San Antonio ; this was the environment of their new estate ; and the man's face in particular beamed with an elation that made him appear ridiculous to the negro porter. This individual at times surveyed them from afar with an amused and superior grin. On other occasions he bullied them with skill in ways that did not make it exactly plain to them that they were being bullied. He subtly used all the manners of the most unconquerable kind of snobbery. He oppressed them ; but of this oppression they had small knowledge, and they speedily forgot that infrequently a number of travelers covered them with stares of derisive enjoyment. Historically there was supposed to be something infinitely humorous in their situation.

"We are due in Yellow Sky at 3:42," he said, looking tenderly into her eyes.

"Oh, are we ?" she said, as if she had not been aware of it. To evince surprise at her husband's statement was part of her wifely amiability. She took from a pocket a little silver watch ; and as she held it before her, and stared at it with a frown of attention, the new husband's face shone.

"I bought it in San Anton' from a friend of mine," he told her gleefully.

"It's seventeen minutes past twelve," she said, looking up at him with a kind of shy and clumsy coquetry. A passenger, noting this play, grew excessively sardonic, and winked at himself in one of the numerous mirrors.

At last they went to the dining-car. Two rows of negro waiters, in glowing white suits, surveyed their entrance with the interest, and also the equanimity, of men who had been forewarned. The pair fell to the lot of a waiter who happened to feel pleasure in steering them through their meal. He viewed them with the manner of a fatherly pilot, his countenance radiant with benevolence. The patronage, entwined with the ordinary deference, was not plain to them. And yet, as they returned to their coach, they showed in their faces a sense of escape.

To the left, miles down a long purple slope, was a little ribbon of mist where moved the keening Rio Grande. The train was approaching it at an angle, and the apex was Yellow Sky. Presently it was apparent that, as the distance from Yellow Sky grew shorter, the husband became commensurately restless. His brick-red hands were more insistent in their prominence. Occasionally he was even rather absent-minded and far-away when the bride leaned forward and addressed him.

As a matter of truth, Jack Potter was beginning to find the shadow of a deed weigh upon him like a leaden slab. He, the town marshal of Yellow Sky, a man known, and feared in his corner, a prominent person, had gone to San Antonio to meet a girl he believed he loved, and there, after the usual prayers, had actually induced her to marry him, without consulting Yellow Sky for any part of the transaction. He was now bringing his bride before an innocent and unsuspecting community.

Of course people in Yellow Sky married as it pleased them, in accordance with a general custom ; but such was Potter's thought of his duty to his friends, or of their idea of his duty, or of an unspoken form which does not control men in these matters, that he felt he was heinous. He had committed an extraordinary crime. Face to face with this girl in San Antonio, and spurred by his sharp impulse, he had gone headlong over all the social hedges. At San Antonio he was like a man hidden in the dark. A knife to sever any friendly duty, any form, was easy to his hand in that remote city. But the hour of Yellow Sky—the hour of daylight—was approaching.

He knew full well that his marriage was an important thing to his town. It could only be exceeded by the burning of the new hotel. His friends could not forgive him. Frequently he had reflected on the advisability of telling them by telegraph, but a new cowardice had been upon him. He feared to do it. And now the train was hurrying him toward a scene of amazement, glee, and reproach. He glanced out of the window at the line of haze swinging slowly in toward the train.

Yellow Sky had a kind of brass band, which played painfully, to the delight of the populace. He laughed without heart as he thought of it. If the citizens could dream of his prospective arrival with his bride, they would parade the band at the station and escort them, amid cheers and laughing congratulations, to his adobe home.

He resolved that he would use all the devices of speed and plains-craft in making the journey from the station to his house. Once within that safe citadel, he could issue some sort of a vocal bulletin, and then not go among the citizens until they had time to wear off a little of their enthusiasm.

The bride looked anxiously at him. "What's worrying you, Jack ?"

He laughed again. "I'm not worrying, girl ; I'm only thinking of Yellow Sky."

She flushed in comprehension.

A sense of mutual guilt invaded their minds and developed a finer tenderness. They looked at each other with eyes softly aglow. But Potter often laughed the same nervous laugh ; the flush upon the bride's face seemed quite permanent.

The traitor to the feelings of Yellow Sky narrowly watched the speeding landscape. "We're nearly there," he said.

Presently the porter came and announced the proximity of Potter's home. He held a brush in his hand, and, with all his airy superiority gone, he brushed Potter's new clothes as the latter slowly turned this way and that way. Potter fumbled out a coin and gave it to the porter, as he had seen others do. It was a heavy and muscle-bound business, as that of a man shoeing his first horse.

The porter took their bag, and as the train began to slow they moved forward to the hooded platform of the car. Presently the two engines and their long string of coaches rushed into the station of Yellow Sky.

"They have to take water here," said Potter, from a constricted throat and in mournful cadence, as one announcing death. Before the train stopped his eye had swept the length of the platform, and he was glad and astonished to see there was none upon it but the station-agent, who, with a slightly hurried and anxious air, was walking toward the water-tanks. When the train had halted, the porter alighted first, and placed in position a little temporary step.

"Come on, girl," said Potter, hoarsely. As he helped her down they each laughed on a false note. He took the bag from the negro, and bade his wife cling to his arm. As they slunk rapidly away, his hang-dog glance perceived that they were unloading the two trunks, and also that the station-agent, far ahead near the baggage-car, had turned and was running toward him, making gestures. He laughed, and groaned as he laughed, when he noted the first effect of his marital

bliss upon Yellow Sky. He gripped his wife's arm firmly to his side, and they fled. Behind them the porter stood, chuckling fatuously.

II

THE California express on the Southern Railway was due at Yellow Sky in twenty-one minutes. There were six men at the bar of the Weary Gentleman Saloon. One was a drummer, who talked a great deal and rapidly ; there were Texans, who did not care to talk at that time ; and two were Mexican sheep-herders, who did not talk as a general practice in the Weary Gentleman Saloon. The barkeeper's dog lay on the board walk that crossed in front of the door. His head was on his paws, and he glanced drowsily here and there with the constant vigilance of a dog that is kicked on occasion. Across the sandy street were some vivid green grass-plots, so wonderful in appearance, amid the sands that burned near them in a blazing sun, that they caused a doubt in the mind. They exactly resembled the grass mats used to represent lawns on the stage. A the cooler end of the railway station, a man without a coat sat in a tilted chair and smoked his pipe. The fresh-cut bank of the Rio Grande circled near the town, and there could be seen beyond it a great plum-colored plain of mesquit.

Save for the busy drummer and his companions in the saloon, Yellow Sky was dozing. The new-comer leaned gracefully upon the bar, and recited many tales with the confidence of a bard who has come upon a new field.

"—and at the moment that the old man fell down-stairs with the bureau in his arms, the old woman was coming up with two scuttles of coal, and of course—"

The drummer's tale was interrupted by a young man who suddenly appeared in the open door. He cried : "Scratchy Wilson's drunk, and has turned loose with both hands." The two Mexicans at once set down their glasses and faded out of the rear entrance of the saloon.

The drummer, innocent and jocular, answered : "All right, old man. S'pose he has ? Come in and have drink, anyhow."

But the information had made such an obvious cleft in every skull in the room that the drummer was obliged to see its importance. All had become instantly solemn. "Say," said he, mystified, "what is this?" His three companions made the introductory gesture of eloquent speech; but the young man at the door forestalled them.

"It means, my friend," he answered, as he came into the saloon, "that for the next two hours this town won't be a health resort."

The barkeeper went to the door, and locked and barred it; reaching out of the window, he pulled in heavy wooden shutters, and barred them. Immediately a solemn, chapel-like gloom was upon the place. The drummer was looking from one to another.

"But say," he cried, "what is this, anyhow? You don't mean there is going to be a gunfight?"

"Don't know whether there'll be a fight or not," answered one man, grimly; "but there'll be some shootin'—some good shootin'."

The young man who had warned them waved his hand. "Oh, there'll be a fight fast enough, if any one wants it. Anybody can get a fight out there in the street. There's a fight just waiting."

The drummer seemed to be swayed between the interest of a foreigner and a perception of personal danger.

"What did you say his name was?" he asked.

"Scratchy Wilson," they answered in chorus.

"And will he kill anybody? What are you going to do? Does this happen often? Does he rampage around like this once a week or so? Can he break in that door?"

"No; he can't break down that door," replied the barkeeper. "He's tried it three times. But when he comes you'd better lay down on the floor, stranger. He's dead sure to shoot at it, and a bullet may come through."

Thereafter the drummer kept a strict eye upon the door. The time had not yet been called for him to hug the floor, but, as a minor precaution, he sidled near to the wall. "Will he kill anybody?" he said again.

The man laughed low and scornfully at the question.

"He's out to shoot, and he's out for trouble. Don't see any good in experimentin' with him."

"But what do you do in a case like this? What do you do?"

A man responded: "Why, he and Jack Potter—"

"But," in chorus the other men interrupted, "Jack Potter's in San Anton'."

"Well, who is he? What's he got to do with it?"

"Oh, he's the town marshal. He goes out and fights Scratchy when he gets on one of these tears."

"Wow!" said the drummer, mopping his brow. "Nice job he's got."

The voices had toned away to mere whisperings. The drummer wished to ask further questions, which were born of an increasing anxiety and bewilderment; but when he attempted them, the men merely looked at him in irritation and motioned him to remain silent. A tense waiting hush was upon them. In the deep shadows of the room their eyes shone as they listened for sounds from the street. One man made three gestures at the barkeeper; and the latter, moving like a ghost, handed him a glass and a bottle. The man poured a full glass of whisky, and set down the bottle noiselessly. He gulped the whisky in a swallow, and turned again toward the door in immovable silence. The drummer saw that the barkeeper, without a sound, had taken a Winchester from beneath the bar. Later he saw this individual beckoning to him, so he tiptoed across the room.

"You better come with me back of the bar."

"No, thanks," said the drummer, perspiring; "I'd rather be where I can make a break for the back door."

Whereupon the man of bottles made a kindly but peremptory gesture. The drummer obeyed it, and, finding himself seated on a box with his head below the level of the bar, balm was laid upon his soul at sight of various zinc and copper fittings that bore a resemblance to armor-plate. The barkeeper took a seat comfortably upon an adjacent box.

"You see," he whispered, "this here Scratchy Wilson is a wonder with a gun—a perfect wonder; and when he goes on the war-trail, we hunt our holes—naturally. He's about the last one of the old gang that used to hang out along the river here. He's a terror when he's drunk. When he's sober he's all right—kind of simple—wouldn't hurt a fly—nicest fellow in town. But when he's drunk—whoo!"

There were periods of stillness. "I wish Jack Potter was back from San Anton'," said the barkeeper. "He shot Wilson up once,—in the leg,—and he would sail in and pull out the kinks in this thing."

Presently they heard from a distance the sound of a shot, followed by three wild yowls. It instantly removed a bond from the men in the darkened saloon. There was a shuffling of feet. They looked at each other. "Here he comes," they said.

III

A MAN in a maroon-colored flannel shirt, which had been purchased for purposes of decoration, and made principally by some Jewish women on the East Side of New York ; rounded a corner and walked into the middle of the main street of Yellow Sky. In either hand the man held a long, heavy, blue-black revolver. Often he yelled, and these cries rang through a semblance of a deserted village, shrilly flying over the roofs in a volume that seemed to have no relation to the ordinary vocal stength of a man. It was as if the surrounding stillness formed the arch of a tomb over him. These cries of ferocious challenge rang against walls of silence. And his boots had red tops with gilded imprints, of the kind beloved in winter by little sledding boys on the hillsides of New England.

The man's face flamed in a rage begot of whisky. His eyes, rolling, and yet keen for ambush, hunted the still doorways and windows. He walked with the creeping movement of the midnight cat. As it occurred to him, he roared menacing information. The long revolvers in his hands were as easy as straws ; they were moved with an electric swiftness. The little fingers of each hand played sometimes in a musician's way. Plain from the low collar of the shirt, the cords of his neck straightened and sank, straightened and sank, as passion moved him. The only sounds were his terrible invitations. The calm adobes preserved their demeanor at the passing of this small thing in the middle of the street.

There was no offer of fight—no offer of fight. The man called to the sky. There were no attractions. He bellowed and fumed and swayed his revolvers here and everywhere.

The dog of the barkeeper of the Weary Gentleman Saloon had not appreciated the advance of events. He yet lay dozing in front of his master's door. At sight of the dog, the man paused and raised his revolver humorously. At sight of the man, the dog sprang up and walked diagonally away, with a sullen head, and growling. The man yelled, and the dog broke into a gallop. As it was about to enter an alley, there was a loud noise, a whistling, and something spat the ground directly before it. The dog screamed, and, wheeling in terror, galloped headlong in a new direction. Again there was a noise, a whistling, and sand was kicked viciously before it. Fearstricken, the dog turned and flurried like an animal in a pen. The man stood laughing, his weapons at his hips.

Ultimately the man was attracted by the closed door of the Weary Gentleman Saloon. He went to it,, and, hammering with a revolver, demanded drink.

The door remaining imperturbable, he picked a bit of paper from the walk, and nailed it to the framework with a knife. He then turned his back contemptuously upon this popular resort, and, walking to the opposite side of the street, and spinning there on his heel quickly and lithely, fired at the bit of paper. He missed it by a half-inch. He swore at himself, and went away. Later he comfortably fusilladed the windows of his most intimate friend. The man was playing with this town ; it was a toy for him.

But still there was no offer of fight. The name of Jack Potter, his ancient antagonist, entered his mind, and he concluded that it would be a glad thing if he should go to Potter's house, and by bombardment induce him to come out and fight. He moved in the direction of his desire, chanting Apache scalp-music.

When he arrived at it, Potter's house presented the same still front as had the other adobes. Taking up a strategic position, the man howled a challenge. But this house regarded him as might a great stone god. It gave no sign. After a decent wait, the man howled further challenges, mingling with them wonderful epithets.

Presently there came the spectacle of a man churning himself into deepest rage over the immobility of a house. He fumed at it as the winter wind attacks a prairie cabin in the North. To the distance there should have gone the sound of a tumult like the fighting of two hundred Mexicans. As necessity bade him, he paused for breath or to reload his revolvers.

IV

POTTER and his bride walked sheepishly and with speed. Sometimes they laughed together shamefacedly and low.

"Next corner, dear," he said finally.

They both put forth the efforts of a pair walking bowed against a strong wind. Potter was about to raise a finger to point the first appearance of the new home when, as they circled the corner, they came face to face with a man in a maroon-colored shirt, who was feverishly pushing cartridges into a large revolver. Upon the instant the man dropped his revolver to the ground, and, like lightning, whipped another from its holster. The second weapon was aimed at the bridegroom's chest.

There was a silence. Potter's mouth seemed to be merely a grave for his tongue. He exhibited an instinct to at once loosen his arm from the woman's grip, and he dropped the bag to the sand. As for the bride, her face had gone as yellow as old cloth. She was a slave to hideous rites, gazing at the apparitional snake.

The two men faced each other at a distance of three paces. He of the revolver smiled and with a new and quiet ferocity.

"Tried to sneak up on me," he said. "Tried to sneak up on me !" His eyes grew more baleful. As Potter made a slight movement, the man thrust his revolver venomously forward. "No ; don't you do it, Jack Potter. Don't you move a finger toward a gun just yet. Don't you move an eyelash. The time has come for me to settle with you, and I'm goin' to do it my own way, and loaf along with no interferin'. So if you don't want a gun bent on you, just mind what I tell you."

Potter looked at his enemy. "I ain't got a gun on me, Scratchy," he said. "Honest, I ain't." He was stiffening and steadying, but yet somewhere at the back of his mind a vision of the Pullman floated : the sea-green figured velvet, the shining brass, silver, and glass, the wood that gleamed as darkly brilliant as the surface of a pool of oil—all the glory of the marriage, the environment of the new estate. "You know I fight when it comes to fighting, Scratchy Wilson ; but I ain't got a gun on me. You'll have to do all the shootin' yourself."

His enemy's face went livid. He stepped forward, and lashed his weapon to and fro before Potter's chest. "Don't you tell me you ain't got no gun on you, you whelp. Don't tell me no lie like that. There ain't a man in Texas ever seen you without no gun. Don't take me for no kid." His eyes blazed with light, and his throat worked like a pump.

"I ain't takin' you for no kid," answered Potter. His heels had not moved an inch backward. "I'm takin' you for a—fool. I tell you I ain't got a gun, and I ain't. If you're goin' to shoot me up, you better begin now ; you'll never get a chance like this again."

So much enforced reasoning had told on Wilson's rage ; he was calmer. "If you ain't got a gun, why ain't you got a gun ?" he sneered. "Been to Sunday-school ?"

"I ain't got a gun because I've just come from San Anton' with my wife. I'm married," said Potter. "And if I'd thought there was going to be any galoots like you prowling around when I brought my wife home, I'd had a gun, and don't you forget it."

"Married !" said Scratchy, not at all comprehending.

"Yes, married. I'm married," said Potter, distinctly.

"Married ?" said Scratchy. Seemingly for the first time, he saw the drooping, drowning woman at the other man's side. "No !" he said. He was like a creature allowed a glimpse of another world. He moved a pace backward, and his arm, with the revolver, dropped to his side. "Is this the lady ?" he asked.

"Yes ; this is the lady," answered Potter.

There was another period of silence.

"Well," said Wilson at last, slowly, "I s'pose it's all off now."

"It's all off if you say so, Scratchy. You know I didn't make the trouble." Potter lifted his valise.

"Well, I 'low it's off, Jack," said Wilson. He was looking at the ground. "Married !" He was not a student of chivalry ; it was merely that in the presence of this foreign condition he was a simple child of the earlier plains. He picked up his starboard revolver, and, placing both weapons in their holsters, he went away. His feet made funnel-shaped tracks in the heavy sand.

Stephen Crane

A TREE, A ROCK, A CLOUD

IT was raining that morning, and still very dark. When the boy reached the streetcar café he had almost finished his route and he went in for a cup of coffee. The place was an all-night café owned by a bitter and stingy man called Leo. After the raw, empty street the café seemed friendly and bright : along the counter there were a couple of soldiers, three spinners from the cotton-mill, and in a corner a man who sat hunched over with his nose and half his face down in a beer mug. The boy wore a helmet such as aviators wear. When he went into the café he unbuckled the chin-strap and raised the right flap up over his pink little ear ; often as he drank his coffee someone would speak to him in a friendly way. But this morning Leo did not look into his face and none of the men were talking. He paid and was leaving the café when a voice called out to him :

"Son ! Hey Son !"

He turned back and the man in the corner was crooking his finger and nodding to him. He had brought his face out of the beer mug and he seemed suddenly very happy. The man was long and pale, with a big nose and faded orange hair.

"Hey, Son !"

The boy went towards him. He was an undersized boy of about twelve, with one shoulder drawn higher than the other because of the weight of the paper-sack. His face was shallow, freckled, and his eyes were round child eyes.

"Yeah, Mister ?"

The man laid one hand on the paper-boy's shoulders, then grasped the boy's chin and turned his face slowly from one side to the other. The boy shrank back uneasily.

"Say ! What's the big idea ?"

The boy's voice was shrill ; inside the café it was suddenly very quiet.

The man said slowly : "I love you."

All along the counter the men laughed. The boy, who had scowled and sidled away, did not know what to do. He looked over the counter at Leo, and Leo watched him with a weary, brittle jeer. The boy tried to laugh also. But the man was serious and sad.

"I did not mean to tease you, Son," he said. "Sit down and have a beer with me. There is something I have to explain."

Cautiously, out of the corner of his eye, the paper-boy questioned the men along the counter to see what he should do. But they had gone back to their beer or their breakfast and did not notice him. Leo put a cup of coffee on the counter and a little jug of cream.

"He is a minor," Leo said.

The paper-boy slid himself up on to the stool. His ear beneath the upturned flap of the helmet was very small and red. The man was nodding at him soberly. "It is important," he said. Then he reached in his hip pocket and brought out something which he held up in the palm of his hand for the boy to see.

"Look very carefully," he said.

The boy stared, but there was nothing to look at very carefully. The man held in his big, grimy palm a photograph. It was the face of a woman, but blurred, so that only the hat and the dress she was wearing stood out clearly.

"See ?" the man asked.

The boy nodded and the man placed another picture in his palm. The woman was standing on a beach in a bathing suit. The suit made her stomach very big, and that was the main thing you noticed.

"Got a good look ?" He leaned over closer and finally asked : "You ever seen her before ?"

The boy sat motionless, staring slantways at the man. "Not so I know of."

"Very well." The man blew on the photographs and put them back into his pocket. "That was my wife."

"Dead ?" the boy asked.

Slowly the man shook his head. He pursed his lips as though about to whistle and answered in a long-drawn way : "Nuuu—" he said. "I will explain."

The beer on the counter before the man was in a large brown mug. He did not pick it up to drink. Instead he bent down and, putting his face over the rim, he rested there for a moment. Then with both hands he tilted the mug and sipped.

"Some night you'll go to sleep with your big nose in a mug and drown," said Leo. "Prominent transient drowns in beer. That would be a cute death."

The paper-boy tried to signal to Leo. While the man was not looking he screwed up his face and worked his mouth to question soundlessly : "Drunk ?" But Leo only raised his eyebrows and turned away to put some pink strips of bacon on the grill. The man pushed the mug away, from him, straightened himself, and folded his loose crooked hands on the counter. His face was sad as he looked at the paper-boy. He did not blink, but from time to time the lids closed down with delicate gravity over his pale green eyes. It was nearing dawn and the boy shifted the weight of the paper-sack.

"I am talking about love," the man said. "With me it is a science."

The boy half slid down from the stool. But the man raised his forefinger, and there was something about him that held the boy and would not let him go away.

"Twelve years ago I married the woman in the photograph. She was my wife for one year, nine months, three days, and two nights. I loved her. Yes..." He tightened his blurred, rambling voice and said again : "I loved her, I thought also that she loved me. I was a railroad engineer. She had all home comforts and luxuries. It never crept into my brain that she was not satisfied. But do you know what happened ?"

"Mgneeow !" said Leo.

The man did not take his eyes from the boy's face. "She left me. I came in one night and the house was empty and she was gone. She left me."

"With a fellow ?" the boy asked.

Gently the man placed his palm down on the counter. "Why naturally, Son. A woman does not run off like that alone."

The café was quiet, the soft rain black and endless in the street outside. Leo pressed down the frying bacon with the prongs of his long fork. "So you have been chasing the floozie for eleven years. You frazzled old rascal !"

For the first time the man glanced at Leo. "Please don't be vulgar. Besides, I was not speaking to you." He turned back to the boy and said in a trusting and secretive undertone : "Let's not pay any attention to him. O.K. ?"

The paper-boy nodded doubtfully.

"It was like this," the man continued. "I am a person who feels many things. All my life one thing after another has impressed me. Moonlight. The leg of a pretty girl. One thing after another. But the point is that when I had enjoyed anything there was a peculiar sensation as though it was laying around loose in me. Nothing seemed to finish itself up or fit in with the other things. Women ? I had my portion of them. The same. Afterwards laying around loose in me. I was a man who had never loved."

Very slowly he closed his eyelids, and the gesture was like a curtain drawn at the end of a scene in a play. When he spoke again his voice was excited and the words came fast—the lobes of his large, loose ears seemed to tremble.

"Then I met this woman. I was fifty-one years old and she always said she was thirty. I met her at a filling station and we were married within three days. And do you know what it was like ? I just can't tell you. All I had ever felt was gathered together around this woman. Nothing lay around loose in me any more but was finished up by her."

The man stopped suddenly and stroked

his long nose. His voice sank down to a steady and reproachful undertone : "I'm not explaining this right. What happened was this. There were these beautiful feelings and loose little pleasure inside me. And this woman was something like an assembly line for my soul. I run these little pieces of myself through her and I come out complete. Now do you follow me ?"

"What was her name ?" the boy asked.

"Oh," he said. "I called her Dodo. But that is immaterial."

"Did you try to make her come back ?"

The man did not seem to hear. "Under the circumstances you can imagine how I felt when she left me."

Leo took the bacon from the grill and folded two strips of it between a bun. He had a grey face, with slitted eyes, and a pinched nose saddled by faint blue shadows. One of the mill workers signalled for more coffee and Leo poured it. He did not give refills on coffee free. The spinner ate breakfast there every morning, but the better Leo knew his customers the stingier he treated them. He nibbled his own bun as though he grudged it to himself.

"And you never got hold of her again ?"

The boy did not know what to think of the man, and his child's face was uncertain with mingled curiosity and doubt. He was new on the paper route ; it was still strange to him to be out in the town in the black, queer early morning.

"Yes," the man said. "I took a number of steps to get her back. I went around trying to locate her. I went to Tulsa, where she had folks. And to Mobile. I went to every town she had ever mentioned to me, and I hunted down every man she had formerly been connected with. Tulsa, Atlanta, Chicago, Cheehaw, Memphis. ... For the better part of two years I chased around the country trying to lay hold of her."

"But the pair of them had vanished from the face of the earth !" said Leo.

"Don't listen to him," the man said confidentially. "And also just forget those two years. They are not important. What matters is that around the third year a curious thing began to happen to me."

"What ?" the boy asked.

The man leaned down and tilted his mug to take a sip of beer. But as he hovered over the mug his nostrils fluttered slightly ; he sniffed the staleness of the beer and did not drink. "Love is a curious thing to begin

with. At first I thought only of getting her back. It was a kind of mania. But then as time went on I tried to remember her. But do you know what happened ?"

"No," the boy said.

"When I laid myself down on a bed and tried to think about her my mind became a blank. I couldn't see her. I would take out her pictures and look. No good. Nothing doing. A blank. Can you imagine it ?"

"Say, mac !" Leo called down the counter. "Can you imagine this bozo's mind a blank !"

Slowly, as though fanning away flies, the man waved his hand. His green eyes were concentrated and fixed on the shallow little face of the paper-boy.

"But a sudden piece of glass on a sidewalk. Or a nickel tune in a music box. A shadow on a wall at night. And I would remember. It might happen in a street and I would cry or bang my head against a lamp-post. You follow me ?"

"A piece of glass..." the boy said.

"Anything. I would walk around and I had no power of how and when to remember her. You think you can put up a kind of shield. But remembering don't come to a man face forward—it corners around sideways. I was at the mercy of everything I saw and heard. Suddenly instead of me combing the countryside to find her she began to chase me around in my very soul. *She* chasing *me*, mind you ! And in my soul."

The boy asked finally : "What part of the country were you in then ?"

"Ooh," the man groaned. "I was a sick mortal. It was like smallpox. I confess, Son, that I boozed. I fornicated. I committed any sin that suddenly appealed to me. I am loathe to confess it, but I will do so. When I recall that period it is all curdled in my mind, it was so terrible."

The man leaned his head down and tapped his forehead on the counter. For a few seconds he stayed bowed over in this position, the back of his stringy neck covered with orange furze, his hands with their long warped fingers held palm to palm in an attitude of prayer. Then the man straightened himself ; he was smiling and suddenly his face was bright and tremulous and old.

"It was in the fifth year that it happened," he said. "And with it I started my science."

Leo's mouth jerked with a pale, quick grin. "Well none of we boys are getting any younger," he said. Then with sudden anger he balled up a dish-cloth he was holding and threw it down hard on the floor. "You draggle-tailed old Romeo !"

"What happened ?" the boy asked.

The old man's voice was high and clear : "Peace," he answered.

"Huh ?"

"It is hard to explain scientifically, Son," he said. "I guess the logical explanation is that she and I had fled around from each other for so long that finally we just got tangled up together and lay down and quit. Peace. A queer and beautiful blankness. It was spring in Portland and the rain came every afternoon. All evening I just stayed there on my bed in the dark. And that is how the science come to me."

The windows in the streetcar were pale blue with light. The two soldiers paid for their beers and opened the door—one of the soldiers combed his hair and wiped off his muddy puttees before they went outside. The three mill workers bent silently over their breakfasts. Leo's clock was ticking on the wall.

"It is this And listen carefully. I meditated on love and reasoned it out. I realized what is wrong with us. Men fall in love for the first time. And what do they fall in love with ?"

The boy's soft mouth was partly open and he did not answer.

"A woman," the old man said. "Without science, with nothing to go by, they undertake the most dangerous and sacred experience on God's earth. They fall in love with a woman. Is that correct, Son ?"

"Yeah," the boy said faintly.

"They start at the wrong end of love. They begin at the climax. Can you wonder it is so miserable ? Do you know how men should love ?"

The old man reached over and grasped the boy by the collar of his leather jacket. He gave him a gentle little shake and his green eyes gazed down unblinking and grave.

"Son, do you know how love should be begun ?"

The boy sat small and listening and still. Slowly he shook his head. The old man leaned closer and whispered :

"A tree. A rock. A cloud."

It was still raining outside in the street : a mild, grey, endless rain. The mill whistle blew for the six o'clock shift and the three spinners paid and went away. There was no one in the café but Leo, the old man, and the little paper-boy.

"The weather was like this in Portland," he said. "At the time my science was begun. I meditated and I started very cautious. I would pick up something from the street and take it home with me. I bought a goldfish and I concentrated on the goldfish and I loved it. I graduated from one thing to another. Day by day I was getting this technique. On the road from Portland to San Diego—"

"Aw shut up !" screamed Leo suddenly. "Shut up ! Shut up !"

The old man still held the collar of the boy's jacket ; he was trembling and his face was earnest and bright and wild. "For six years now I have gone around by myself and built up my science. And now I am a master. Son. I can love anything. No longer do I have to think about it even. I see a street full of people and a beautiful light comes in me. I watch a bird in the sky. Or I meet a traveler on the road. Everything, Son. And anybody. All stranger and all loved ! Do you realize what a science like mine can mean ?"

The boy held himself stiffly, his hands curled tight around the counter edge. Finally he asked : "Did you ever really find that lady ?"

"What ? What say, Son ?"

"I mean," the boy asked timidly. "Have you fallen in love with a woman again ?"

The old man loosened his grasp on the boy's collar. He had turned away and for the first time his green eyes had a vague and scattered look. He lifted the mug from the counter, drank down the yellow beer. His head was shaking slowly from side to side. Then finally he answered : "No, Son. You see that is the last step in my science. I go cautious. And I am not quite ready yet."

"Well !" said Leo. "Well, well, well !"

The old man stood in the open doorway. "Remember," he said. Framed there in the grey damp light of the early morning he looked shrunken and seedy and frail. But his smile was bright. "Remember I love you," he said with a last nod. And the door closed quietly behind him.

The boy did not speak for a long time. He pulled down the bangs on his forehead and slid his grimy little forefinger around the rim of his empty cup. Then without looking at Leo he finally asked :

"Was he drunk ?"

"No," said Leo shortly.

The boy raised his clear voice higher. "Then was he a dope fiend ?"

"No."

The boy looked up at Leo, and his flat little face was desperate, his voice urgent and shrill. "Was he crazy ? Do you think he was a lunatic ?" The paper-boy's voice dropped suddenly with doubt. "Leo ? Or not ?"

But Leo would not answer him. Leo had run a night café for fourteen years, and he held himself to be a critic of craziness. There were the town characters and also the transients who roamed in from the night. He knew the manias of all of them. But he did not want to satisfy the questions of the waiting child. He tightened his pale face and was silent.

So the boy pulled down the right flap of his helmet and as he turned to leave he made the only comment that seemed safe to him, the only remark that could not be laughed down and despised :

"He sure has done a lot of traveling."

Carson McCullers

AUGUST 1999 :

THE EARTH MEN

WHOEVER was knocking at the door didn't want to stop.

Mrs Ttt threw the door open."Well?"

"You speak *English* !" The man standing there was astounded.

"I speak what I speak," she said.

"It's wonderful *English* !" The man was in uniform. There were three men with him, in a great hurry, all smiling, all dirty.

"What do you want ?" demanded Mrs Ttt.

"You are a *Martian* !" The man smiled. "The word is not familiar to you, certainly. It's an Earth expression." He nodded at his men. "We are from Earth. I'm Captain Williams. We've landed on Mars within the hour. Here we are, the *Second* Expedition ! There was a First Expedition, but we don't know what happened to it. But here we are, anyway. And you are the first Martian we've met !"

"Martian ?" Her eyebrows went up.

"What I mean to say is, you live on the fourth planet from the sun. Correct ?"

"Elementary," she snapped, eyeing them.

"And we"—he pressed his chubby pink hand to his chest—"we are from Earth. Right, men ?"

"Right, sir !" A chorus.

"This is the planet Tyrr," she said, "if you want to use the proper name."

"Tyrr, Tyrr." The captain laughed exhaustedly. "What a *fine* name ! But, my good woman, how is it you speak such perfect English ?"

"I'm not speaking, I'm thinking," she said. "Telepathy ! Good day !" And she slammed the door.

A moment later there was that dreadful man knocking again.

She whipped the door open. "What now ?" she wondered.

The man was still there, trying to smile, looking bewildered. He put out his hand. "I don't think you *understand*—"

"What ?" she snapped.

The man gazed at her in surprise. "We're from *Earth* !"

"I haven't time," she said. "I've a lot of cooking today and there's cleaning and sewing and all. You evidently wish to see Mr Ttt ; he's upstairs in his study."

"Yes," said the Earth Man confusedly, blinking. "By all means, let us see Mr Ttt."

"He's busy." She slammed the door again.

This time the knock on the door was most impertinently loud.

"See here !" cried the man when the door was thrust open again. He jumped in as if to surprise her. "This is no way to treat visitors !"

"All over my clean floor !" she cried. "Mud ! Get out ! If you come in my house, wash your boots first."

The man looked in dismay at his muddy boots. "This," he said, "is no time for trivialities. I think," he said, "we should be celebrating." He looked at her for a long time, as if looking might make her understand.

"If you've made my crystal buns fall in the oven," she exclaimed, "I'll hit you with a piece of wood !" She peered into a little hot oven. She came back, red, steamy-faced. Her eyes were sharp yellow, her skin was soft brown, she was thin and quick as an insect. Her voice was metallic and sharp. "Wait here. I'll see if I can let you have a moment with Mr Ttt. What was your business ?"

The man swore luridly, as if she'd hit his hand with a hammer. "Tell him we're from Earth and it's never been done before !"

"What hasn't ?" She put her brown hand up. "Never mind. I'll be back."

The sound of her feet fluttered through the stone house.

Outside, the immense blue Martian sky was hot and still as a warm deep sea water. The Martian desert lay broiling like a prehistoric mud pot, waves of heat rising and shimmering. There was a small rocket ship reclining upon a hilltop nearby. Large footprints came from the rocket to the door of this stone house.

Now there was a sound of quarreling voices upstairs. The men within the door stared at one another, shifting on their boots, twiddling their fingers, and holding onto their hip belts. A man's voice shouted upstairs. The woman's voice replied. After fifteen minutes the Earth men began walking in and out the kitchen door, with nothing to do.

"Cigarette ?" said one of the men.

Somebody got out a pack and they lit up. They puffed slow streams of pale white smoke. They adjusted their uniforms, fixed their collars. The voices upstairs continued to mutter and chant. The leader of the men looked at his watch.

"Twenty-five minutes," he said. "I wonder what they're up to up there." He went to a window and looked out.

"Hot day," said one of the men.

"Yeah," said someone else in the slow warm time of early afternoon. The voices had faded to a murmur and were now silent. There was not a sound in the house. All the men could hear was their own breathing.

An hour of silence passed. "I hope we didn't cause any trouble," said the captain. He went and peered into the living room.

Mrs Ttt was there, watering some flowers that grew in the center of the room.

"I knew I had forgotten something," she said when she saw the captain. She walked out to the kitchen. "I'm sorry." She handed him a slip of paper. "Mr Ttt is much too busy."She turned to her cooking. "Anyway, it's not Mr Ttt you want to see ; it's Mr Aaa. Take that paper over to the next farm, by the

blue canal, and Mr Aaa'll advise you about whatever it is you want to know."

"We don't want to know anything," objected the captain, pouting out his thick lips. "We already *know* it."

"You have the paper, what more do you want ?" she asked him straight off. And she would say no more.

"Well," said the captain, reluctant to go. He stood as if waiting for something. He looked like a child staring at an empty Christmas tree. "Well," he said again. "Come on, men."

The four men stepped out into the hot silent day.

Half an hour later, Mr Aaa, seated in his library sipping a bit of electric fire from a metal cup, heard the voices outside in the stone causeway. He leaned over the window sill and gazed at the four uniformed men who squinted up at him.

"Are you Mr Aaa ?" they called.

"I am."

"Mr Ttt sent us to see you !" shouted the captain.

"Why did he do that ?" asked Mr Aaa.

"He was busy !"

"Well, that's a shame," said Mr Aaa sarcastically. "Does he think I have nothing else to do but entertain people's he's too busy to bother with ?"

"That's not the important thing, sir," shouted the captain.

"Well, it is to me. I have much reading to do. Mr Ttt is inconsiderate. This is not the first time he has been this thoughtless of me. Stop waving your hands, sir, until I finish. And pay attention. People usually listen to me when I talk. And you'll listen courteously or I won't talk at all."

Uneasily the four men in the court shifted and opened their mouths, and once the captain, the veins on his face bulging, showed a few little tears in his eyes.

"Now," lectured Mr Aaa, "do you think it fair of Mr Ttt to be so ill-mannered ?"

The four men gazed up through the heat. The captain said, "We're from Earth !"

"I think it very ungentlemanly of him," brooded Mr Aaa.

"A *rocket* ship. We came in it. Over there !"

"Not the first time Ttt's been unreasonable, you know."

"All the way from Earth."

"Why, for half a mind, I'd call him up and tell him off."

"Just the four of us ; myself and these three men, my crew."

"I'll call him up, yes, that's what I'll do !"

"Earth. Rocket. Men. Trip. Space."

"Call him and give him a good lashing !" cried Mr Aaa. He vanished like a puppet from a stage. For a minute there were angry voices back and forth over some weird mechanism or other. Below, the captain and his crew glanced longingly back at their pretty rocket ship lying on the hillside, so sweet and lovely and fine.

Mr Aaa jerked up in the window, wildly triumphant. "Challenged him to a duel, by the gods ! A duel !"

"Mr Aaa—" the captain started all over again, quietly.

"I'll shoot him dead, do you hear !"

"Mr Aaa, I'd like to *tell* you. We came sixty million miles."

Mr Aaa regarded the captain for the first time. "Where'd you say you were from ?"

The captain flashed a white smile. Aside to his men he whispered," *Now* we're getting someplace !" To Mr Aaa he called, "We traveled sixty million miles. From Earth !"

Mr Aaa yawned. "That's only *fifty* million miles this time of year." He picked up a frightful-looking weapon. "Well, I have to go now. Just take that silly note, though I don't know what good it'll do you, and go over that hill into the little town of Iopr and tell Mr Iii all about it. *He's* the man you want to see. Not Mr Ttt, he's an idiot ; I'm going to kill him. Not me, because you're not in my line of work."

"Line of work, line of work !" bleated the captain. "Do you have to be in a certain line of work to welcome Earth men !"

"Don't be silly, everyone knows *that* !" Mr Aaa rushed downstairs. "Good-by !" And down the causeway he raced, like a pair of wild calipers.

The four travelers stood shocked. Finally the captain said, "We'll find someone yet who'll listen to us."

"Maybe we could go out and come in again," said one of the men in a dreary voice. "Maybe we should take off and land again. Give them time to organize a party."

"That might be a good idea," murmured the tired captain.

The little town was full of people drifting in and out of doors, saying hello to one another, wearing golden masks and blue masks and crimson masks for pleasant variety, masks with silver lips and bronze eyebrows, masks that smiled or masks that frowned, according to the owner's dispositions.

The four men, wet from their long walk, paused and asked a little girl where Mr Iii's house was.

"There." The child nodded her head.

The captain got eagerly, carefully down on one knee, looking into her sweet young face. "Little girl, I want to talk to you."

He seated her on his knee and folded her small brown hands neatly in his own big ones, as if ready for a bed-time story which he was shaping in his mind slowly and with a great patient happiness in details.

"Well, here's how it is, little girl. Six months ago another rocket came to Mars. There was a man named York in it, and his assistant. Whatever happened to them, we don't know. Maybe they crashed. They came in a rocket. So did we. You should see it ! A *big* rocket ! So we're the *Second* Expedition, following up the First ! And we came all the way from Earth..."

The little girl disengaged one hand without thinking about it, and clapped an expressionless golden mask over her face. Then she pulled forth a golden spider toy and dropped it to the ground while the captain talked on. The toy spider climbed back up to her knee obediently, while she speculated upon it coolly through the slits of her emotionless mask and the captain shook her gently and urged his story upon her.

"We're Earth Men," he said. "Do you believe me ?"

"Yes." The little girl peeped at the way she was wiggling her toes in the dust.

"Fine." The captain pinched her arm, a little bit with joviality, a little bit with meanness to get her to look at him. "We built our own rocket ship. Do you believe *that* ?"

The little girl dug in her nose with a finger. "Yes."

"And—take your finger out of your nose, little girl—*I* am the captain, and—"

"Never before in history has anybody come across space in a big rocket ship," recited the little creature, eyes shut.

"Wonderful ! How did you know ?"

"Oh, telepathy." She wiped a casual finger on her knee.

"Well, aren't you just *ever* so excited ?" cried the captain. "Aren't you glad ?"

"You just better go see Mr Iii right away." She dropped her toy to the ground. "Mr Iii will like talking to you." She ran off, with the toy spider scuttling obediently after her.

The captain squatted there looking after her with his hand out. His eyes were watery in his head. He looked at his empty hands. His mouth hung open. The other three men stood with their shadows under them. They spat on the stone street...

Mr Iii answered his door. He was on his way to a lecture, but he had a minute, if they would hurry inside and tell him what they desired...

"A little attention," said the captain, red-eyed and tired. "We're from Earth, we have a rocket, there are four of us, crew and captain, we're exhausted, we're hungry, we'd like a place to sleep. We'd like someone to give us the key to the city or something like that, and we'd like somebody to shake our hands and say 'Hooray' and say 'Congratulations, old man !' That about sums it up."

Mr Iii was a tall, vaporous, thin man with thick blind blue crystals over his yellowish eyes. He bent over his desk and brooded upon some papers, glancing now and again with extreme penetration at his guests.

"Well, I haven't the forms with me here, I don't *think*." He rummaged through the desk drawers. "Now, where *did* I put the forms ?" He mused. "Somewhere. Somewhere. Oh, *here* we are ! Now !" He handed the papers over crisply. "You'll have to sign these papers, of course."

"Do we have to go through all this rigmarole ?"

Mr Iii gave him a thick glassy look. "You say you're from Earth, don't you ? Well, then there's nothing for it but you sign."

The captain wrote his name. "Do you want my crew to sign also ?"

Mr Iii looked at the captain, looked at the three others, and burst into a shout of derision. "*Them* sign ! Ho ! How marvelous ! Them, oh, *them* sign !" Tears sprang from his eyes. He slapped his knee and bent to let his laughter jerk out of his gaping mouth. He held himself up with the desk. "*Them* sign !"

The four men scowled. "What's funny ?"

"*Them* sign !" sighed Mr Iii, weak with hilarity. "So very funny. I'll have to tell Mr Xxx about this !" He examined the filled-out form, still laughing. "Everything seems to be in order." He nodded. "Even the agreement for euthanasia if final decision on such a step is necessary." He chuckled.

"Agreement for *what* ?"

"Don't talk. I have something for you. Here. Take this key."

The captain flushed. "It's a great honor."

"Not the key to the city, you fool !" snapped Mr Iii. "Just a key to the House. Go down that corridor, unlock the big door, and go inside and shut the door tight. You can spend the night there. In the morning I'll send Mr Xxx to see you."

Dubiously the captain took the key in hand. He stood looking at the floor. His men did not move. They seemed to be emptied of all their blood and their rocket fever. They were drained dry.

"What is it ? What's wrong ?" inquired Mr Iii. "What are you waiting for ? What do you want ?" He came and peered up into the captain's face, stooping. "Out with it, you !"

"I don't suppose you could even—" suggested the captain. "I mean, that is, try to, or think about..." He hesitated. "We've worked hard, we've come a long way, and maybe you could just shake our hands and say 'Well done !' do you—think ?" His voice faded.

Mr Iii stuck out his hand stiffly. "Congratulations !" He smiled a cold smile. "Congratulations." He turned away. "I must go now. Use that key."

Without noticing them again, as if they had melted down through the floor, Mr Iii moved about the room packing a little manuscript case with papers. He was in the room another five minutes but never again addressed the solemn quartet that stood with heads down, their heavy legs sagging, the light dwindling from their eyes. When Mr Iii went out the door he was busy looking at his fingernails...

They straggled along the corridor in the dull, silent afternoon light. They came to a large burnished silver door, and the silver key opened it. They entered, shut the door, and turned.

They were in a vast sunlit hall. Men and woman sat at tables and stood in conversing groups. At the sound of the door they regarded the four uniformed men.

One Martian stepped forward, bowing. "I am Mr Uuu," he said.

"And I am Captain Jonathan Williams, of New York City, on Earth," said the captain without emphasis.

Immediately the hall exploded !

The rafters trembled with shouts and cries. The people, rushing forward, waved and shrieked happily, knocking down tables, swarming, rollicking, seizing the four Earth Men, lifting them swiftly to their shoulders. They charged about the hall six times, six times making a full and wonderful circuit of the room, jumping, bounding, singing.

The Earth Men were so stunned that they rode the toppling shoulders for a full minute before they began to laugh and shout at each other :

"Hey ! This is more *like* it !"

"This is the life ! Boy ! Yay ! Yow ! Whoopee !"

They winked tremendously at each other. They flung up their hands to clap the air. "Hey !"

"Hooray !" said the crowd.

They set the Earth Men on a table. The shouting died.

The captain almost broke into tears. "Thank you. It's good, it's good."

"Tell us about yourselves," suggested Mr Uuu.

The captain cleared his throat.

The audience ohed and ahed as the captain talked. He introduced his crew ; each made a small speech and was embarrassed by the thunderous applause.

Mr Uuu clapped the captain's shoulder. "It's good to see another man from Earth. I am from Earth also."

"How was that again ?"

"There are many of us here from Earth."

"You ? From Earth ?" The captain stared. "But is that possible ? Did you come by rocket ? Has space travel been going on for centuries ?" His voice was disappointed. "What—what country are you from ?"

"Tuiereol. I came by the spirit of my body, years ago."

"Tuiereol." The captain mouthed the word. "I don't know that country. What's this about spirit of body ?"

"And Miss Rrr over here, she's from Earth, too, *aren't* you Miss Rrr ?"

Miss Rrr nodded and laughed strangely.

"And so is Mr Www and Mr Qqq and Mr Vvv :"

"I'm from Jupiter," declared one man, preening himself.

"I'm from Saturn," said another, eyes glinting slyly.

"Jupiter, Saturn," murmured the captain, blinking.

It was very quiet now ; the people stood around and sat at the tables which were strangely empty for banquet tables. Their yellow eyes were glowing, and there were dark shadows under their cheekbones. The captain noticed for the first time that there were no windows ; the light seemed to permeate the walls. There was only one door. The captain winced. "This is confusing. Where on Earth is this Tuiereol ? Is it near America ?"

"What is America ?"

"You never heard of America ! You say you're from Earth and yet you don't know !"

Mr Uuu drew himself up angrily. "Earth is a place of seas and nothing but seas. There is no land. I am from Earth, and know."

"Wait a minute." The captain sat back. "You look like a regular Martian. Yellow eyes. Brown skin."

"Earth is a place of all *jungle*," said Miss Rrr proudly. "I'm from Orri, on Earth, a civilization built of silver !"

Now the captain turned his head from her and then to Mr Uuu and then to Mr Www and Mr Zzz and Mr Nnn and Mr Hhh and Mr Bbb. He saw their yellow eyes waxing and waning in the light, focusing and unfocusing. He began to shiver. Finally he turned to his men and regarded them somberly.

"Do you realize what this is ?"

"What, sir ?"

"This is no celebration," replied the captain tiredly. "This is no banquet. These aren't government representatives. This is no surprise party. Look at their eyes. Listen to them !"

Nobody breathed. There was only a soft white move of eyes in the close room.

"Now I understand"—the captain's voice was far away—"why everyone gave us notes and passed us on, one from the other, until we met Mr Iii, who sent us down a corridor with a key to open a door and shut a door. And here we are..."

"Where are we, sir ?"

The captain exhaled. "In an insane asylum."

It was night. The large hall lay quiet and dimly illuminated by hidden light sources in the transparent walls. The four Earth Men sat around a wooden table, their bleak heads bent over their whispers. On the floors, men and women lay huddled. There were little stirs in the dark corners, solitary men or women gesturing their hands. Every half-hour one of the captain's men would try the silver door and return to the table. "Nothing doing, sir. We're locked in proper."

"They think we're really insane, sir ?"

"Quite. That's why there was no hallabaloo to welcome us. They merely tolerated what, to them, must be a constantly recurring psychotic condition." He gestured at the dark sleeping shapes all about them. "Paranoids, every single one ! What a welcome they gave us ! For a moment there"—a little fire rose and died in his eyes—"I thought we were getting our true reception. All the yelling and singing and speeches. Pretty nice, wasn't it—while it lasted ?"

"How long will they keep us here, sir ?"

"Until we prove we're not psychotics."

"That should be easy."

"I *hope* so."

"You don't sound very certain, sir."

"I'm not. Look in that corner."

A man squatted alone in darkness. Out of his mouth issued a blue flame which turned into the round shape of a small naked woman. It flourished on the air softly in vapors of cobalt light, whispering and sighing.

The captain nodded at another corner. A woman stood there, changing. First she was embedded in a crystal pillar, then she melted into a golden statue, finally a staff of polished cedar, and back to a woman.

All through the midnight hall people were juggling thin violet flames, shifting, changing, for nighttime was the time of change and affliction.

"Magicians, sorcerers," whispered one of the Earth Men.

"No, hallucination. They pass their insanity over into us so that we see their hallucinations too. Telepathy. Auto-suggestion and telepathy."

"Is that what worries you, sir ?"

"Yes. If hallucinations can appear this "real" to us, to anyone, if hallucinations are catching and almost believable, it's no wonder they mistook us for psychotics. If that man can produce little blue fire women and that woman there melt into a pillar, how natural if normal Martians think *we* produce our rocket ship with *our* minds."

"Oh," said his men in the shadows.

Around them, in the vast hall, flames leaped blue, flared, evaporated. Little demons of red sand ran between the teeth of sleeping men. Women became oily snakes. There was a smell of reptiles and animals.

In the morning everyone stood around looking fresh, happy, and normal. There were no flames or demons in the room. The captain and his men waited by the silver door, hoping it would open.

Mr Xxx arrived after about four hours. They had a suspicion that he had waited outside the door, peering in at them for at least three hours before he stepped in, beckoned, and led them to his small office.

He was a jovial, smiling man, if one could believe the mask he wore, for upon it was painted not one smile, but three. Behind it, his voice was the voice of a not so smiling psychologist. "What seems to be the trouble ?"

"You think we're insane, and we're not," said the captain.

"Contrarily, I do not think *all* of you are insane." The psychologist pointed a little wand at the captain. "No. Just *you*, sir. The others are secondary hallucinations."

The captain slapped his knee. "So *that's* it ! That's why Mr Iii laughed when I suggested my men sign the papers too !"

"Yes, Mr Iii told me." The psychologist laughed out of the carved, smiling mouth. "A good joke. Where was I ? Secondary hallucinations, yes. Women come to me with snakes crawling fom their ears. When I cure them, the snakes vanish."

"We'll be glad to be cured. Go right ahead."

Mr Xxx seemed surprised. "Unusual. Not many people want to be cured. The cure is drastic, you know."

"Cure ahead ! I'm confident you'll find we're all sane."

"Let me check your papers to be sure they're in order for a 'cure.' " He checked a file. "Yes. You know, such cases as yours need special 'curing.' The people in that hall are simpler forms. But once you've gone this far, I must point out, with primary, secondary, auditory, olfactory, and labial hallucinations, as well as tactile and optical fantasies, it is pretty bad business. We have to resort to euthanasia."

The captain leaped up with a roar. "Look here, we've stood quite enough ! Test us, tap our knees, check our hearts, exercise us, ask questions !"

"You are free to speak."

The captain raved for an hour. The psychologist listened.

"Incredible," he mused. "Most detailed dream fantasy I've ever heard."

"God damn it, we'll show you the rocket ship !" screamed the captain.

"I'd like to see it. Can you manifest it in this room ?"

"Oh, certainly. It's in that file of yours, under *R*."

Mr Xxx peered seriously into his file. He went "Tsk" and shut the file solemnly. "Why did you tell me to look ? The rocket isn't there."

"Of course not, you idiot ! I was joking. Does an insane man joke ?"

"You find some odd senses of humor. Now, take me out to your rocket. I wish to see it."

It was noon. The day was very hot when they reached the rocket.

"So." The psychological walked up to the ship and tapped it. It gonged softly. "May I go inside ?" he asked slyly.

"You may."

Mr Xxx stepped in and was gone for a long time.

"Of all the silly, exasperating things." The captain chewed a cigar as he waited. "For two cents I'd go back home and tell people not to bother with Mars. What a suspicious bunch of louts."

"I gather that a good number of their population are insane, sir. That seems to be their main reason for doubting."

"Nevertheless, this is all so damned irritating."

The psychologist emerged from the ship after half an hour of prowling, tapping, listening, smelling, tasting.

"*Now* do you believe !" shouted the captain, as if he were deaf.

The psychologist shut his eyes and scratched his nose. "This is the most incredible example of sensual hallucination and hypnotic suggestion I've ever encountered. I went through your 'rocket,' as you call it." He tapped the hull. "I hear it. Auditory fantasy." He drew a breath. "I smell it. Olfactory hallucination, induced by sensual telepathy." He kissed the ship. "I taste it. Labial fantasy !"

He shook the captain's hand. "May I congratulate you ? You are a psychotic genius ! You have done a most complete job ! The task of projecting your psychotic image life into the mind of another via telepathy and keeping the hallucinations from becoming sensually weaker is almost impossible. Those people in the House usually concentrate on visuals or, at the most, visuals and auditory fantasies combined. You have balanced the whole conglomeration ! Your insanity is beautiful complete !"

"My insanity." The captain was pale.

"Yes, yes, what a lovely insanity. Metal, rubber, gravitizers, foods, clothing, fuel, weapons, ladders, nuts, bolts, spoons. Ten thousand separate items I checked on your vessel. Never have I seen such a complexity. There were even shadows under the bunks and under *everything* ! Such concentration of will ! And everything, no matter how or when tested, had a smell, a solidity, a taste, a sound ! Let me embrace you !"

He stood back at last. "I'll write this into my greatest monograph ! I'll speak of it at the Martian Academy next month ! *Look* at you ! Why, you've even changed your eye color from yellow to blue, your skin to pink from brown. And those clothes, and your hands having five fingers instead of six ! Biological metamorphosis through psychological imbalance ! And your three friends—"

He took out a little gun. "Incurable, of course. You poor, wonderful man. You will be happier dead. Have you any last words ?"

"Stop, for God's sake ! Don't shoot !"

"You sad creature. I shall put you out of this misery which has driven you to imagine this rocket and these three men. It will be most engrossing to watch your friends and your rocket vanish once I have killed you. I will write a neat paper on the dissolvement of neurotic images from what I perceive here today."

"I'm from Earth ! My name is Jonathan Williams, and these'—"

"Yes, I know," soothed Mr Xxx, and fired his gun.

The captain fell with a bullet in his heart. The other three men screamed.

Mr Xxx stared at them. "You continue to exist ? This is superb ! Hallucinations with time and spatial persistence !" He pointed the gun at them. "Well, I'll scare you into dissolving."

"No !" cried the three men.

"An auditory appeal, even with the patient dead," observed Mr Xxx as he shot the three men down.

They lay on the sand, intact, not moving.

He kicked them. Then he rapped on the ship.

It persists ! *They* persist !" He fired his gun again and again at the bodies. Then he stood back. The smiling mask dropped from his face.

Slowly the little psychologist's face changed. His jaw sagged. The gun dropped from his fingers. His eyes were dull and vacant. He put his hands up and turned in a blind circle. He fumbled at the bodies, saliva filling his mouth.

"Hallucinations," he mumbled frantically. "Taste. Sight. Smell. Sound. Feeling." He waved his hands. His eyes bulged. His mouth began to give off a faint froth.

"Go away !" he shouted at the bodies. "Go away !" he screamed at the ship. He examined his trembling hands. "Contaminated," he whispered wildly. "Carried over into me. Telepathy. Hypnosis. Now *I'm* insane. Now *I'm* contaminated. Hallucinations in all their sensual forms." He stopped and searched around with his numb hands for the gun. "Only one cure. Only one way to make them go away, vanish."

A shot rang out. Mr Xxx fell.

The four bodies lay in the sun. Mr Xxx lay where he fell.

The rocket reclined on the little sunny hill and didn't vanish.

When the town people found the rocket at sunset they wondered what it was. Nobody knew, so it was sold to a junkman and hauled off to be broken up for scrap metal.

That night it rained all night. The next day was fair and warm.

Ray Bradbury : *The Martian Chronicles*, 1950

BIOGRAPHICAL NOTES

ASIMOV, Isaac (1920-   )

Known as the father of modern science fiction. Born in Russia, later moved to the United States where he became a naturalized citizen in 1928. Although originally a professor of biochemistry, he soon devoted all his time to writing, and is one of the most prolific writers of our time. One critic states that he has written more books on more subjects than any other contemporary writer—touching on fields such as biology, physics, general sciences as well as science fiction. He produces one book every six weeks, with 200 titles in print. Best known works : *Pebble in the Sky* (1950), *Foundation Trilogy* (1951-1952), *An Intelligent Man's Guide to Science* (2 vols., 1960) which concerns evolutionary theory. *Inside the Atom* (1961) is representative of his books for high school students.

BRADBURY, Ray (1920-   )

After a high-school education and much reading of sensational fiction and comic papers, he began to contribute stories to pulp magazines, graduating after a few years to better class periodicals. He became best known—and seriously regarded by intellectuals—as a writer of science fiction with *The Martian Chronicles* (1950), *The Golden Apples of the Sun* (1953), *Fahrenheit 451* (1953), etc.

BUCHWALD, Art (1925-   )

A well-known contemporary humorist whose columns in the *Washington Post* are syndicated to a great number of newspapers throughout the U.S. to the delight of millions of readers.

CAPOTE, Truman (1924-   )

A remarkable stylist and a New York socialite, Capote had published several collections of short stories, including *Breakfast at Tiffany's* (1958), when he produced *In Cold Blood* in 1966. The book sold some 3-million copies and was later made into a film. Since then Capote has written a number of television plays.

CHOPIN, Kate O'Flaherty (1851-1904)

Lived in St Louis, New Orleans and on a plantation near Cloutiersville (La). Mrs Chopin began writing after the death of her husband in 1882 and published two collections of stories : *Bayou Folk* (1894) and *A Night in Acadie* (1897) which were quickly recognized as major additions to the local-color genre. She is remembered for her lush description of Louisiana scenes, her sympathetically realistic delineation of Creole and Cajun characters and society and her finely wrought plots.

CRANE, Stephen (1871-1900)

Born in New Jersey, He first worked as a newspaper reporter in New York. His masterpiece *The Red Badge of Courage* (1895) subtitled "An Episode of the American Civil War" met with immediate success. It shows a remarkably convincing study of a young soldier's fear and compensating courage on the battlefield. This was not the product of personal experience (for Crane was not born at that time) but of his reading. Crane afterwards spent several years as a war correspondent in Mexico, Cuba and Greece. He died of consumption in Germany.

DOCTOROW, E.L. (1931-   )

He was born in New York and educated at Kenyon College and Columbia University. His novels include *Welcome to Hard Times* and *The Book of Daniel*. *Ragtime,* a best-seller for months, was the literary event of 1975.

DOS PASSOS, John (1896-1970)

Came to prominence with *Manhattan Transfer* (1925) in which he first developed a literary style that was revolutionary in its combination of naturalism and the stream-of-consciousness technique. A portrayal in hundreds of brief episodes of the many-faceted life of New York City, the book reflected his radical outlook on life, which found a fuller expression in his major work, the trilogy *U.S.A.*, comprising *The 42nd Parallel* (1930), *1919* (1932) and *The Big Money* (1936).

EMERSON , Ralph Waldo (1803-1882)

A New England essayist and poet, he became the central figure of the Transcendentalist spirit of intellectual independence from all obstacles to originality, and exerted through his lectures and writings a strong and long-lasting influence on American philosophy.

GIOVANNI, Nikki (1943-   )

Born in Knoxville, Tennessee, she has published several volumes of poetry and teaches creative writing at Rutgers University. Explicitly concerned with the black revolution, she has been very outspoken on the problems of the black woman and is critical of the pattern of the black family in which the husband beats his wife and children and deserts his family because he has problems with the outside world.

KEROUAC, Jack (1922-1969)

Born in Lowell, Mass., in a French-speaking family of Canadian origin, he did a variety of casual jobs before entering Columbia where he met poets and intellectuals such as Allan Ginsberg and Neal Cassady. From 1943 to 1950 he roamed through the U.S. and Mexico. *On the Road,* his most famous novel, was written during a frantic three weeks in 1951, the first of a series published in quick succession. His success has outlasted the beatnik subculture of which he was the acknowledged spokesman in prose.

KING, Martin Luther, Jr. (1929-1968)

A Baptist pastor in Montgomery, Alabama, he came into public view in 1955 when he led a successful boycott by the black community of Montgomery's segregated buses, which led to the Supreme Court's ruling against racial discrimination in transportation. Elected president of the Southern Christian Leadership Conference in 1957, he developed a nonviolent but active strategy of massive confrontation against injustice, which climaxed in the march on Washington in 1963. Later criticized by more militant black activists, he was awarded the Nobel Peace Prize in 1964. He was shot to death by a sniper in Memphis in 1968.

KRAMER, Jane (1938-   )

Born in Rhode Island, Kramer is a journalist and writer. She is the New Yorker's European reporter and is known for her articles and books treating political, sociological and intellectual trends both in the U.S. and abroad. Works include : *Honor to the Bride, Unsettling Europe* (on immigrants in Europa) and *The last Cowboy.*

LERNER, Max

Author, academic and syndicated columnist. Since 1974 Emeritus Professor of Human Behavior at the U.S. International University at San Diego. At one time Managing Director of the Encyclopedia of Social Sciences, Professor of Political Science (Harvard University), Professor of American Civilization (Ford Foundation), Professor of American Civilization and World Politics (Brandeis University).

LINCOLN, Abraham (1809-1865)

Born in a log cabin in Kentucky, Lincoln grew up in the poverty of a frontier family eventually to become the 16th president of the U.S. in March 1861. His election triggered the secession of 7 Southern states and the Civil War broke out in April 1861. Reelected by a large majority in 1864, he was shot while attending a theater performance only 3 days after General Lee's surrender at Appomatox.

McCULLLERS, Carson (1917-1967)

Born in Georgia, she was a Guggenheim Fellow in 1942-3 and in 1946 and also received an award from the American Academy of Arts and Letters in 1945. Her most famous novels are *The Heart is a Lonely Hunter* (1940), *Reflections in a Golden Eye* (1941), *The Member of the Wedding* (1946) and *The Ballad of the Sad Café* (1951).

MILLER, Arthur (1915-   )

Playwright and author who was raised in modest circumstances and had to combine his studies with full-time jobs in order to get a university degree. His first successful play, *All My Sons,* was performed in 1947, *Death of a Salesman* in 1949. In *The Crucible* (1953), his account of the Salem witch trials closely paralleled political events of the McCarthy anti-Communist crusade. Other productions included plays such as *A View from the Bridge* (1955), *After the Fall* (1964) and *The Price* (1968). Miller also wrote the screenplay for *The Misfits,* in which the main female character was played by Marilyn Monroe, whom he had married in 1956 and eventually divorced in 1960.

NASH, Ogden (1902-1971)

A school teacher who had to leave after one year because of harassment by his fourteen-year-old pupils, Ogden Nash began contributing his verse—a unique and eccentric variety of words and rhymes—to numerous magazines in the late 1920s, and subsequently joined the staff of the *New Yorker*. His verse reflected on little boys, women's hats, salads, diets and literature, and these poems appeared in various collections, the best known of which are perhaps *The Face is Familiar, Parents Keep Out* and *You Can't Get There From Here*.

PACKARD, Vance (1914-   )

A sociologist whose interests led him into the work done by the motivational-research people in the U.S., he started collecting material on the subject in the early fifties. He was the inventor of the concept of the "affluent society". Apart from *The Naked Society*, his impact-making studies include *The Hidden Persuaders, The Status-Seekers, The Waste-Makers* and *The Pyramid-Climbers*.

SAGAN, Carl (1934-   )

Born in New York, Sagan was first an astrophysicist and then joined the faculty of Cornell University as a professor of Astronomy and Space Sciences. He worked as an experimentor for various U.S. government space missions to Venus and Mars and is consultant to the National Academy of Sciences. His extremely popular television serial *Cosmos* established his reputation for vulgarisation of the world of science.

STEINBECK, John (1902-1968)

A highly successful novelist, whose books include *Tortilla Flat, Cannery Row, In Dubious Battle, Of Mice and Men, The Grapes of Wrath* and *East of Eden*, Steinbeck, who was awarded the Nobel Prize for Literature in 1962, showed throughout his work a deep interest in sociology, which prompted him to write a series of perceptive essays and eventually led him on a huge investigating tour of the U.S., that is recorded in *Travels with Charley* (1962).

THURBER, James Grover (1894-1961)

Humorist and cartoonist, with a pen equally facile and whimsical in writing or drawing. A long-time contributor to the *New Yorker*, Thurber was a prolific writer of short-stories, and produced many collections, among which are *Fables for our Time* and *The Thurber Carnival*. His most famous short story, "The Secret Life of Walter Mitty", created a character that became a prototype at the same time as the story itself became a part of American tradition.

TOFFLER, Alvin (1928-   )

Toffler has been an editor of *Fortune* and a Washington correspondent. He has written for numerous periodicals such as *Life*, and is the author of *The Culture Consumers*. He is a specialist of the "sociology of the future" and as such has taught courses at some of the most prestigious universities.

WAUGH, Evelyn Arthur St John (1903-1966)

Born in London, educated at Lancing and Oxford ; studied art, worked on the *Daily Express* and mixed with high society. *Decline and Fall* (1928) immediately gave him the position he retained to the end of his life as England's leading satirical novelist. Though his books have many brilliantly comic passages, his satire was frequently directed at too obvious targets, such as the press lords in *Scoop* (1938), while in *The Loved One* (1948) on American commercialization of bereavement, the satirical point is overworked and soon exhausted.

WRIGHT, Richard (1908-1960)

A Negro born on a Mississippi plantation, Wright struggled through a difficult childhood, educated himself, and in the 1930s worked with the Federal Writer's Project. During this period he was involved with the Communist party which he later left in disillusionment. His novel, *Native Son* (1940) was a Book-of-the-Month Club selection, and established his fame. His folk history of the American Negro, *Twelve Million Black Voices* (1941) was followed by his autobiography, *Black Boy* (1945). His last novels were *White Man Listen* (1956) and *The Long Dream* (1958).

GRAMMATICAL AND COMMUNICATIVE INDEX

C A N A D A

Lake Superior

MICHIGAN

Lake Huron

Lake Michigan

MINNE-SOTA

WISCONSIN

Minneapolis

Milwaukee

Chicago

IOWA

ILLINOIS

MIS-SOURI

Kansas City

St Louis

ARKANSAS

ARKANSAS R.

RED R.

MISSISSIPPI

LOUISIANA

New Orleans

Galveston

uston

GULF OF MEXICO

Quebec

Montreal

Ottawa

ST LAWRENCE RIVER

MAINE

VERMONT

NEW HAMPSHIRE

MASSA-CHUSETTS

Boston

RHODE ISLAND

CONNEC-TICUT

NEW YORK

Toronto

L. Ontario

Lake Erie

HUDSON R.

New York

Philadelphia

Baltimore

DELAWARE

MARYLAND

NEW JERSEY

DELAWARE RIVER

ALLEGHENY MTS.

PENNSYLVANIA

INDI-ANA

OHIO

Pittsburg

Cincinnati

WEST

VIRGI-NIA

Washington

POTOMAC R.

OHIO R.

KENTUCKY

TENNESSEE RIVER

APPALACHIANS

VIRGINIA

NORTH CAROLINA

SOUTH CAROLINA

TE-NNESSEE

Memphis

MISSIS-SIPPI

ALABAMA

GEORGIA

Atlanta

FLORIDA

Miami

ATLANTIC OCEAN

MISSISSIPPI R.

MISSOURI R.

ILLUSTRATION CREDITS

Addressograph-Multigraph Corporation for *Life La Photographie* for page 151 ; Mark Antman for pages 84, 85, 92, 97, 121, 142, 147, 152, 156 and 158 ; Robert Bishop for page 80 ; Black Star, Declan Haun for page 11 ; Charles Moore for page 208 ; F. Boutin for pages 90 and 223 ; Michel Cabaud for pages 111 and 196 ; Cahier du Cinéma for pages 101 and 216 ; CBS entertainment for page 166 ; Columbia Pictures Company for page 218 ; Jean-François Défossé for pages 41, 87, 105, 109, 164 and 222 ; Diners Club for pages 128 and 129 ; Randall Enos for page 205 ; Field Newspaper Syndicate for B.C. cartoon for page 221 ; Carlos Freire for page 104 ; Gamma, David Burnett for pages 198-199 ; Bernard Charlon for page 201 ; Connolly for page 53 ; Robert Frank for page 103 ; Owen Franken for page 59 ; Susan Greenwood for page 53 ; L Gubb for page 177 ; Hayton for page 198 (top left) ; J.P. Laffont for pages 85 and 124 ; Catherine Leroy for page 18 ; Sheldon Moskowitz for page 184 ; SAS for page 23 ; Etienne Montès for page 84 ; J.P. Pairreault for page 213 ; Jim Pozanik for page 48 ; Leie Skorgeors for page 60 ; Walker for page 194 ; The Gospel Tract Society for page 124 ; IBM for page 206 ; Magnum, René Hurri for page 80 ; Charles Harbutt for page 146 ; Gilles Pérès for page 163 ; Marc Riboud for page 117 ; Burk Uzzle for pages 30-31 ; Larry Morris for page 46 ; From *Vintage Thurber* by James Thurber. The collection © 1963 Hamish Hamilton Ltd., London for page 190 ; Hammermill Paper Group for page 149 ; L.M.D. for page 214 ; Mad Magazine © 1976 and 1975 by E.C. Publications Inc. Reprinted by permission for pages 138, 139 and 228 ; Newsweek, © 1972 reprinted by permission for pages 130 and 131 ; The Newyorker Magazine for 4 cartoons, Alain © 1940, 1968 for page 221 ; Chas. Addams © 1955 for page 118 ; Carl Rose © 1935, 1963 for page 175 ; O. Soglow © 1939, 1965 for page 153 ; New York Historical Society for page 49 ; Opera Mundi for cartoon Blondie for page 113 ; Peabody Museum of Salem, Massachusetts for page 35 ; A.D. Peters and Co Ltd., reprinted by permission for page 125 ; Jean-Michel Ploton for pages 34, 73, 89, 114 and 123 ; Rinehart and Winston for cartoon from *Call Me When You Find America* for page 43 ; Norman Rockwell for page 110 ; Karen O'Rooke for page 85 ; Harold Smith for page 85 ; Sygma, Tony Corrody for pages 83 and 84 ; J.P. Laffont for pages 172, 173 and 211 ; J.P. Laffont-Owen Franken for page 21 ; Tiziou for page 29 ; United Feature Syndicate for page 112 ; United Press International, Inc. for page 77 ; USIS for pages 24, 55, 63, 154 and 157 ; Mireille Vautier for pages 107 and 220 (left) ; The Washington Post for page 44.

Whilst every effort has been made to trace the owners of copyright, in a few cases this has proved impossible and we take the opportunity to offer our apologies to any authors whose rights may have been unwittingly infringed. We have been unable to trace the copyright holders of material appearing on pages 94, 145, 170 and 215 and would be grateful for any information that could help us trace them.

ACKNOWLEDGEMENTS

We are grateful to the following for permission to reproduce copyright material :
Apple Magazine for extract of an article by Isaac Asimov ; Associated Book Publishers Ltd. for extract from *The Loved One* by Evelyn Waugh Published by Chapman and Hall Ltd. and extract from *The Multinationals* by Christopher Tugendhat published by Eyre and Spottiswoode Ltd. ; American Heritage Publishing Co Inc. for excerpt from *The Penguin Book of the American West* by David Lavender, © 1965 by publishers and reprinted with permission ; Author's agent for extract from *First Person America*, reprinted by permission of Ann. Banks, © 1981 Ann. Banks ; Author's Agents for extract from *The Martian Chronicles : August 1999* by Ray Bradbury ; Reprinted by permission of A.D. Peters and Co Ltd. Colorific Photo Library for excerpts from *Loving America* by Henry Grunwald, © 1965 by Arthur Hailey Ltd. Reprinted by permission ; André Deutsch for extract from *On the Road* by Jack Kerouac ; E.P. Dutton and Co Inc. for extract from *Hotel* by Arthur Hailey, © 1965 by Arthur Hailey Ltd. Reprinted by permission ; André Deutsch for extract from *On the Road* by Jack Kerouac ; E.P. Dutton and Co Inc. for extract from *Touch the Earth : Self-Portrait of Indian Existence* by T.C. McLuhan, © 1971 by T.C. McLuhan. Reprinted by permission of the publishers ; Hamish Hamilton Ltd. for extract from *In Cold Blood* by Truman Capote, © 1965 by Truman Capote, and extract from "The Thurber Carnival" from *Vintage Thurberly* by James Thurber. Excerpt from pages 1-3 of *American Hunger* by Richard Wright, © 1944 by Richard Wright, © 1977 by Ellen Wright. By permission of Harper and Row, Publishers, Inc. ; Little Brown and Co for extract from *The New Centurions* by Joseph Wambaugh, © 1970 by Joseph Wambaugh ; Author's agent for extract from *Bachelorhood* by Philip Lapate ; reprinted by permission. MacMillan Administration (Basinstoke) Ltd. for extract from *Ragtime* by E.L. Doctorow ; MacMillan Publishing Co Inc. for extract from *Manchild in the Promised Land* by Claude Brown, © Claude Brown 1965 ; David McKay Co. Inc. for extract from *The Naked Society* by Vance Packard, 1964 ; Author's Agents and the estate of the late Carson McCullers for "A Tree, a Rock, a Cloud" from *The Ballad of the Sad Cafe* by Carson McCullers, published by Barrie and Jenkins Ltd. ; William Morrow and Co Inc. for extract from *The Other Woman* by Rona Jaffe. Reprinted by permission of the publishers, © 1972 by Rona Jaffe. Reprinted by permission of the publishers, © 1972 by Rona Jaffe and extract from *Grand Canyon : Today and all its Yesterdays* by Joseph Wood Krutch ; The Nation for excerpt from article "A Four-Day Work Week" from *The Nation*, 1st March 1975 ; National Geographic Magazine for excerpt from article "A Walk Accross America" by P.G. Jenkins in *National Geographic*, April 1977 ; *New York Herald Tribune* for excerpt from article "Winter 1970-71" by Art Buchwald in *New York Herald Tribune* ; The New York Times for excerpt from article "Anchorage Alaska" in *The New York Times*, © 1977. Reprinted by permission ; W. Norton and Co Inc. for extract from *Enterprising Women* by Caroline Bird, with permission of publishers, © 1976 by Caroline Bird ; Mrs John Dos Passos for extract from *The 42nd Parallel* by John Dos Passos. © by Elizabeth Dos Passos. Reprinted by permission ; G.P. Putnam's Sons for extract from *The Days of Martin Luther King Jr.* by Jim Bishop ; Random House for specified excerpts from pages 339, 342 and 345 of *Who Speaks for Earth* by Carl Sagan ; Random House Inc. for extract from *Division Street : America* by Studs Terkel, © 1967 by Studs Terkel. Reprinted by permission of Pantheon Books, a division of Random House Inc. ; *Science Digest* for article from "Space Hardware Comes to Earth" in *Science Digest*, Dec. 1976, © 1976 The Hearst Corporation ; Jesse Schwartz for an interview with the Mayor of Palos Heights ; excerpts from *The Forgotten Warriors* by Lance Morrow. © 1981 Time Inc. All rights reserved. Reprinted by permission from Time ; Time Inc. for article "The World Is Blue-Jean Cou Now" from *Life* © 1972 Time Inc. Reprinted with permission ; © 1980 by Kate Moody, reprinted by permission of Times Books, the New York Times Book Co Inc., excerpted from *Growing Up On Television* by Kate Moody ; Transworld Feature Syndicate (UK) Ltd. for excerpts from "You Have a New Brother" by Mary Ann O'Roark in *McCall's*, May 1976 ; US News and World Report for excerpts from articles "From Gadgets to People" and "Two Views of 4-Day Work-Week" in *US News and World Report*, Nov. 8th 1976 and May 3rd 1971 ; The Viking Press Inc. for extract from *Death of a Salesman* by Arthur Miller, © 1929 © 1977 by Arthur Miller, extract from *America and Americans* by John Steinbeck, © 1966 by John Steinbeck, All rights reserved and extract from *Travels With Charley* by John Steinbeck, © 1961, 1962 by the Curtis Publishing Co Inc. © 1062 by John Steinbeck. All reprinted by permission of the Viking Press ; A.P. Watt and Son and the estate of the late Ogden Nash for extract from "The Terrible People" by Ogden Nash from *Collected Poems 1929 On* by Ogden Nash ; Author's Agents for extract from *Cinema* by Thomas Wiseman, © 1964 by Thomas Wiseman and reprinted by permission, published by Cassell and Co Ltd.

Whilst every effort has been made we have been unable to trace copyright holders for the following : song (text only) *City of New Orleans* by Steve Goodman, extract from *Overload* by Arthur Hailey, extract from *Superpower* by Robert Hargreaves, extract from *Midnight Cowboy* by James Leo Herlihy, article by David Henshaw in *The Listener*, extract from *The Last Cowboy* by Jane Kramer, extract from "The View from Providence" by Joseph Nocera, extract from *The San Francisco chronicle*, extract from *Chicano* by Richard Vasquez and an article "The Faces of America" in *The Washington Post* and any information which would enable us to do so would be appreciated.

I.M.E. - 25-Baume-les-Dames - Dépôt légal Septembre 1983 - N° éditeur 8560